PHILOSOPHICAL THEMES IN MODERN EDUCATION

Robert S. Brumbaugh
Yale University

Nathaniel M. Lawrence
Williams College

UNIVERSITY
PRESS OF
AMERICA

LANHAM • NEW YORK • LONDON

University Press of America,® Inc.

4720 Boston Way
Lanham, MD 20706

3 Henrietta Street
London WC2E 8LU England

This edition published in 1985 by
University Press of America, Inc.,
by arrangement with Houghton Mifflin Company

Library of Congress Cataloging-in-Publication Data

Brumbaugh, Robert Sherrick, 1918-
  Philosophical themes in modern education.

  Reprint. Originally published: Boston: Houghton
Mifflin, 1972, c1973.
  1. Education—Philosophy—Addresses, essays.
lectures. I. Lawrence, Nathaniel Morris, 1917-
II. Title.
LB41.B89   370'.1   1985   85-11267
ISBN 0-8191-4718-4 (pbk. : alk. paper)

CONTENTS

ART CREDITS

The authors wish to thank the Williams College 1900 Fund for several grants which aided in preparing the manuscript.

PREFACE

Themes have no life of their own. Someone has a thought, a vision, a synoptic understanding, and he places it before others. They modify, adopt, adapt, continue, and pass along; the theme outlives its owners and users. But it is not thereby separate or, through periods of time, exactly self-identical. The themes we identify and explain in this book are such themes. They are given concretely, in the thoughts of men who subscribed to and defended them. This is appropriate for a book on education, since education is primarily a relation among persons.

This collection of essays has, as the reader will see, a complementary function in relation to a previous study.[1] It aims at exploring themes of high significance in educational theory, themes which have left their mark on how human beings bring oncoming human animals into human existence. Our former study was an investigation of the educational thought of six exceptional philosophers, for each of whom his thoughts on education were part of a total philosophic understanding. Some of the authors in the sequel are philosophers, some not, but each—even authors whom the reader may never have heard of before —has exerted a profound influence on philosophy of education. The two books together thus compose a very substantial presentation of the vast inheritance, including that of men still living, of the philosophical foundations of educational thought and practice. If only one of these books is used, the other should be kept as a background reference.

For something better than a month the two authors of this book enjoyed that rare luxury, an unimpeded time free of all care in which to work out the book's final form. On an island in sight of Samos and—when the heat rises a bit—the Turkish shore, the spirit of Greek liberty still prevails as does the ancient conception of education for the improvement of man and for no other reason. There is no visible law on Ikaria, no government authority in evidence, no officials, save a few young soldiers placed there as part of their two years of military service. But they came with the Colonels, and it was the same before the Colonels came to power. There is a strong tradition of right and wrong, of sharing and of ownership (the passer-by may pick one bunch of grapes, not two). There are strong hatreds and fast friendships, and always the Odyssean love of strangers. On the eastern tip of Ikaria, along a white strand, Odysseus may have taken refuge from the storm that drove him away from Menelaos.[2] In Armenistis we took refuge, as we both had done before, from our own storms. There we listened to a man with a sixth-grade education tell us of the niceties of his language and the baffling diversity of its dialects with all the control of a practiced pedagogue and linguist. There also we listened to accounts of the island and its people. These were given simply because knowledge is good in itself, and the strangers, as teachers, would understand that. There one of us learned most of the Greek he knows from an island woman of endless patience and acute discrimination (she had had five years of schooling) and a bit more from ten-year-old Polyxene, whose unaffected and delicate attention to the mainland accent was the pride of her household.

Ikaria, like all of Greece, lies in a doldrum, surviving on the last of a brilliant tradition. This is not Greece's finest hour. Yet that calm conviction—for all it is undermined by poverty and derailed from political expression by a depressing government—that it is good to teach and learn because men are bettered thereby is very much present. We remember that undramatic island atmosphere, in this last week of February 1972, when the reports coming out of the President's visit to China are of a once great university—Peking—brought to its knees as a three-year technical school with classes from eight till six; when from our own capital the hoarse demagogic curse of the chairman of the House Committee on Armed Services proclaims that those American universities who will have no ROTC will get no government aid. So this book is, strangely, dedicated to Ikaria and to its people with affection: to its resonance for the birth of Western civilization and the educational ideal, without which civilization and Oriental despotism are indistinguishable.

γία το νησί Ικαρία, νὰ ζήσετε

R.S.B.
N.M.L.

NOTES

1. R. S. Brumbaugh and N. M. Lawrence, *Philosophers on Education*, Boston, 1963.
2. Mauricio Obregon, *Ulysses Airborne*, New York, 1971, p. 55.

INTRODUCTION

This fractured time! Free schools, open classroom, voucher system, performance contracting, competency-based education, busing, community control, Head Start, property-tax base, teachers' union, strike!

Education has always been the favorite plaything of ideologues and activists, but it is hard to remember a time when the Ideas and the Activisms were more aggressively pushed than they are today. Every nostrum, every pet scheme, every private vision of a New Palladium is hawked daily in the public prints. And the professional, to say nothing of the lay parent, is bewildered by this seemingly endless and mindless peddling of cure-alls.

What we forget, but always return to, is the fact that there is such a thing as *knowledge,* that there is an act called *learning,* and that knowledge and learning have become the vital center of human personality. Some steady thinking about these basic ingredients is a continuing need in these days of special pleading.

Fortunately, some of our more thoughtful predecessors in the "knowledge industry"—Freud, Neill, Skinner, Piaget, Bruner—have already addressed themselves to these troublesome matters. Building on basic work in epistemology by the Greeks and the Romans, as well as Descartes, Locke, and Hume, these modern students of the educative process have, in our contemporary idiom, "put it all together." They have turned off the hucksters and instead delivered theories of man and the world which build connections between the chaotic character of natural events and the inner order of man's plans for himself. These theories have been articulated through the medium of various themes of discourse: Knowledge as Information, as Illumination, as Understanding, as Analysis. Learning as Self-Realization, as Behavioral Conditioning, as Psychic Growth.

This book is a study of these major themes. It is an exercise for the modern teacher in building linkages between the experience of the raw recruit fidgeting in the third row and the experience of the mature adult capable of disciplined performance in the outside world. As a transitional piece between exotic, esoteric theory on the one hand and concrete pedagogical strategy on the other, this volume is supremely relevant to an educational epoch now so much in love with quick trips, fast bucks, and easy solutions. It is a concordat of steady and deliberate thinking on the complicated business of educating the young.

Here, Messrs. Brumbaugh and Lawrence explain the basic ideas which hold up the institution of the school. But then they move on. How do these ideas get translated into programs for the development of boys and girls into full human beings? To find the answer, the authors examine the pedagogical systems of the major contemporary thinkers in Europe and America named above. Through a close inspection of these systems and the minds which have produced them, we begin to see how the epistemological traditions of classical philosophy thematically reappear in modern form and get translated into real-life programs of learning for today's youngsters.

This book is immediately appropriate for courses in the foundations of education, the philosophy of education, and the history of educational ideas. There is no professional today who can afford to remain ignorant of the major strategists who have shaped the American educational experience. Here is where the student of education can acquire a working knowledge of these individuals and of the earlier theories on which they built their designs for a genuinely human education.

Van Cleve Morris
University of Illinois at Chicago Circle

PART ONE

THEORIES OF LEARNING
AND KNOWLEDGE

THE TEACHING ANIMAL

Among the many fields of philosophy, one belongs squarely in the public domain. This field is philosophy of education. It is everybody's property—though some misuse it—because education is everyone's concern. The reason is obvious: individual men are helpless animals; only by sharing in an educational continuum do they attain human maturity.

This fact is worth examining. Individually, man is born helpless. Few men ever completely overcome this helplessness. Those who do attain relative independence do so with the help of others since no innate mechanism brings man automatically to human adulthood. For example, feral children, reared out of society, never even learn the upright posture, the human gait. They travel seminocturnally, alternating from two to four feet. By contrast, a bird which has never seen other birds, parents, or nest will learn to fly. Moreover, a bird reared apart from all contact with bird sounds still sings a primitive but usually recognizable version of the song of his own species. But apparently children reared away from human society lose their humanity in the first few years. The period for acquiring that most distinctive behavioral trait of *homo sapiens,* human language, is not long; it has largely vanished in ten years.[1] A race of such creatures, surviving a world catastrophe, might precariously reproduce the human *animal* and perhaps start the evolution of man all over again. But would such languageless creatures *be* men?

Through language we are human. We communicate, we share knowledge, and we store knowledge. Our physiological capacities for making sounds and hearing them, for writing symbols and reading them are biologically inherited. But the life of language is outside individual bodies. We are not born with any primitive species song. Language abides in society generally. We socially inherit language, art, know-how, technology, spirituality, and the like. Thus to say that men are essentially social is not merely to say that they have fellow-feeling, are companionable, or can assist one another, but also to say that they cannot become human beings outside the society which is trustee for their humanity. At least for human beings the inheritance of acquired characteristics is not debatable. It is as obvious as the inheritance of

4

the opposed thumb by which we hold tools. We share with our contemporaries a responsibility from the past for the future. It is hardly surprising that most people have ideas about the education of the young.

We have all been educated and all of us educate, formally or informally. When this process of eliciting and actualizing human capacities begins is hard to say. However, a mother certainly becomes an educator with the baby whose hunger leads him to yell and who, spasmodically and blindly, gropes and finds a nipple. If she has no convictions about, say, permissivism and discipline (which might be just as well), she will shortly develop them. Should she, for example, endure all conceivable pain from vigorous nursing and abandon all habits of regular sleep for the sake of demand feeding to give her child a feeling of security? Or should she teach the child early that life depends on discipline, regularity, and habit—and incidentally get some rest? What she does will be a declaration of educational policy, regardless of whether she even talks about child guidance. And policy easily turns into theory. When her well-fed child screams for no apparent reason, she may even come to believe in original sin—the willful rebellion against all good and all order—only to find when the child rolls over that original sin is an open safety pin.

Bachelors and spinsters, however, are not exempt from the role of educator. Every child is undeveloped by definition and reaches toward some development. The child reaches out for attitudes, ideas, feelings, values—in short, for growth. It is the child who thus casts everyone and everything with which he comes into contact in the role of teacher. His delight, his eagerness, his excitement, his curiosity are invitations to the world: *teach me.* The adult, vis-à-vis a child, instinctively takes up a teaching posture, even if the child is nothing to him and he couldn't care less about "teaching." That teaches the child something, too. Even in adult society, men continue to learn—or, alternatively, to *reinforce* their convictions about men and the world—from one another.

The difference between the furtive, grunting, feral child and a person is society. The entire social process is education in its primary and therefore informal sense. Formal education differentiates itself only gradually from this social mass, even with well-defined schools, curricula, professional teachers, and so on, for the school itself is in constant interaction with society. This is true not just because teachers are also members of society, but because society includes school boards and elected educational officials. Most people are willing to discuss how children ought to be brought up not simply because we share and store and communicate knowledge, but also because we interact collectively as an educational whole. It may be doubted that anyone who

says he is disinterested in education has really understood what education is.

Nonetheless, formal education, in a time of awakened public interest, suffers from a grave kind of neglect. Until quite recently our interest in education has largely been directed to crying present school
problems. Schools are bulging. School budgets can hardly be wrung
out of increasingly taxed homeowners. School and society collide on
the problems of legally required busing. School curricula face the fact
that there is twice as much for the student to learn but the length of
time for learning is still the same. Urban schoolchildren at nine die of
drug overdose. The Vietnamese war has placed the value—and the
values—of formal education in chronic doubt. Student unrest has
steadily filtered to the secondary school level and may go deeper. Far
from thinking that these pressing problems—and only a few have
been mentioned—should be pushed aside, we think that they should
occupy even larger parts of the public awareness. They are where the
action is. Nonetheless, man's view of his own nature is where the
thinking is. In the end, what men think human nature is underlies how
they handle educational problems.

Educational development and reform undertaken apart from the
questions of what it is that is being educated and why and whereto
and how is pointless. One is reminded by such shallow efforts at educational reform of the alchemists who searched for the "philosopher's
stone," which would change baser metals to gold on contact. The
alchemists hoped to change one kind of matter to another without
knowing what matter is. If we wish to reform the education of man,
we should ask, "What *is* man?" The answer is hard and even ultimately evasive, but we do not gain by postponing or shelving the question. Perhaps there is no immutable human essence—or precious little
that resists conditioning. B. F. Skinner, for example, seems to argue
this way. For him, "human engineering" (an offshoot of his pigeon
conditioning) reveals the human animal as infinitely plastic, moldable
by "reinforcement" into predetermined forms. So different a man as
Sartre would agree, but on the ground that if men are free then they
must be at center ambiguous—self-shaping. Or perhaps the phases of
human development follow well-defined norms that can hardly be advanced or exchanged with one another. Piaget seems to think this is
so. The question still remains behind all educational philosophy:
"What is man?"

PHILOSOPHERS AND PHILOSOPHIES

In a previous book,[2] the authors examined the thought of six leading philosophers whose philosophy includes in each case a more or less explicit philosophy of education. We chose these men—two classic figures, two from the Enlightenment, and two who lived through the first half of the twentieth century—because of their impact upon and their embodiment of philosophical convictions about man and his self-betterment in society. The book sprang from our teaching experience and, more particularly, from teaching seminars in the philosophy of education. Our conviction that these are the great philosophers of the Western tradition in philosophy of education remains unchanged. Yet there is much in current variegated educational theory and practice which does not trace directly to them. The complexity of modern issues leaves too many open spaces in the tough network of ideas gained from these six great philosophers. The reason is clear: avowed professional philosophers are not the only articulate source of philosophy of education. Somewhere between the massive sets of ideas that arise more or less unreflectively from society generally and explicit professional philosophies of education lies a large body of reasonably coherent convictions about human nature. Such convictions operatively have the force of philosophy of education. In addition, there are persistent ideas, not ascribable to individual thinkers, about human beings and their education in our culture which have received some impetus from (not necessarily first-line) philosophers. Often these ideas have been warmly received and carefully worked out by important thinkers who have not counted themselves as philosophers. And this is as it should be.

We have chosen to call these rich sources of significant thought about education *Philosophical Themes in Modern Education.* Whether or not philosophers, in the narrow sense of the term, are involved is then of secondary interest. What we will be examining will be prominent themes—on the basis either of their real importance or of the seriousness with which they are accepted, or both—as expounded by theologians, philosophers, psychologists—anyone who has given the ideas credence. Thus our present book presupposes and leads back to the discussion of aims and philosophies in *Philosophers on Education.*

Twentieth-century work in philosophy and in language analysis has exposed a little noticed yet obvious feature of discussions about education: there is a tendency for a theorist to take one example or situation as a "typical" case of what is under discussion—teaching, for example, or learning, or subject matter—and then to assume that all other cases can be explained by using this type case as a model. One amusing example of this effect was a debate between John Dewey and Robert Maynard Hutchins in the 1930's over "learning." All of Dewey's examples were taken from the kindergarten, all of Hutchins' from the graduate school. Each generalized from his own "typical case." Dewey treated the scholar as an overgrown kindergartener, while Hutchins treated the kindergartener as a sort of deprived potential scholar.

Commonly, however, it is not our special interest in some age group but rather some particular subject matter that leads us to prefer one model of "learning" over another. Learning the art of mathematical proof is very different from learning history by a study of artifacts and documents. And both of these have only a little in common with learning how to speak a foreign language or how to do carpentry or how to appreciate a painting. The differences are so marked that more is confused than is clarified by a wholesale extension of a single notion.

Our special interests tend to make us feel that certain kinds of learning are more "basic," "real," "natural," etc., than others. Suppose a high school has offices arranged so that divisions and departments are all located together: every teacher has a sort of home base and feels less and less at ease as he moves away from it. Our colleagues begin to talk about unfamiliar things, perhaps language tapes or potters' wheels or something called truth sets, each reflecting a slightly different technology and idea of learning. The debate between users of different models is likely to continue until we realize that its basis lies in our differences of competence and in our preferences for subject matter.

Underneath our preferences and our professional competence there is always an at least partly formed philosophy, a theory of reality. A "realistic" program for education reflects a commitment to what is genuinely "real." For example, classical atomic theory, from Democritus to Newton, holds that the world is best understood as a vast array of tiny bits of ultimate stuff in motion. These particles follow laws which cause them to act as regularly as does a machine, for example a clock. The universe is a vast mechanism. Nothing "really" exists but machines made up of material parts. To the extent that he believes what he says, the atomist will, of course, look at the student as a very complex machine, and it will seem clear to him that learning is best understood by analogies to a computer. On the other hand, someone who holds that nature as a whole behaves more as if she were a complex of living organisms, each with its own growth pattern and its own subjective search for satisfaction, will think of the learning process in a quite different way. Stephen Pepper discerns four distinct models that different philosophers take as type cases of "reality": the machine, the organism, the diagram, and the work of fine art.[3] This set of models (he calls them "root metaphors") exactly matches the set of four philosophic systems frequently recognized and sometimes labeled as Platonism (the world representable as diagram), Aristotelianism (the world conceived in terms of living organisms), atomism (the world explained as a mechanical system of elements), and process philosophy (the world considered as a work of art, with new qualities emerging as it advances).

However, what is crucial for this discussion is not so much these classifications in the abstract as the effect models and systems have in concrete educational attitudes and theories. We have already cited the contrasting notions of learning that result from taking mathematics as the exclusive model, as opposed to making the exclusive model history. As long as we assume that only one model and one framework must be the key to all theories and tactics, the result will be a contradiction. For example, the mathematician and the historian will be wholly unable to agree on the importance of a large library. On the other hand, once we are aware of the limitations of using any model by itself and treat alternatives as complementary, we find that each has certain advantages and proper uses of its own.

No matter what development of twentieth-century philosophy we follow, we find ourselves talking about this phenomenon of models, of conceptual frames, of alternative definitions when we try to relate philosophy and educational theory. An analytic philosopher, for example, will be interested in distinguishing the different meanings of such words as "teaching" and "education" in various contexts. An existentialist will probably be more interested in finding an exact description of the way it feels to "learn something," and the different sorts of very concrete experience this general term covers. A systematic philosopher —for example, a Platonist who admires Whitehead—will be more concerned with the logic of systems that transforms and relates conceptual frameworks. But all three should agree on the importance of what kind of model we look to if we are to have a sound insight into education.

The second part of this book emphasizes systematic views of human nature. The first part is a set of case studies of models, i.e. paradigms shaping educational thought and their development and conflict with one another from Greece into the modern era. The same basic models are still at work in contemporary educational thought and practice, but a number of classical assumptions have been discarded; as a result, modern theories of education are likely to be somewhat complex blends of older, more single-minded views.

When we have studied the four main paradigms in various historical settings, we will be ready to look at their occurrences and conflicts in the twentieth century. For reference, it may be useful to offer some further characterization of what these key models are. The idea of education as a matter of memory, with the learner a kind of center for "storage" and "retrieval" of information, is what Pepper would call taking the machine as key metaphor. The conceptual frame in which this idea fits most naturally is some version of the atomic theory, with elements acting on each other in tight causal chains—like the gear train of a clock. It seems that this mind-set works excellently for purposes of technology and for some kinds of natural science. But it doesn't do much justice to creativity, to aesthetic experience. If we take the work of fine art, rather than the clock, as model, we find ourselves emphasizing novelty, the bringing forth of novel potentialities. Here the aim of education is appreciation and exercise of creativity and originality. Inquiry will be stressed, rather than information. The conceptual background that goes naturally with *this* foreground model is that of modern process philosophy (Hartshorne, Weiss, Whitehead, et al.) or modern existentialism. If one looks for a classical anticipator of this approach, almost the only candidate is Socrates, with his persistent questioning and his refusal to offer or accept dogmatic answers.[4] Even so, that is only one facet of the historical Socrates—and there is no one else like him.

A third model that plays its part in philosophy and educational theory is biological or medical. It takes as its key metaphor the growth and behavior of individual organisms, specimens which by and large follow the same stages as they become mature. The art of medicine which takes this standpoint is clearly different either from the mechanic's craft (though Descartes wanted to reduce it to the latter) or from the artist's domain of emerging novelty and individuality. As thinkers oriented in this way, we are concerned with life cycles and life histories—of plants, animals, persons, perhaps stars—with the delicate balance of functions that makes life and adaptation possible. The conceptual scheme that is the natural framework for this type of thinking is the Aristotelian philosophy, with its explanations which work so elegantly in zoology extended to astronomy and poetry. The most interesting contribution here is probably the insistence that different skills and concepts come at different and predictable stages of "maturity" or "normal development"; that is where they belong, and it would be a mistake to try to hasten or retard them.

But the Aristotelian model, with its schemes for classifying specimens, does not adapt very well to the world of mathematics and pure formal logic. Aristotle did not like mathematics, and the brilliant mathematician Descartes found no virtues in Aristotle. The world of the equation and the diagram is a Platonist's domain. (Learning here consists in gaining insight into form and structure, and in many respects Descartes was a Platonist.) But it is not like the artist's free creation. The numbers and figures, spaces and fields of mathematics are not something we *create,* but an objective system which we *discover.* Learning is a personal, introspective affair: we may help the learner by suggesting a method of ordering ideas, but beyond that he must be motivated to try to "see" or recognize forms. The introspection is not subjective, nor does it deal with private feelings. It comes from personal effort directed toward objective logical truths. Clearly, classical Platonism is the conceptual system that best backs up this notion of the diagram as key metaphor.[5] Perhaps what is most surprising about this fourth model is how much it can leave out as accidental to "education." The student, given pencil and paper, can work by himself; he needs no distracting conversation, no experimentation with an external world, no creativity of a kind that goes beyond systematic logical discipline. Of course, particularly for questions of ethics, we assume that once someone has this pure insight, he will be able to step back into the concrete context of nature and society and easily apply it.

To sum up, then, we are going to be talking about four "root metaphors": the diagram, the organism, the work of art, and the machine. Each of these matches a conceptual system: Platonism, Aristotelianism, process, and atomic mechanism, respectively. Each leads to a different set of suggestions for things to do, criteria of success, and things to notice when we are teaching.

The foregoing is itself a somewhat abstract account. Here are four examples, each following a particular kind of paradigm, of ways of "learning" something.

FOUR KINDS OF LEARNING

LEARNING AS RECOGNITION OF FORM

Suppose we try to prove that "the difference between a number written normally and the same number with its digits reversed is always a multiple of nine." [6] Now, what you do here is to look for an insight that gives a formal and necessary relation. There is no need to go to the library. Pencil and paper are a help but not a necessity. Group conversation, activity, and division into committees are beside the point. If the solution of this sort of problem is a paradigm of learning, as it apparently was for Plato and St. Augustine and Descartes, then the key is learning a proper form of thought.

LEARNING AS STORAGE AND RETRIEVAL OF INFORMATION

Suppose, on the other hand, that you are in the museum at Mesa Verde, Colorado, in front of the case of unidentified artifacts labeled "What are they?" You are allowed to take them back to school or college with you. What do you do now? Well, the first thing, of course, is to handle the things and look at them. One is a hollowed bone with a notch in the side. You blow it and get a rather weak, high-pitched whistling sound. Not a very good whistle, but it could be one. You look at the notch carefully to see if it might be an accidental break, rather than a deliberate cut; no, the edges are sharp and straight. There is a small hole bored in the other end, suggesting that it was carried on a string. Now it is time to put your mind to work. Were there other whistles definitely identified in the museum? Do Southwestern Indians today use them for ritual, musical, or signaling purposes? How much historical identity can we establish between pre-Columbian and post-Columbian Indians in this region? Did the Mesa Verde Indians use thongs or string to carry small tools or ornaments around? Were there, perhaps, different roles in the ritual that required different sound effects? Each one of these questions is a result of your relating the information you have to the problem at hand—and *here* you will find yourself really grateful for that half-forgotten course in locating information in the library. Obviously, the more you "know" and "learn," the better your solution of this problem will be.

This type of learning is quite different from the first one. In mathematics, to test the theorem which is to be proven for all cases, experiments until doomsday are inadequate and irrelevant; you have to *see* the proof. This second view of learning as probable reasoning about presented facts is the model case that underlies the theory of teaching emphasized in the Greek Sophists and John Locke.

LEARNING AS HABIT AND EXPERIENCE

Now take another problem. Suppose you are in a school that has just set aside a large plot of land for a school garden. The students need to work in groups. You need to allocate space, locate crops, design experiments, and arrange a roster for needed work, as Russian children do. Here it is very doubtful if either pure reason or pure reference library reading will solve the problem. What is needed is some plan that will be operable and, more important, self-correcting, so that you learn as you go along. Evidently, this sort of organizing and planning viewed as a kind of learning will be very different in feeling and operation from either the pure formal type or the mastery-of-information sort. There are critics who claim that this sort of experience ought not to count as learning at all. Others think it is the typical pattern of all learning. Both views are extreme; it is one of the ways in which students (and adults) learn. One of the major aims of our contemporary high school education, of course, is to teach students to become effective democratic citizens by learning of just this sort. Directing attention to this kind of learning was one of the major contributions of American pragmatism in its application to educational theory. We might call this learning by direct experience as opposed to learning by indirect experience.

LEARNING AS AESTHETIC INSIGHT

Consider still a fourth kind of learning situation. There is a form of Japanese poetry, the haiku, which aims at a maximum aesthetic impact within a length of seventeen syllables. Here is a classical example:

> On a bare branch
> A solitary crow
> Evening in autumn
>
> —BASHŌ

Basho painted a picture to go with this poem: the autumn evening spreads out, orange and unbroken, in the background; in the foreground the lonely crow is huddled on his branch, very black and very small. Now, do you learn anything from reading the poem and visualizing the image it presents? One of us once asked a senior seminar in zoology whether this verse had taught them anything about crows. Sixteen said no, two said yes. Perhaps it was a poor question; but we think most of us would agree that one learns something from an aesthetic image or experience; the dissenters are either wholly insensitive or unskilled in using language correctly. Learning through this kind of aesthetic insight can also be taken as the best example of what education ought to try for in its techniques. The methods and materials will differ in very important ways between this fourth model and the other three. We can't afford to ignore the importance of engagement and individual authenticity on the part of the student. Such engagement is more like aesthetic awareness than mastery of method, material, or practical organization.

The interplay of these diverse models of learning with differential emphasis on objectives (some examples of which we explored in *Philosophers on Education*) and with the different techniques teachers have devised—diagram, dialogue, textbook, lecture, laboratory, workbook, and so on—is a key to the complex historical discussion of organization, form, and material in education.

We turn now to prime examples of how the use of paradigmatic models for the ideas of teaching and learning have both clarified our understanding of education and created problems for it.

FORM, EXPERIENCE, AND SOME PHILOSOPHERS

As an example of the identification of education with information, we will discuss Hippias, one of a group of philosophers who were the first professional educators in Western civilization. They mark a phase in the appearance of urban society, the release of some of the father's tutelage of his sons to professionals who claimed excellence in the training of the young. Hippias, by his own account, knew everything and gave a course in memorizing.

For the complementary view of education as knowledge of form—that is, knowledge of the essences and inner workings of things, both of the self and of the world, rather than a possession of a kind of world book of facts—we turn to St. Augustine. Augustine's philosophy is a fusion of respect for the total inwardness of the soul and its search for God, with the beauty and structure of the world which He had created.

Between St. Augustine and Descartes there was a return to Aristotelian principles, this time blended with Christian doctrine for all things spiritual. The result is St. Thomas' monumental *Summa Theologica,* a work of the thirteenth century. On the secular side this work follows Aristotle rather closely, emphasizing habit in ethical education and observation in science—that is, discovery of principles from experience as opposed to forcing experience to conform to rational conviction. But the very comprehensiveness of St. Thomas' Aristotelianism, with the answers to all questions laid out carefully, and the reasons given, led in time to complacent and dogmatic authoritarianism. By the time of Descartes, in the seventeenth century, the Aristotelianism of the schools was largely dead, repetitious, and formulaic. Secular challenge to it amounted to heresy, since it had been welded to an elaborate Christian theology that the Church had forged over centuries of doctrinal struggle and did not propose to submit to further critique. The attack upon Galileo was a case in point; everyone "knew" that the planets moved in crystal spheres, with the earth at the world's center, heaven at its perimeter, and hell beneath the ground. The terminology of this science was used to evade substantive answers to scientific questions. In a sense scholasticism had succeeded too well. The schools, possessing the only common language in Europe—Latin—and the only international authority—Christianity—almost had authoritarianism thrust upon them. *Someone* had to represent order. *Something* had to be consultable for the right answers. The very comprehensiveness of the *Summa Theologica* precluded answers from another authority, another source.

A revolutionary resurgence of formalism, usually taken by historians as the birth of modern philosophy, appeared in the work of René Descartes. Descartes set about a project that was nothing less than a complete reeducation of the West: Aristotelian scholasticism was to be replaced by a return toward the Augustinian psychology of inwardness and introspection, coupled with an acceptance of the new mathematical, materialistic physics of Copernicus, Kepler, and Galileo. Descartes' work rested finally upon a "new method" which he had "discovered" and applied with unsurpassed success in mathematics. Roughly, it was the systematic discovery of inescapable basic truths, placed together in a logical framework and elaborated into conclusions which are absolutely certain. The emphasis was on what the mind must think, not on the richness of experience. The method was, at bottom, formal: that of Euclid's geometrical reasoning. The mastery of the mathematical method would, it seemed to Descartes, create and extend a new science and a new philosophy. Reasonably enough, the Aristotelian faculty of the Sorbonne failed to share the young mathematician's enthusiasm for popular and total demolition of their position. Descartes left the modern world a heritage of ideas which by now are no longer controversial new theses. The most important of these are the common sense distinction between mind and body and the less obvious notion of matter as mere propertyless "extension." His method—which required sharp distinctions—created insoluble problems, so long as the sharpness of the distinctions was retained. His project—of reeducating Europe— succeeded remarkably well in advancing the new science of Copernicus and Galileo and in discrediting the fossilized Aristotelianism of his philosophic contemporaries.

By the end of the seventeenth century, however, observation and experience, as opposed to dominantly logical reflection, had found a new champion in the person of the English philosopher, John Locke, by training a doctor of medicine and by temperament far more an Aristotelian than a Platonist. Locke's *Two Essays on Civil Government* influenced the development of the American democracy more than any other single source. They were required reading at Harvard when John Hancock, John Quincy Adams, and Samuel Adams were there; ideas and even phrases from the writings of Locke play a prominent part in the Declaration of Independence and the Constitution. Locke wrote two other works, one technical and one popular, that had as strong an impact on the theory of knowledge and learning as did his political works on political theory.

Locke's *Of Education* hit his readers with the combined impact of

Emily Post, Benjamin Spock, and John Dewey. And in the background, for admirers interested in the more theoretical foundation of
his views, was the monumental *An Essay Concerning Human Understanding*. The *Essay* profoundly influenced subsequent philosophy,
psychology, and education. It set the tone of the British empiricist tradition. Locke's work may be fairly regarded as a foundation block, if
not the cornerstone, of associationist phychology. For our comparison
of philosophies of education the most important aspect of Locke's psychology of understanding is his initial assumption that knowledge consists of activities—operations of synthesis, analysis, and comparison of
ideas generated in our minds by things outside those minds. With Descartes, Locke distinguishes between "primary" and "secondary" qualities in things. Primary qualities are the properties of extension, shape,
resistance, and motion. These have so great a stability and invariance
among different observers that they may be properly taken as "objective" qualities of things. Secondary qualities are more variable: color,
flavor, and so on, are "subjective" properties projected by the human
observer whose senses have been stimulated by emanations of "imper-
ceptible bodies" from objects. Hence ideas of secondary qualities are
not good facsimiles of the things. They do not resemble the external
things that gave rise to them.

So far, this might seem very Aristotelian; but in his very first chapters Locke diverges from the Aristotelian tradition at a crucial point.
For Aristotle and St. Thomas the inmost natures of things can be discovered by the joint use of perception and reason. Thus knowledge of
the external world is possible. But for Locke, as he pursues his line of
thinking, these inmost natures—"essences"—seem to escape us. Our
knowledge is confined to our ideas and these are confined to our
mind. At his most skeptical Locke confesses that every external object
is, at bottom, "an *x*, I know not what."

With skepticism about the external world comes skepticism about
language. Thinkers in the classical tradition, including St. Augustine,
regarded the proper use of language as embodying the meanings that
are found in nature. But Locke, with his acute awareness of the limitations of human knowledge did not: if there are real essences they remain unknown. Human knowledge is limited to nominal essences, to
the *names* of clusters of characteristics. An apple is sweet, seeded, round
ish, red, etc. But meanings—like that of "apple"—are substantially
subject to human decision. Each of the above characteristics is altera-
ble in apples. Plenty of them are not sweet, some freakishly appear
without seeds, and so on. How many of these properties can an apple
be without? This is a matter of useful convention. Is the haw of the
hawthorne an apple? Is a willow a tree or a bush?

An example that illustrates his point is the platypus, discovered and classified a century after Locke published the *Essay*. Is the platypus a mammal? It has an incompletely four-chambered heart. It bears fur but has a duck-like beak. Its brain resembles a reptilian brain in some respects more than the usual mammalian brain. Like reptiles and birds it lays eggs. It suckles its young, like mammals, but its milk ducts are not gathered into localized breasts or udders surmounted by teats. Shall we make it a separate class of animals resembling mammals or a special subclass of mammals? The latter decision was chosen, and the "monotremes," including a relative of the platypus called the echidna, were created. "Created" is not too strong a term. Nature's boundaries are blurred, as in trees and bushes. Definitions are human and a matter of language. Meanings are imposed by men. At most nature provides clues.

This was the rising philosophical spirit in Europe, an emphasis at once on the inherent limitations of reason and understanding and on the sense of the opportunities for expanding knowledge through patient observation, classification, and the finding of useful principles of order. For Locke there are no "innate" ideas; these—or the raw materials for them—we acquire from our experience. The richness of experience, the amount of information we possess—this determines the wealth of our knowledge and incidentally keeps our admittedly human decisions from being whimsical or arbitrary. In greatly simplified terms, the eighteenth century was a century of freedom: freedom from the authority of church, monarch, and formal reason. The monarch was no substitute for the rights of men, the church no substitute for conscience, and reason no substitute for experience. All of these views Locke held.

The implications for education of the new model of learning are evident. First, the mind must be filled with appropriate ideas, gained through sense experience; then it must learn which combinations of ideas constitute the meanings of the words we use. Complex ideas can be clarified and understood by breaking them down into their simple components, and much of Locke's *Essay* undertakes this analytic work. It would seem that, in principle, the most complex processes of thought can be explained as many repetitions of simple operations with elementary ideas which are conjoined, contrasted, compared, etc. And from this tradition, clearly, the notions of a well-stocked mind and the need to "cover the material" as an educational ideal follow.

One important theme that runs through our study is the relation of theory and practice, of the true and the useful. Correlated with this is the question of the importance of firsthand experience as a way of giving meaning to abstract concepts and patterns of order. From the

Greek Sophists through the medieval scholastics, there were groups of
thinkers who thought that education should include some knowledge
of the arts and crafts and that contact with things should supplement
the learning of names. But the general common-sense view separated
practical and theoretical knowledge quite sharply, taking the theoretical to be a sort of spectator's vision of the truth—objective, self-satisfy-
ing, and if not opposed to, at least very different from, the view of the
world as a theater of action. On the other hand, it was often assumed
that someone who was thoroughly trained in theory and the theoretical approach would automatically be able to transfer his insights and
methods, and would be more effective than someone who was not so
trained on the level of the practical. (This is the nonmalicious idea behind Shaw's famous crack: "Those who can, do; those who can't,
teach.") This way of thinking, of course, set the school apart from
everyday life in society and restricted the notion of "education" to the
training in theory that went on in the school. Descartes and Locke
each contributed something to the modification of this scheme. Descartes was tremendously excited by the mastery of nature that applied
science offered and by the possibility of new discoveries through experiment with special apparatus. Locke was convinced that the content of
education should ultimately be measured by the criterion of its usefulness for an English gentleman, and on this basis he even suggested
courses in accounting, for example, as a desirable part of the curriculum.

In Part One we shall be showing the strengths and weaknesses of
four approaches to what constitutes knowledge and accordingly four
views of the nature of the learning process. The positive case for each
constitutes an ideal that we do in point of fact pursue. But none is adequate by itself; none is universal. No more does any philosopher or
theoretician of ideas attempt to make it so. Each defines a process and
a result that we must include in any educational system. Without such
understanding, no one is in a position to think about a total curriculum nor to judge and use the technology which has already begun to
appear in every level of teaching technique.

THE IDEA OF DEVELOPMENT

A further new twentieth-century conception in psychology and philosophy has had implications for educational theory at least as important
as our new self-consciousness about language and method. This is the
idea of *developmental process* as it appears in both science and cosmology. The "process" scheme of concepts is the one that forms a nat-

ural background to the foreground model of "reality" as being like the creation of a work of art. The idea that our universe might be a field of process, with new species and qualities constantly being created and with an open future, was first scientifically accepted as Darwin presented it in *The Origin of Species* and *The Descent of Man*. But outside biology, scientists and philosophers were for the most part not interested in using the developmental metaphor on a grand scale. Its lack of closure seemed aesthetically unsatisfying; its lack of a final set of fixed species and types seemed to make scientific classification arbitrary; its open future seemed to make the value of past experience or history problematic for treating new situations. Even Hegel, in the nineteenth century, thought that a divine mind would see a dialectical pattern in history, though a human one could only confront process. But the scientific theory of evolution, a new tempo of life thanks to a new speeded-up technology, and a new aesthetic sense not at odds with open form combined to make the process conceptual scheme attractive. And the work of many philosophers since 1900, particularly A. N. Whitehead and his admirers, has shown how one can build a systematic "process philosophy."

The implications of process philosophy are no less startling for educational theory and design than for aesthetics and zoology. For planners and theoreticians until the present century it had seemed reasonable to identify the way a finished product was structured with the stages of process by which it had come to be. To understand the stages of growth or learning, if that were so, would require only a conceptual analysis of a "mature" adult or a deductive system of geometry. But a logical and temporal sequence may not be the same; this possibility is particularly clearly illustrated by considering two approaches to a work of fine art. The critic works with objects already finished: he can show that the opening image of a net in the *Agamemnon* is necessary to anticipate the later choral odes on the web of Fate. He *cannot* show when that image occurred to Aeschylus as he was designing the play; that creation has another sequence of its own. In fact, it may be that the image of the net suggested itself at the very end of the author's thought. In the same way, the classical theorist would study "human excellence," moral and intellectual, by examining adult type specimens and then treating a maturing child as a deprived approximation who may take on items of "form" in some logical order.

In other contexts, as well as the aesthetic or ethical, it is easy to equate the structure of something complete with the stages of its emergence or construction. The teacher does this when he or she pictures learning as something that can be measured and evaluated after it has been completed by various testing techniques. The mathematician does the same thing when he assumes that the ideas *he* finds "simplest" (perhaps "set"?) are those which should be taught first to the beginning student.

In a universe where all development is programed in advance, equating temporal and logical sequence seems reasonable. But in a world of process where there is more freedom, creativity, and eccentricity, the only way to find out how things come about in time is to observe them; there is no easy a priori substitute. This puts a new stress on psychology and physiology as disciplines to which the educator must turn.

Not only does the new emphasis on process lead us to turn to empirical work in psychology and physiology for an understanding of the way a person learns, matures, and so on; it is accompanied by a new psychological theory which requires the turn to be made in a nonclassical way. Roughly until Freud (there were a few exceptions), it was assumed that each individual was completely conscious of his ideas, feelings, and motives. This assumption comes naturally, and it is probably very fortunate for psychology in the West that it was not questioned earlier. But the inconsistencies of behavior and introspection required a new theory in which *unconscious* desires and processes played a major part. No longer could a Descartes, asking the question "What am I?" jauntily answer, "A substance the essence of which is thought." Beneath the conscious rationalizations and rationalities may lie deep attitudes directing attention and behavior: roles that I feel I should play, likes and dislikes for my teachers and peers, a developing erotic maturity, repressed drives to satisfy all possible appetites at the same time. And all of this must be taken into account by education, in one way or another. The old paradigms remain, but now the older conceptual analyses are supplemented by studies of development that add a further dimension, so that the role of the standard models is no longer so easily identified.

Of course, one thing that can be done, given the fact that in any case introspective reports must be checked and interpreted by an outside therapist or theorist, is to discount them altogether. From the standpoint of educational technology, conceived as externally observable modification of behavior, this is the only sensible move. It matches exactly the basic model of the mechanism which has been one of the persistent key approaches in Western thought. This is the line that B. F. Skinner has taken.

Most of us are too tender minded to agree with Skinner. We are fascinated by the technological power of his operant conditioning and programing techniques; but we want some attention to the inner feelings of insight, effort, and closure that differentiate "learning" from sheer unconscious "conditioning" or "training." And so we move to an opposite extreme and wonder how Skinner's work relates to the ideas of Neill. Offhand, one might think that it does not relate at all: neither author has more than a few passing remarks about the other. Such a lack of communication is, however, a familiar one between theorists using "mechanist" and those using "creative art" paradigms. Neill is concerned with the development of subjective authenticity; with individual self-creation, an unfolding not channeled and hampered by a neurotic society. The last thing he wants to see is a "social-engineering" type of external modification of behavior. We have too much of that already, he is sure, and only by sensitivity, respect for individuality, and relaxation of pressure can we avoid being crushed by it. His school's children will learn when they are ready: but the readiness is a state of mind, not a stage in biological-psychological development. (Maybe when they are ready some of Skinner's programs can play a minor role in teaching them.) It is worth noticing that when Skinner is reporting his most interesting work his writing is entirely objective and technical; Neill at his most interesting becomes anecdotal and autobiographical. The latter reminds one of St. Augustine in his *Confessions,* the former of Descartes at work proving that animals are mere machines.

The paradigm of the organism, with its life cycle and stages of growth, seems to match the work of Jean Piaget. His careful accounts of concept formation, with stages coming at roughly the same levels of accumulated experience and physical maturity, remind one of Aristotle in his *Parva Naturalia* or Locke in *Some Thoughts Concerning Education.* And although Piaget tests all guesses and patterns by experiment, he still holds an Aristotelian (or a Lockean or a medical) belief that a logical analysis of concepts sheds some light on the age at which a young human being can form them. An interesting contrast with Skinner here is the difference between a "concept" for Piaget and an "item" of input for Skinner. The concept requires an organism to construct it by various "operations"—the concept of time, for example, is much more than a conditioned reflex to certain positions of a hand on the clock.

Piaget's work brings out two things that are not so clear if one uses other paradigms: the first, that there is a correlation of "readiness" to form concepts—of "morality," "number," "time," whatever—and biological maturity; the second, that there is a stage when a concept is clear and functions well in a *simple* context but gets mixed up or lost in a complex one. Ordinarily we would assume that a child either has or does not have, say, a concept of "greater than" or "older than." This, however, is not the case. In the course of his work Piaget introduces some interesting classifications of complex concepts into their components and some interesting experiments to see whether the concept can be applied in a concrete situation requiring action and decision.

The pure Platonic formalist model, with number line and diagram, finds its admirers primarily in the field of mathematics; the School Mathematics Study Group materials are an excellent example. But Freud is also close to an Augustinian version of Platonism, in which education becomes a kind of therapy and self-knowledge a way to self-realization. However, with Freud, the Platonic forms in their ethical role appear as subjective, internalized standards which we feel we ought to respect. Too much of a gap between our performance and our notion of the way we ought to perform leads to neurosis, in his view. The role of insight and inquiry, which is another strand of the Platonic heritage, is picked up by Bruner in his work with cognitive studies; the place that roles and attitudes play is developed further by Erikson.

The need now is for educational theorists and practitioners who appreciate this contemporary work to select the perspective from it that is most relevant to the problems and aims at hand.

NOTES

1. The "Wild Boy of Aveyron," found at about age nine or ten, learned a handful of naming words under the diligent, loving guidance of Père Itard. See Jean-Marc G. Itard, *The Wild Boy of Aveyron*, trans. G. and M. Humphrey, New York, 1962.

2. *Philosophers on Education: Six Essays on the Foundations of Western Thought*, Boston, 1963.

3. Stephen Coburn Pepper, *World Hypotheses*, Berkeley, Calif., 1942. The map of four alternative conceptual systems was explored in N. P. Stallknecht and R. S. Brumbaugh, *The Compass of Philosophy*, New York, 1952. A final set of transformation rules making these frameworks mutually intelligible has been suggested by R. S. Brumbaugh, "Cosmography," *Review of Metaphysics* XXV (1971): 337–347. For the role that the concept of paradigms has played in the recent history and philosophy of natural science, see Carl Kordig. *The Justification of Scientific Change*, Dordrecht, Holland, 1971. It is interesting to note that, whereas in the natural sciences one preferred model succeeds another, in philosophy all four systems tend to persist and find defenders in every period, though of course style and dominant emphasis change.

4. But this generalization must be qualified by noting that the process conceptual schemes had occupied a subordinate role—among philosophers and pedagogues, if not among mystics and artists—from the invention of philosophy right down to their sudden dominance in the twentieth century.

5. Classical Platonism rather than modern, because some modern Platonists ac-

cept this account for structures but not for value questions. Plato, on the other hand, was convinced that by inquiry one could come to ethical insights—for instance, that property is less important than justice for human excellence—with the same certainty that one could see the theorem of Pythagoras work out in geometry.

6. The clue is, of course, that with our positional notation a number with digits ab represents $10a$ plus $1b$, so that its reverse . . .

1

Knowledge as Skill and
Used Information: Hippias

In the fifth century B.C. there occurred a revolution in the conception of education which signaled a major shift in cultural and political history. Education traditionally had been a conditioning to conformity, not for the sake of stifling individuality but for the sake of conserving time-tested values. Respect for family, for one's people, and for the gods all entailed memorial observances and behavior whose form and meaning had to be learned from one's elders. Education has always been a means of conserving time-tested values so that humanity will not have to recapitulate its past experience in complete detail for each new child. In each generation the great questions are: "How much novelty will the old beliefs stand?" and "What traditional values are still good for us?" [1] But two new conceptions of education appeared in fifth-century Greece: (1) education as acquiring skill and storing information—as know-how and facts; (2) education as "liberal"—learning how to generalize and how to apply generalizations to individual decisions and judgments.

Much of what we call intelligence is rooted in the conflict of the old education with these new ideas. Various factors in this conflict still typify the Western mind more than the Eastern one: (1) a notion of individual identity rather than a collective role in the society; (2) the written word, making it possible to capture, hold, and abstract ideas in a way that the heroic stories of the early oral tradition did not do; (3) a sudden change in social conditions making traditional education badly out of date. It was by no means inevitable that the idea of education as intellectual development would win out in fifth-century Greece, but it did. It *was* perhaps inevitable that the expectations would be exaggerated and that a course would be set which later history was to prove too optimistic. The limitations of the method of observation/generalization/application would appear in the future. The contest of the old and the new was not yet a clear collision of the models or paradigms we discussed in the introduction to Part One, but it did create problems and questions.

The central issue is very much with us today. Should we reconsider the inclusion of "vocational" work in our secondary schools? Should we insist on a certain amount of rote memorization of information as part of our curricular material? Skills, memorization, and the like require little social interaction. At the level of theory, should we agree with Skinner that education is a branch of human engineering, most effective when one can program operant conditioning, say with a Skinner box as mechanical tutor? And should that program vary, depending on the skills needed by society at a given time? Or is Neill right in his insistence that human freedom and dignity develop only when the individual is protected from the pressures to conform imposed not only by a specially designed conditioning machine but also by ordinary modern society?

The same questions confronted the ancient Athenian who was interested in education. When he looked about him for "wise men" who might advise him or teach his sons, he found two different models: one, the brilliant Sophist, Hippias of Elis; the other, Socrates the Athenian. The reason we know as much as we do about Hippias is that as often as not he, not Socrates, was taken to be the ideal "intellectual." This so outraged Socrates' admirer Plato and his Academy that they composed two dialogues between Socrates and Hippias—imaginary conversations, a confrontation of two ideals—aimed at setting straight the balance as they saw it.[2] It is admittedly a hostile portrait, but the characterization brings out quite nicely the claims that can be urged for "intellectual insight" as against "reception and recall of information" or "training."

It may be useful to provide a little historical background at this point for these problems. In fifth-century Athens a sudden cultural change—a result of an expanding empire, expanding trade, flourishing fine arts, experiments in democracy—had left the traditional "education" far behind. That tradition was based on the oral transmission of culture as recorded in the poetry of Homer: it had no room for individuality as against the Homeric hero who did not see himself as apart from his society, and its values were those of a warlike feudal age, not well suited to an urban civilization. The Sophists—"wise men"—professional teachers, appeared on the scene, offering instruction in skills that would lead to individual success. These skills were, roughly, public speaking, legal case pleading, and cultural information.[3] The emphasis had swung to extreme individualism, with the argument that what was "natural" was for everyone to put his selfish interest ahead of everything else; social restraints were "conventions." Socrates changed the main course of Greek thought when he realized that, for all of their talk about self-interest, or self-realization, neither the Sophists nor anyone else had discovered the nature of a human "self." Whatever such a self was, he thought, it seemed to be responsible for its choices, to be able to reason, to use intelligence, and to be happy when it chose wisely. In that case, the cultivation of "mind" was obviously the main target for education, whether through study of mathematics, ethics, or astronomy, for mind could grasp the general patterns—"forms"—that contribute to our self-realization and make possible choosing what we really want.

Hippias was, like his fellow Sophists, a traveling teacher of literature, public speaking, and law. These were the skills a young man in this period needed to get ahead; and success, measured in prestige and wealth, was the explicit objective of this basic education. Beyond this, however, Hippias claimed that he himself knew everything. To prove the point, he starred in his own Olympic Games Quiz Program. He invited the audience to ask him any questions they wanted to, and he never failed to have the answer. He gave great public lectures on fields ranging from literary criticism to astronomy and evidently made his material clear and entertaining, for he "made as large a fortune as any other two Sophists together." The history of education is probably indebted to Hippias for the invention of the book of reference, ancestor to our almanac, encyclopedia, and handbooks of chemistry and physics.[4] In addition to these excellences, he was interested and skilled in handicrafts: at one of his appearances at Olympia he wore clothing and jewelry he had made for himself.[5] No wonder his contemporaries were dazzled.

But how far can "intelligence" be identified with conditioned skill in crafts or with training in the storage and retrieval of individual items of fact? (Today we would ask the same question, but instead of individual items of fact, we would work with "bits" of information.) The answer is not entirely clear; it seems to depend on some previous question that "intelligence" is needed to resolve. For questions of fact —say, the date and birthplace of Cardinal Bessarion—clearly the best prescription is to "look it up in the encyclopedia." For other questions, it seems equally clear that reference books are largely irrelevant. Such questions as "What is a human self?" or "What is ethical excellence?" seem to be of this type. Here reference books can offer only a catalogue of opinions or definitions of words.

How much virtue there is in reference books—or in monumental reference libraries—is still a point where humanists are sharply divided. Some think that the development of the library of Alexandria was one of the all-time great advances in educational technology. Oth-

ers think it introduced a new notion of "scholarship" that was an intellectual disaster. But in the Academy, in this early stage of optimistic
intellectualism, there was no division of opinion. They thought Hippias wrong about everything: the aims of education, the value of sheer
information, the notion that ethics could be taught by memorized
rules—and his notion that he was the wisest man of his day!

"Hail, handsome Hippias . . ." begins the *Hippias Major,* as Socrates greets Hippias in the Athenian Agora and prepares to ask him
about the nature of handsomeness and beauty.[6] Hippias relates to Socrates his own successes and achievements, including his feats of intellectual athleticism at Olympia, and adds that his city keeps entrusting
him with diplomatic missions because he is so wise. But, Socrates
asks, will Hippias answer some questions that perplex him about the
nature of the beautiful; not make a speech about it? Hippias would
prefer to lecture, but agrees. Well, then, what is beauty? Gold! says
Hippias; gold is beautiful. Socrates doubts this identification of beauty
with gold; wouldn't any man think a human mistress more beautiful
than a golden one? Hippias agrees. So, gold is not the same as or the
cause of beauty, Socrates goes on. After a tedious set of examples—
which Hippias unsuccessfully tries to turn into a solo lecture on
aesthetics—Hippias gets the point. Well, look at it another way. Take
a kitchen spoon. Isn't a spoon beautiful when it is perfectly designed
to perform its function? Yes, Hippias agrees to that. And a horse is a
beautiful horse when he is built for speed and durability, which are
the horse's function? Yes, Hippias agrees. In general, Hippias, Socrates
now asks, what conclusion shall we draw about the relation of beauty
to functional form? "I haven't a clue," Hippias replies, and the discussion ends.[7]

The main point is obviously the unsuitability of Hippias' methods
and ideas as patterns of inquiry; he is unable to generalize, as opposed
to listing particular items—his initial identification of beauty with
gold is a case in point. In spots the *Hippias Major* is tedious reading,
and many critics doubt that Plato himself would have written anything so pedestrian. But the author, whoever he was, must have had
some historical basis for this exasperated portrait of an animated encyclopedia, and even Plato might have done it in a mood of sufficient irritation.

Now suppose that Hippias were given a chance to reply to this sat-
ire. What would he have said in a criticism of Socrates? First off, he
would no doubt point out the futility of the "Socratic method" of inquiry as an educational technique. If no one knows the answer to a
question, what good does further speculation do? In the absence of an
authority, the right answer wouldn't be recognized even if it were

stumbled upon.[8] Discussion may be good for provoking interest, but it is not the way to get precise answers. Yes, we may imagine Socrates to rejoin, this is true of *some* questions—precisely the kind Hippias answers in his performances. But *other* questions, particularly those involving planning and evaluating, or causal explanation, can't be "answered" in this way. For example, can the nature of human excellence be found by consulting books of facts? Hippias would think it can. But isn't what one gets a list of examples, rather than the essence of human excellence which the examples share?

This notion of a textbook definition of "excellence" is the basic idea under attack in the Academy's second portrait of Hippias in action, the *Hippias Minor*. Hippias has been discussing Homer as a guide to right action. A young Greek will find three models in the Homeric epics: Achilles is the bravest of the Greeks, Nestor the wisest, and Odysseus the "shrewdest." [9] In response to Socrates' question—Which is best?—Hippias chooses Achilles. Why? Because Odysseus is a liar. (Nestor is left out in the following conversation.) Hippias is representing three ideas which come under Academic attack. First, rather conventionally, he assumes that the conduct of a hero of the Mycenaean Age is still a possible model for a young urban Athenian. Second, he assumes that ethics is best taught by literature. Third, he seems to believe (this is shown in his reason for preferring Achilles) that right and wrong actions can be determined by concrete situational directions, so that a memorized list of these will be a guide to moral behavior.[10] "Never lie!," "Don't sing in the street!," and so on, would constitute such a set of rules for conduct. Now, it seemed clear to Socrates that "values" or "standards of excellence," whatever they might be, were not specific physical things or situations nor were they, strictly, even wholly embodied in such particular cases. A sign of this, he thought, was that there are exceptional cases in which *any* rigid situational rule goes counter to what a good person ought to do. "Never tell an untruth" is a case in point; until we see why not, it lacks ethical content; once we do see the rationale behind the rule, we recognize that there are cases where we ought not to apply it. (Actually, Hippias' implied rule makes a stronger claim than our English translation shows, for the Greek word for "lie"—*pseudos*—applies to any statement that is not literally true: popularized science, dreams, myths, and so on.[11])

Socrates promptly sets a lively logical puzzle in motion by disagreeing with Hippias; he claims that the man who lies deliberately is better than the one who lies involuntarily. Achilles tells lies too, Socrates points out. Yes, but not deliberately, counters Hippias; when he says something in the heat of passion this is very different from the calculated prevarications of Odysseus. Now, in saying that a deliberate liar

is a better man than an inadvertent one, Socrates is at the same time
telling a deliberate lie and proving himself a better man in debate
than Hippias. But in Hippias' sense of the word "better"—of excellence as compounded of conformity and power or skill—the statement
holds, and Hippias finds that he has lied involuntarily in his initial
description of the three Homeric heroes.[12] Again the conversation is
complicated by Hippias' difficulty in following an inductive generalization. The thrust is perfectly clear to the reader, long before Hippias
feels it. If to be good is to be able to do something well, and to be bad
is to be unable to do it, then only an expert can deliberately give a
poor performance; the nonexpert is poor involuntarily. This works for
running, calculation, lyre playing, and so on; finally, by generalization,
Socrates suggests that it holds for justice as well. Only a good man
could be wicked deliberately, so the deliberately unjust person is "better" than the inadvertent one.

The interesting thing about Socrates' half-playful "lie" is that his argument with Hippias appears to be an instance in which the lie is
true; Socrates, comparing himself to Odysseus, comes out ahead of
Hippias, who emulates Achilles. We find this result already anticipated in the opening speeches when Hippias and Socrates both agree
that Hippias is wise: the falsehood is involuntary on Hippias' part,
ironic in Socrates' agreement.

Underneath the clumsy banter (which here again is so clumsy that
many refuse to attribute the dialogue to Plato), there is a solid body of
Socratic conviction about what genuine knowledge is: (1) Mere facts
lack the power to guide action and thus cannot pass for knowledge.
The world is full of facts. Some facts are more valuable than others. It
is as having values that they sponsor or provoke action. After all, the
form of all forms is called "The Good" in *The Republic* and "The
Beautiful" in *The Symposium*. These are value terms and are two different names for the ultimate lure for *both* knowledge and action. (2)
Even "knowledge" embodied in action, e.g. in a skill or craft, is not necessarily knowledge, though it may be admirable. (3) Even abstract reasoning or the gift of a fine memory similarly may not be knowledge,
though they are admirable. (4) Genuine knowledge cannot be divorced from the subject of what is best for man, and therefore how a
man ought to live.

The *Hippias Minor* is an implied critique of the equation of goodness with success. It turns out that factual knowledge, conformity to
convention, and technical skill and prowess are ethically neutral. They
have little to do with personal worth, and what good is knowledge
that contributes little or nothing to personal enrichment? It seems,
then, that there must be other meanings and criteria proper to a dis-

cussion of human excellence. Hippias himself might have trouble in following a discussion of them, but some of his colleagues also wanted to know what these other criteria are.[13]

The question of criteria is a tantalizing one. It seems quite clear that a computer will be morally indifferent to the figures fed into it: it will be equally good in finding maximum casualties from fallout and maximum effectiveness for an antityphoid world health program. It does not make it clear, however, whether one is "good" and the other "bad." For one thing, if we believe the Sophists, every culture seems to attach its own definitions to words such as "good" and "bad," and each individual apparently chooses his actions by computing what will be most likely to further his personal interest—wealth, power, and prestige.[14] "Common sense," whether ancient or modern, that thinks "human nature" infallibly dictates standards of right and wrong, good and bad, is shown to be mistaken by the vast cultural differences in societies as close together as those of ancient Greece, Egypt, and Persia.[15] The Sophist can add, to the discomfiture of the "It's just plain human nature" moralist, that "standards" in business and law are conventional and arbitrary.[16] The Greek Sophists had shocked their contemporaries by arguing in just this way, against the uncritical admiration of the Homeric code of conduct. Today, one of the first-run products of early college education is the discovery of the relativity of behavioral norms from nation to nation. Today's sophomore reacts sophistically to this discovery.[17] He confuses ethical insight, which is forward looking in a progressive society, with guides to conduct, which are inherently conservative and serve as public norms summarizing past community standards.[18]

Over against this superficial cultural relativity, however, there is the possibility that *every* human being has or is an inner "self," concerned with decisions, able to grasp unchanging patterns (those of mathematics are nonvalue examples), aspiring to some kind of immortality, and best realizing its pursuit of the ideal when it has qualities of wisdom, justice, temperance, and courage. This was the insight Socrates had; the Academy made it more precise and general by asserting that there is a common "essential form" of humanity, which all human beings share and which motivates us all as a goal, even though we may not be *fully* aware of its existence or power.[19] Our freedom, responsibility, concern, and creativity are all properties of human existence which the Sophists found difficult to explain; so, posing as "realists" against this "idealism," they were forced to try to explain them away. History has made an ironic point here. The Sophists, who by their own account of social relativism would have little to say to us, are in fact all but unknown by the modern world. By their account, Socrates should be similarly obscure. But his conception of values as transcultural—at least as constant objects of search and inquiry—has immortalized him.[20]

Plato himself was apparently never quite satisfied that he had refuted and reeducated the Sophists, even when he was writing the imagined conversations in which they figure. This is not surprising, for his position and theirs differ at almost every point, making discussion inconclusive. Even when there is verbal agreement, it turns out that the two parties have been using the same word in different senses. (For example, Hippias' and Socrates' different senses of "better" in the *Hippias Minor*.)

In the contest for domination of later educational practice and theory, the Academy won out. With an able assist from its daughter school, the Lyceum, the doctrine and the model of education as intellectual power—development of our capacities for generalization, deduction, and grasp of abstract form—dominated the field for two millenia. In the background of this victorious model, a number of assumptions are present, with most of which the Sophists would disagree. For example, the "intellectualist" models talk about "insight," a subjective grasp of form, where the Sophists would prefer to talk about "performance"—measured by standard true-false tests. The Academy also believes that there *are* objective "forms"—criteria which we can discover and apply to questions of value and of fact. The Sophists hold that truth is wholly culturally relative, except for the "natural" tendency of everyone to seek his own profit. The Sophists think of "ideas" as lists or as mental pictures; the Academy appeals to mathematical examples to show that there is a difference in kind between, let us say, the single idea of "triangularity" and an imagined row of many different triangles. Both refer to learning as a kind of "memory" —in the background here is the Greek oral tradition, with its invocations to the Muses who are to "remind" the poet. But for the Sophist, it is memory of what some authority has said; for the Academy, memory of an innate idea, latent in the mind, perhaps from a vision prior to our present incarnation.

Thus in the consideration of Sophistry and its early critics a clear issue emerges, and an argument is begun which still goes on. The analogy of the student's mind to a computer, with items in "storage," is tempting. We often add to the temptation by giving students the examinations we do. But is it true that thinking consists merely of rapid sequences of simple operations with these stored facts? It does describe one kind of learning and knowing. Does it describe all kinds? The best? If so, what of the training—e.g. in mathematics—in the art of generalization? Or of the power to overcome complacency about ethical standards? Or of aesthetic sensitivity, as our cities and the means of mobility among them become uglier? Perhaps the computerizable world, the world of "bits" of information, catalogues of fact—however vast and however indispensable—is only the antechamber of knowledge for men and societies alike.

NOTES

1. It follows that whoever would encourage change, revolution, etc., must either have a strong sense of history or suppose himself possessed of supernormal if not superhuman insight. Hence the word "visionary."

2. Translations of the two dialogues in question, the *Hippias Major* and the *Hippias Minor*, will be found in E. Hamilton and H. Cairns, eds., *Plato: Complete Works*, New York, 1961. They are included as Plato's in the great Alexandrian "edition" of Plato; but so are other works which are certainly not authentic, so this is no guarantee of Plato's authorship. For the contents of the arrangement by Thrasyllus and a brief discussion of the question of the authenticity of the two dialogues, see R. S. Brumbaugh, *Plato for the Modern Age*, New York, 1962, pp. 192–195, 198–205, 223. For the present discussion we need assume only that the dialogues were written by someone in the Early Academy who wanted to point up the contrast between Hippias and Socrates and whose literary portrait matches very well our other information about Hippias himself and the new sophistic educational movement he represented.

3. For the Sophists and their place in Greek thought, see, for example, M. Untersteiner, *The Sophists*, trans. K. Freeman, New York, 1954. (But this should be read with some caution—compare R. Levinson's review of this book in *Review of Metaphysics* VIII (1955): 271–272.) A general account is in R. S. Brumbaugh, *The Philosophers of Greece*, New York, 1964, pp. 112–123. The actual evidence, collected in H. Diels-W. Kranz, *Die Fragmente der Vorsokratiker* (10th ed., Berlin, 1961), is translated with comments in K. Freeman, *Ancilla to Pre-Socratic Philosophy* (Oxford, 1948) and *Companion to Pre-Socratic Philosophy* (Oxford, 1948). One crosscheck we have is the portrait of Hippias by Plato in the unquestionably authentic dialogue *Protagoras*. An achievement in pure mathematics which the Academy did *not* care to commemorate and which was in fact atypical of sophistic education is discussed by Sir Thomas Heath, *History of Greek Mathematics*, vol. I, Oxford, 1921, pp. 182, 226–230. The reader must remember, however, that even hostile exaggeration must have enough resemblance to an original to make it recognizable.

4. See Freeman, *Companion*, p. 3.

5. From the *Hippias Minor*. In general, in estimating the attitude of Plato and Aristotle to "arts and crafts" we should keep in mind that the Sophists as a group seem to have proposed substituting skills that were useful for "liberal education" in philosophy and science. The downgrading of all "servile arts" by Aristotle and Plato may therefore be less an ingrained "aristocratic class bias" than a polemical counterattack on a lopsided curricular proposal.

6. That inspired beginning alone is a strong suggestion that Plato himself and not some younger imitator is the author. What follows in this paragraph is a paraphrase of the *Hippias Major;* it is not documented sentence by sentence.

7. This *is* mentally incompetent but in that historical setting not the sheer imbecility that it would amount to today. For the problem Socrates and Plato faced in breaking the spell of the oral tradition in favor of a new method of generalization, see the brilliant study of Eric Havelock, *Preface to Plato*, Cambridge, Mass., 1963.

8. This is exactly what a young "sophisticate," Meno, urges against Socrates' notion that they might share an inquiry into the nature of "virtue," though neither knows for certain what this nature is. Compare the treatment of Plato's *Meno* in R. S. Brumbaugh and N. M. Lawrence, *Philosophers on Education,* Boston, 1963, Chapter 2.

9. And far from being alone in this idea, Hippias has the whole common sense of the contemporary educational system on his side. From H. D. F. Kitto's *The Greeks* (Baltimore, 1960) to W. Jaeger's *Paideia: The Ideals of Greek Culture* (trans. Gilbert Highet, 3 vols., Oxford, 1939–1945), a clear picture emerges of an educational system trying to teach "excellence" by a combination of specific directives and the example of Homeric heroes.

10. A view that Plato attacks most strongly in Book I of the *Republic.* It is odd, though true, that the Sophists agreed that value judgments are context-dependent as between cultures, or even between classes within Greek culture, but apparently thought rigid situational rules could be prescribed for "right action" within one role in one class in one culture. Compare the Sophist Gorgias' catalogue of proper "virtues" for men, women, slaves, and so on, which his student Meno refers to in the beginning of Plato's *Meno* (71c).

11. There is an extensive literature on this point, focused on the "royal lie"—all men are brothers—which Plato proposes in the *Republic* that his citizens be told. The lie goes on in the "Myth of Metals" to explain natural differences of ability by a piece of popularized genetics. Compare *pseudos* in H. G. Liddell, R. Scott, and Sir H. Jones, *Greek Lexicon,* 9th ed., Oxford, 1940, p. 2021.

12. The different implied definitions of "lying" and "better" are the key to this argument. There is no reason to think that Plato changed his mind later, or that the deliberately unjust man Socrates conjures up cannot (in Hippias' sense of justice) exist. Hippias has implicitly equated "truth" with literal accuracy of statement and "better" with superior (ethically neutral) skill. The author of this dialogue apparently had been delighted by the liar paradox and thought up his own more complex variation: "Epimenides the Cretan says that all Cretans are liars."

13. The question occurs, explicitly or implicitly, over and over again in Plato's set of dialogues in which Socrates encounters the Sophists and their admirers. If the unfinished conversation, the *Cleitophon,* which occurs along with the two *Hippias* dialogues in the Academy papers, is by Plato himself, it suggests the urgency of the question and also suggests that nothing less than the entire *Republic* is an adequate answer to it.

14. Compare Thucydides: "Of Gods we believe, and of men we know, that by their nature they seek for power whenever they can."

15. Compare Herodotus' *History.* The oddities of other cultures were a subject of comment from very early times, but the Sophists were probably the first thinkers to see the implications for the simple-minded view that whatever is local custom is "natural."

16. A point a classical Athenian would have seen particularly clearly, as the government attempted one device after another to set up conventional standards defining "fair trade," "fair election," and "fair trial." A relatively new study of philosophical ideas and archaeological finds bearing on this point will be found in R. S. Brumbaugh, *Ancient Greek Gadgets and Machines,* New York, 1966, pp 50 75.

17. Sixty-odd years ago, William G. Sumner's *Folkways* (Boston, 1911) was a really illuminating surprise. Since then we have no history of sophomores to give us objective data, though one should be written.

18. This is hardly a scholarly footnote. But it seems to us that "the Establishment" has done as much as it could to abet this confusion. Why does it consider long hair a sign of inner moral decadence or effeminacy (compare Samson)? What the older generation considers realistic and possible is what was possible and realistic two decades ago, not necessarily now. See Plato's *Laws* for an exposition of the limit of enlightened utopian imagination for a "realistic" ideal colonial city in the fourth century B.C.

19. Plato has caught this point so well in the *Symposium* that Western thought has since had little to add except footnotes and ethological observations.

20. For example, the recent Broadway play by Sherwood Anderson, *Barefoot in Athens;* also recent books: H. Spiegelberg, ed., *The Socratic Enigma* (New York, 1967), and L. Versenyi, *Socratic Humanism* (New Haven, Conn., 1963).

2

Knowledge as Inner Illumination: St. Augustine

Universal secular education is a relatively recent invention. Special skills, crafts, and trades were, of course, often taught in isolation. But the idea that men can be adequately educated, apart from religious instruction, has not been held by much of mankind for very long. The reason is clear. Men, as far back as we can even guess their mode of existence, have associated their psyches—their inmost personal selves—with the divine. My spirit is a gift from or a part of a greater spirit or spirits. These spiritual beings are immortal, beyond my life; they require reverence, awe, and worship.

The great cave paintings of the Aurignacian period, for example, are almost universally interpreted as religious. The people who made them buried their dead under the floors of the caves they lived in. Their work may date from 17,000 B.C., three times as long ago as the beginning of history itself. It represents the first great wave of aesthetic achievement in human development, as well as being among the first religious representations. It embodies values beyond the use-value of tools and weapons. Eventually men came to believe, with some cause, that religion—in the form of the church as an institution—threatens the liberty and progress of mankind when it enters the secular domain. But for the bulk of human history, education is the betterment of the psyche, and the psyche bears an essential relation to the divine.

Christian education begins with the teachings of Jesus of Nazareth. But the life, the sayings, and the deeds of Jesus, as we know them, are largely direct spiritual pedagogy. They contain techniques of teaching: analogy, simile, metaphor, parable, and many others, but no explicit theory of teaching. St. Paul's teaching again was largely directed toward a cleansing of the spirit against the time of an oncoming Return and an Apocalypse. The first great pedagogue—a teacher with educational theories—in Christianity is St. Augustine.

St. Augustine's views of man and the world intimately shape his remarks on education. There are two main sources for these views: the philosophy of Neo-Platonism, which he studied before his final conversion, and Christianity. Though Augustine saw it as a philosophy, Neo-Platonism was itself regarded by many of its adherents as a religion, and for three centuries it played the part of competitor with Christianity. It is an elaboration of one side of Platonic formalism, or the idea of knowledge as insight through inner reminiscence of form. But given the impersonality of the Roman Empire, the sense of individual futility, and a loss of the engaged energy of the Greek world of Plato's time, this Platonic view served largely as a strategy of consolation and escape.

On first encounter, the modern reader is likely to feel that this remote Platonism—intellectual, ascetic—has nothing to offer our current scene. But further study shows that there are many important similarities between the concerns of younger people today and the Neo-Platonic reaction to being caught in a meaningless, materialistic world, lost in space, unable to revolt effectively or to conform authentically.

In Neo-Platonism, as expressed by Plotinus, one of the great metaphysicians and mystics of all time, the whole of reality is to be conceived as a single entity: The One.[1] This is vastly—inexpressibly—superior to perceptible things and our finite minds, which are but parts of it, and we can apprehend this ultimate reality only spiritually, inwardly, by the mystical "ecstasy" of direct union with it.[2] From The One, all other things proceed by "emanation." Remaining itself unchanged, its being overflows like a light source shining into darkness, and this being, somewhat mixed now with plurality and unreality, becomes *Nous*, divine or cosmic Mind.[3] In this Mind, the Platonic forms exist as timeless "ideas": the perfect patterns which are imitated by things in the lower orders. The next emanation below Mind is the realm of Soul. This includes both a single World Soul, which moves and directs nature, and our individual human souls, which exist within the World Soul on this level. Finally, far from the source, as the light of The One is dim and approaches darkness, the last emanations constitute the shadowy domain called "Matter," a blind, flickering existence in the darkness of physical space and time. Men, however, in spite of their materiality as composites of mind and body, have an innate inner impulse to leave the material world and to return to a higher, more abiding reality.[4]

The philosophic revolt against the materialistic Roman society could hardly be expressed more strongly; the declaration of the sheer unreality of the physical world was a rejection of the values of that contemporary culture. At the same time, this declaration carried with it the implication that the mind is independent of the body—a fact that, it was argued, can be directly experienced in certain states of meditation—and that the body is unreal and unimportant. But here an ethical and educational problem arises: it is possible for a soul to become erotically attached to its body and to fall in love with physical beauty. This is a fall, an error, a failure of *eros* to mature normally and focus on its proper objects: *Nous* and The One. But care, affection, and therapy are needed, as well as pure cognitive argument, to correct and avert this narcissistic fall of the soul, enchanted by some material reflection.

Unlike our aim of study and research today—human progress—the goal of Plotinus was to recover a lost, never quite realized perfection: to escape and to return "yonder" to our true home. In realizing its true identity with The One, the human soul would finally lose its individuality and be released from a cycle of rebirth and suffering which carries most of us from one incarnation into another.[5] This idea sounds very like some doctrines of Indian religion, and there may be some—if tenuous—causal connection. Plotinus knew enough about the Sages of India and their ideas to want to go there, even at the price of joining a military campaign—though his plan was not successful.

This later Platonism is evidently carrying the Platonic model of learning as "introspective grasp of form" to its final limit. Plato was not entirely clear in his dialogues and may well himself have been undecided about the kind and degree of independent existence the changing world of sensible objects and individual persons has.[6] Plotinus, however, is perfectly clear in holding that the particular instances have *no* reality apart from the general form they instantiate. To understand cats, I must be reminded of the form of catness, so that this innate idea is present to my mind. But once I have grasped this form, I know what cats *really are,* and there is no point in further observation of concrete individual cats, which are only imperfect emanations or projections of this form. Space, time, and matter have only a thin reality when we contrast them to mind, form, and soul; the *form* is all the cat really is, with nothing left over to constitute *real* individuality or individual identity. Matter comes and goes—forms abide.[7]

This picture of graded levels of reality, with one single highest Being at the vertex of a hierarchy running from one to many and from form to matter, was very well suited to the religious consciousness of the West.[8] In particular, it included a religiously satisfying notion of the soul as immaterial and immortal, of a creative power sustaining and responsible for the existence of finite beings, of a world constantly trying to attain an intuited perfection. The view also offered an explanation of evil that was very appealing to this same religious consciousness. For evil is a result of a mixture of nonbeing with being, a result of matter imperfectly incarnating form; consequently, it is a purely negative thing. The philosopher can see that all evil is privation—a mere lack—hence unreal. Evil is the differential between lesser and greater goods.[9] The One, or in other religious adaptations, God, is not the author or creator of evil.

The physical world, to which Western science keeps paying so much attention, is thus only a parade of phantasms, of tokens; reality is only to be known by inner illumination of the innate ideas we have, glimpses of an ideal order. The key to explanation and understanding is to grasp these ideas and to locate each one properly in the hierarchical order which they occupy. For this purpose, an extended education is necessary; it will involve dialectic and mathematics and meditation, but its early stages should consist in reading Plato. (This is by no means a bad prescription for beginning liberal education.) Evidently, attention to the body or to such transient distractions as wealth or power in any given finite incarnation (for, as we have noted, the soul is immortal and may live one life after another) is mere distraction, a waste of time. The Neo-Platonic Academy offered no courses in cosmetology, business administration, or the theory of gladiatorial contests (the Roman anticipation of our courses in football).

The differences in vocabulary between Neo-Platonism and modern philosophy—not to mention modern general conversation—and the Neo-Platonists' use of Plato's dialogues as religious revelation, which the modern reader is not about to accept, hides the profound similarities between Plotinus and sensitive young intellectuals today. But a simple correction shows that the two share an interest in Oriental religion and transcendental meditation and a desire—very well expressed in the writings of Norman O. Brown—for an escape from the neurotic character of "civilized" human time. In addition, the two share a distaste for the materialism of their contemporary cultures and a conviction that "social engineering" and "objective scientific study" are *not* the route to effective interpersonal communication.

If we look for the arguments that Plotinus himself brought to support his position, we will find him appealing to aesthetic, religious, and mystical experience; he is more a phenomenologist than an empirical scientist or a logician. Perhaps the most important phenomenon is that we desire immortality and that we sometimes have a keen sense of the unreality of the material world, bringing with it a homesickness we cannot explain for some other home "yonder." Evidently, these feelings are not the gear-train processes or responses of a mechanism; only a soul or self, which is always aware that it is something more than a body and something less authentic than it might become, can have such feelings as these. Clocks do not worry because they aren't keeping accurate time! And this point holds even though physical states—changes in bodily mechanism—may be related to and may even induce these psychological feelings.

Another interesting point of similarity between Plotinus and the young person in search of "meaning" today in a world he sees as materialistic to the core is the appeal of the idea of a "commune." At one time, Plotinus secured the grant of a tract of land on which he planned to develop a "city of philosophers." (The name of the community would naturally enough have been Platonopolis.) For various reasons, however, that project was not realized; perhaps sufficient government subsidy was not available.

From what we have said, it is clear that Neo-Platonism concentrates on our experience as viewed subjectively rather than on outward behavior. The primary appeal is to introspective data, a useful reminder to later theorists: the subjective side to learning is easily overlooked because objective performance is so much more easily and accurately measured. Hippias, for example, with his equation of knowledge with information plus skill, found the joy of it in outer display and competition and did not appeal to inner enrichment.

A further consideration in defense of the introspective standpoint is the nature of "concepts." If these are, as the Platonic tradition claims, something quite different in kind from particular mental pictures, they cannot be treated simply as physical impressions coming into a mind that is passive and simply receives them mechanically. Genuine concepts require active reflection and critical thought for their formation.[10]

To return to St. Augustine: training in a mystical, inwardly oriented cosmology was less common in his world than was preparation for a professional career. The schools for orators and lawyers had continued the technical, extroverted, and this-worldly work of the Greek Sophists, with renewed attention to the arts of language and the techniques of persuasion. Grammar, logic, literature, and some mathematics had a part in this Roman curriculum of professional education; elaborate and "impractical" theories of the self or a world of Platonic forms did not.

St. Augustine himself trained as a young man in these secular schools to become a teacher of rhetoric.[11] As a young student living in North Africa he had gone to a school in Madaura where he mastered Latin literature and style. He did not, however—thanks in part to the severity of the teacher of the subject—learn Greek. At the age of seventeen he went to Carthage where he soon was one of the leading students in the metropolitan school of rhetoric. His youth in Carthage was very worldly: he had a mistress there, was passionately fond of the theater, and had strong ambitions for a professional career. At the age of nineteen he began to read philosophy, something that had been omitted from his literary studies until then. He did not finally become a Christian until the age of thirty-one, after a progressive renunciation of worldly skills, ambitions, and responsibilities. St. Augustine's account of his life in the *Confessions* is the story of his conversion to Christianity and his increasing sense of dependence on God, as things of this world failed to satisfy him.[12] As a young teacher of rhetoric he had not liked the Bible because its literary style had seemed poor to him and its ideas unsophisticated. But reading it as allegory, with the philosophy of Neo-Platonism firmly in mind, gave him new insight: he found that the Bible was capable of sound philosophic interpretation, and he set about using his secular tools for its explication and for religious instruction.

One reason for our fairly extensive development of the Neo-Platonic view of Plotinus is to show that St. Augustine could not entirely reconcile it with his own ideas of Christian education. In particular, Christianity has an entirely different role for love: God loves the souls He has created, and they should love Him and also love one another. There is a community of believers who share a special affection for one another and a special concern for each others' salvation. This modification of the austere view of The One leads to ideas that have counterparts today: it seems just these values of concern and community that many young people are trying to realize in their designs for communes, their experiments with transfer groups, sometimes in their concern with religion and with education.

A further difference between Plotinus and Augustine is that the Augustinian world is a product of divine creation, not an eternal emanation of The One. It contains traces of God's ideas of order—measure, weight, and number—but since the created physical universe is only inert matter, it does not count as very important or even interesting in Augustine's view. What does count is the right direction of the soul's love. The soul must come to recognize its dependence on God and must focus its affection on Him by introducing a disciplined right order into its attitudes, concepts, and value scales. Such a right order comes from the inner grasp of the *forms* (Platonic forms, now reinterpreted as ideas in the mind of God), which are the necessary conditions of intelligibility, beauty, truth, and virtue.

There is dramatic tension in the Augustinian universe; teaching and learning play their part in the drama. Mankind, having fallen from grace, can hope still for individual salvation as human history moves from the Incarnation to the Last Judgment. It is a world of risk; it is unlike the cool, timeless Neo-Platonic hierarchy of form or the eternal cosmic cycle of Greek cosmology; it is an onstage comedy or tragedy. It is also, like the tragedy onstage, a scene of individual decision and responsibility: each of us will be judged on his own merits, and each is responsible for his attitudes and choices.

In this setting, the teacher's attitude and affection for the student should set the example that will turn the student's love as well as his thought in the right direction. This matter of attitude is at least as important as the teacher's competence in handling form. Yet in the final analysis, the learning is the student's: he "learns" through an inner light, and this illumination can't be "put into" a soul from the outside. The teacher, then, for all his concern is merely a cooperator with God. Yet in that cooperation, the teacher may be a very subtle therapist, supporting the student's morale, removing blocks to learning, offering a model for emulation.

There has always been an element of mystery and drama in teaching, and Augustine's view of the teacher does this justice. In fact, in many ways his teacher has the same function that a psychoanalyst later has in Freud's theory. The Platonic paradigm of pure form tends to change, as we consider the process of teaching, into something more like our paradigm of the creation of a work of art. For the Augustinian Christian, it is crucial to see that education is not simply a matter of *information* but of *transformation* leading to new attitudes, new intellectual insights, and a new cosmic destination.

On the other hand, though pure reason may be only a small part of the complex that is a human self, it is like the conning tower of a submarine rather than the tip of an iceberg, as it extends up into the world of timeless form. For conscious thought acts directly to order, sublimate, and change the unclear lower ambitions, appetites, and desires (which, while unclear, are not "unconscious" in this tradition). Thus what a student learns by grasping form becomes internalized and changes his psychic structure. Logic, for example, is not merely to be seen as a set of rules for external manipulation of arguments: it is a pattern of consistency in ordering, which disciplines our thoughts, evaluations, and practical decisions. Thus a strongly formalist idea of education is the dominant paradigm in this tradition, because it is thought to hold the key to psychotherapy.

To the end of establishing a right order in the soul, the liberal arts developed in the secular schools are the best discipline. The idea behind these liberal arts traces back to the conflict between Plato and the Sophists which we discussed in the preceding chapter. When, in his *Republic,* Plato turned his attention to a higher education that would suit the intellectual development of ideal rulers, he suggested an ideal curriculum of arithmetic, plane geometry, solid geometry, theoretical astronomy, and harmonics or ratio theory (rather misleadingly, this mathematical study is called "music" in its ancient and medieval Latin versions). At the end of this course, having learned how to think rigorously, his scholars would move on to a final course of dialectic, about which little is told us, but which would no doubt deal with words rather than with quantities and would try to build some sort of rigorous social and legal theory. Aristotle's works on language, the monumental *Organon* with its study of the logical uses of language and the *Rhetoric* which treats originally and interestingly the persuasive uses of language, offered new materials for linguistic study. These two disciplines, logic and rhetoric, were taken as liberal arts, running parallel to the mathematical studies. The logic and rhetoric were to be preceded by "grammar," an interesting amalgam of semantics, syntax, and metaphysics. This set of seven studies—the trivium of grammar, logic, and rhetoric and the quadrivium of arithmetic, geometry, astronomy, and music—came to be accepted as the definitive set of disciplines which a free man would need to make his decisions wisely.

St. Augustine had planned to write a treatise on each of these seven liberal arts, but only two of the set are extant: his dialogue on music, *De Musica,* and his treatment of grammar, which, however, he entitled *De Magistro—On the Teacher.*[13] Augustine does not use the dialogue form as Plato had done, to recreate a shared inquiry; nor does he use it as Cicero had, to report urbane but inconclusive conversation. It is rather more like the Aristotelian lecture: a tool for instruction, with an authority who knows the answers presenting them to the student in rigorous order and asking questions to be sure the student is paying attention. The mystery, the concern, even the humor that lie in the background of teaching seem at first to be pretty much kept in the background in these two books focused on form.

Yet there is a difference between the two treatises in this respect: in the *De Musica,* where the *magister* is defining music (as "the art of moving well") to a *discipulus,* the disciple turns out to be human, after all. He anticipates what his teacher is about to say, jumps in, and gets it wrong; he claims to have a rather better formula for defining music than his teacher's, but it proves to be neither better nor even a definition of music; he forgets what he has just been told three minutes earlier and has to have that part of the lesson repeated again. So beneath its austere formality, the *De Musica* is not so bad an illustration of realistic pedagogy.

The *De Magistro,* however, is entirely serious. Augustine introduces a concrete element of concern and love between student and teacher by structuring the work as a dialogue between himself and Adeodatus, his fifteen-year-old son. But he has complex purposes behind this grammar lesson and wants no foreground noise to interfere: in this first textbook of the proposed series on the liberal arts, two things are being presented at once. As is clear from the content, Augustine is giving his son a survey of "grammar"—for the most part, what we would today call semantics or theory of signs. But, as we believe the title *(Concerning the Teacher* rather than *On Grammar)* was meant to emphasize, the dialogue also argues for a definite model of teaching and learning, which the whole instruction in liberal arts presupposes. Ultimately, the best description of the Augustinian learning model is that "Christ, the Master, teaches within." But leading up to that, a vigorous secular argument is offered to prove that the ability to use signs at all is a distinctively human faculty. Our handling of language is a result of innate cognitive skills, inner illumination, and insight that make an evident absurdity of the theory that reduces education to the sort of behavioral modification one finds in animal training or the sort of mechanical operation one finds in programed marionettes. The teacher and the school are dealing with a being which has a soul—an inner self—and a capacity for insight.

If this more general framework is indeed part of the intention of the *De Magistro,* its title is not misleading, though many of its readers have been disappointed by the apparent concentration on details of Latin grammar. In fact, the very choice of grammar as subject matter to illustrate general points about learning has a twentieth-century feeling: a dominant theme of twentieth-century philosophy has been the power and importance of language in culture, education, everyday life, and everywhere else. And at the moment educational theorists are being told by one group of students of linguistics that in fact a child's ability to learn language rests on innate cognitive powers that make it in no way comparable to any ability to learn possessed by animals or machines. If that "cognitivist" case is finally demonstrated, the proposition that man is a sign-using animal may be a way of distinguishing human as opposed to other animal mentality. But it is not only the professional linguists who argue that recognizing a sign requires an interpreter able to grasp its significance and that this knowledge is wholly different from perceiving the sign as a physical event or object. Michael Polanyi, for example, in discussing different ways of knowing, contrasts physical reality and human interpretation by comparing the properties of a painted arrow seen simply as a physical fact and seen as showing the way to a subway exit or shuttle line.[14]

To prove that there is no type of communication that does not require interpretation by an intelligent being, St. Augustine must show that this is the case for every kind of sign and interpretation. Even the case of teaching by performance, he argues, still requires this sort of intelligent interpretation. The teacher, when asked the meaning of "walk," may show it by walking; but the student must still grasp which features of the performance are "meant" to define the name (for example, if the teacher walks first slowly and then briskly, the student must grasp the likeness—which is what walking means—and also the difference between walking and sauntering or hurrying). The conclusion is that learning must be a reminder to the student of meanings he grasps by some inner insight; without that special intelligence, signs—linguistic and other—would be merely meaningless physical objects or events. As it is, the Augustinian regards the whole created world as a kind of sign pointing to God as its divine cause, to His creative power and divinely planned patterns of order.

In this revived Platonism, the true, the good, and the beautiful alike owe their value to the presence of organized *form*. Explanation and clear communication require forms that are grammatically correct and logically coherent. Poetry and persuasion, too, create pleasure and conviction by observing proper form. Once one has learned how to check the logical reasoning in any kind of content in terms of logical rules, one can check any other kind. If A implies B, and B implies C, then A implies C. A, B, and C can be beliefs, factual claims, or judgments of value. Logical form is universal. So is aesthetic form: once the literary critic has recognized the power of transposition and omission as tests of the unity of a work as a whole, he can explore the unity of a piece of literature in any genre. But to get a clear vision of these pervasive forms, it is necessary to separate them from accidents of particular content and to recognize that they apply *analogically* across certain type lines.

Now this observation of the power of pure form has, historically, repeatedly suggested an interesting educational project. If good form stays the same for *any* content, why can't teachers speed up learning by presenting it abstracted from *every* content? Logic, for example, could be reduced to general patterns such as A implies B, no S's are P's, whenever a happens, then b happens, and so on. It is interesting to notice that in at least the two pedagogical works extant, St. Augustine is too wise an educator to try out the "pure form" shortcut. (Whether he would have done so in arithmetic or geometry is hard to say.) The experiment, whenever it has been tried—and this has been often—yields a different result from the one expected: while pure form is independent of *any specific* content (tragedy can be illustrated by a work of Aeschylus or Eugene O'Neill, for example), it can only be appreciated and put to use when it is taught with *some* such content. Thus the wisdom of Augustine in using Vergil's poetry to raise questions of grammar, rather than trying to develop a scheme of *pure form* alone.[15]

The reader interested in the theory of signs may find in a monograph of Charles Morris an interesting modern systematic treatment.[16] It is also interesting that the three distinct ways in which verbal signs can function, in Morris' view, are among the distinctions in sign function recognized in the *De Magistro*. Some signs, according to the *De Magistro*, are significant through relation to other signs. Morris describes their function as *syntactic*. Words like "and" and "or" are examples. Other signs indicate things and classes, both abstract and concrete. Morris calls this a *semantic* dimension of sign functioning. Proper and common nouns work in this way. Still other signs introduce the attitude of speaker or writer, or act to cause an emotional response from the reader or hearer—they function in a *pragmatic* dimension. As an example, the word "if" may introduce an attitude or state of mind on the part of the user which the interpreter is expected to share. The *De Magistro* theory further distinguishes between words which function by indicating something directly and those which function only in context—"syncategorematically." The word "nothing" is an example. By the time of Morris' analysis, the notion of these diverse kinds of function was taken for granted; but when Socrates, Hippias, and their contemporaries were just becoming analytic in their approach to language, the question of "what sort of thing 'nothing' indicates" was a real puzzler.[17] In every case Augustine and his son examined, whether they were dealing with a conjunction of concepts, a notion of value, an attitude—for instance of expectation—there was active thought involved in sign functioning, *a person behind the word.*[18]

Men have become men through language. It binds them together socially; it provides them with a common past through the resources of racially entertained understanding. St. Augustine's advances in the analysis of language were thus not mere shrewdness in the scrutiny of one set of human tools among many others, but they were progress in self-awareness. For early Christian thought, man and nature are separate acts of God's creation. In Greek thought, however, man is wholly within nature. For the Greek, therefore, language has its natural function in the mirroring of reality—whether literally, metaphorically, or mythically. But in the Judeo-Christian account of the world, men do not belong to nature save by God's fiat. Their language can thus be understood as something *added* to the natural scene from their own independence. That human mentality is engaged not merely in probing and reflecting reality but in constituting and contributing to it as well represents a new phase in human self-understanding. Men reflect not just the timeless order of nature, but in some small way the creative power of God. Even when education becomes secularized, the Augustinian insight remains. The conception of language as not simply portraying or presenting but as creating originated in the beginning of the Christian era. Later features of European civilization made it unique in history: a widespread creative technology in invention, the construction of new sciences, experimentation in new forms of art and drama, and in our own century experimentation in nonrepresentational art.

NOTES

1. Plotinus (204–269 A.D.) is the great expounder of Neo-Platonism. A mystic, a great teacher and lecturer, but an unwilling author, he finally did write down his teaching in six sets of nine essays called the *Enneads*, trans. S. MacKenna, 2d ed. rev. B. S. Page, New York, 1957. In The One, Neo-Platonism takes over and, most scholars agree, radically modifies an idea from the *Parmenides* in which Plato suggests that if "the one"—the form which gives things their unity and identity—is in fact wholly separate from everything else, it cannot be known, named, or even said to "be." The Neo-Platonists accept this reasoning but still hold that The One does exist in some eminent way *beyond* being and knowing and that all other things come from it as source and depend on it for identity.

2. Notice, however, that this is true in only one respect: insofar as things are *real*—unchanging, universal—they share in The One; but their materiality, mutability, and multiplicity attaches to them only insofar as they have an admixture of *unreality*.

3. Plotinus thus finally grounds his philosophy in mystical experience; he had himself experienced the union with The One which he describes. But his is an austere mysticism preceded by rigorous intellectual discipline.

4. A good account of Plotinus will be found in B. A. G. Fuller, *History of Greek Philosophy*, New York, 1923. The high point of Plotinus' system is usually taken to be *Ennead VI*, in which he writes on The Good and The One.

5. Plotinus takes Plato's myths of reincarnation literally; only the purified soul can return "yonder" to its home; the others must undergo another incarnation, another round of immortality. Plotinus catches here the feeling of alienation and homesickness that everyone feels at some time in the transient physical world. "The Soul," as he puts it, "is a traveler who sleeps every night in another inn."

6. In fact, there is an inner tension between the logical statements Plato makes about the status of "becoming" and the dramatic use of myth and dialogue which keeps its vividness and concreteness before us. The final answer must be found by reconciling the two portraits of Socrates and accounts of the "forms" in the nearly contemporary two dialogues, the *Phaedo* (a favorite of Roman Neo-Platonists) and the *Symposium* (the favorite of Renaissance Platonism).

7. A detailed study of this question will be found in I. M. Crombie, *An Examination of Plato's Doctrines*, Oxford, 1967, vol. II.

8. Compare A. N. Whitehead, *Religion in the Making*, New York, 1926.

9. B. A. G. Fuller, *The Problem of Evil in Plotinus*, Cambridge, 1912. St. Augustine develops this interpretation of evil. Actually, this is typical of Plotinus' version; but by the fifth century Proclus had recast the position and its defense in a form that depends mainly on very austere formal dialectic for its appeal, transforming it into a logical rather than an aesthetically oriented position.

10. One classical view held that "impressions" are images similar in quality to the objects that are their causes. This runs into such strong theoretical objections (What possible way do we have, for example, of telling what these causes are like and whether our impressions are similar to them?) that it has to be modified extensively to become consistent. (This problem troubled Locke, also; see Chapter 4.)

11. We get an idea of this type of education from such works as Quintillian's *Institutes* and Cicero's *On the Rhetorician*.

12. The *Confessions* is a remarkably sensitive work which succeeds beautifully in directly communicating Augustine's increasing sense of dependence on God. Readers differ violently as to the significance and validity of this development; compare, for example, Bertrand Russell's negative appraisal, *History of Western Philosophy* (New York, 1945, pp. 352–366), with the introduction in John A. Mourant, *Introduction to the Philosophy of St. Augustine* (University Park, Pa., 1964). For the reader interested in medieval philosophy, a classic source is E. Gilson, *La philosophie au moyen age* (Paris, 1944). R. McKeon, *Selections from Medieval Philosophers* (2 vols., New York, 1929) is an excellent sampling of treatments of the problem of knowledge through the period. More recently, F. Copleston's volume on medieval history in his *History of Philosophy* (New York, 1946–) is an excellent brief treatment.

13. We will concentrate on the *De Magistro* (trans. G. Leckie, New York, 1938) and the *De Musica* (trans. L. C. Taliaferro, Annapolis, Md., 1939) in bringing out a fundamental point of St. Augustine's educational theory because these are technical works focused specifically on education, and because they do not rest on shared Christian faith and experience for their validity but seem open to dialogue with any educator. St. Augustine's other works are more profound but presuppose much more in the way of shared religious experience on the part of the reader.

14. In a 1966 lecture at Yale University. Wittgenstein, in influential if cryptic reflection on the nature and limits of language, uses the distinction between what a statement or sign "says" and what it "shows" to arrive at a more negative conclusion than Polanyi's.

15. A similar problem of form and content arises in Chapter 3. In modern philosophy the question arises of whether I can be "conscious" but not "conscious *of*" anything. Clearly I can be conscious without thinking of *any one* selected item— say, a fox. But could I be if my thought were devoid of *every* specific item of content? In the seventeenth century there was a tendency to assume that such consciousness *was* possible; in the twentieth we tend to say that it is *not.*

16. C. W. Morris, *Foundations of the Theory of Signs,* Chicago, 1938. This is a particularly good contemporary work to read as an introductory or companion piece to the *De Magistro.*

17. These examples—the kinds of signs, the meaning of "if," the problem posed by the word "nothing"—are, of course, Augustine's.

18. And for St. Augustine the "word" presupposes divine illumination as well as a person. For him the step from human self-consciousness to awareness of God was a simple and direct one; from the world the step to awareness of God was simply a case of recognizing the created world as a "sign." Thus an Augustinian might well find our phrase "a person behind the word" a simple and natural way of saying what we mean and at the same time a reflection of one of the most important parts of the Christian doctrine of the Holy Trinity.

3

Paradigms in Collision: Descartes

The modern period of philosophy was ushered in by the work of a brilliant seventeenth-century Frenchman, René Descartes, a mathematician equally enthusiastic about the Augustinian notions of a self and soul and the new materialistic model which Galileo had used for his science of physics. The result was a revolt in both physics and psychology against an establishment that had committed itself to an oversimplified, dogmatic Aristotelian view. The revolution was to shape Western common sense for three centuries or more—not simply what everyone recognized as sensible ideas about specific areas, such as education or ecology, but basic presuppositions that applied to all of these special areas. Unfortunately, that common sense juxtaposes an inner light and individual freedom in psychology with a pure mechanistic determinism in physics—a physics which, in Descartes' view, includes neurology and physiology. This leads to a drastic mind-body, or spirit-matter, dualism which theory cannot bridge and which encourages taking only one side and ignoring the other. The implications and limits of the mechanism paradigm for educational theory come out particularly clearly when we see it in collision with the freedom-and-dignity alternative. At present, we have temporarily found other models which avoid the Cartesian split; Whitehead and Dewey offer two of them. But we are in danger of heading right back into Cartesian dualism again, as some of our contemporary theorists take the mechanistic model as the only right one, others the insight view.

From the new mathematical physics, Descartes' philosophy draws the idea of *objective* reality as embodied in matter—the extended stuff of the outer world which we feel, hear, and see. But from the older Augustinian psychology, with its idea of the privacy of an inward, nonmaterial self, his system derives its idea of *subjective* reality. The objective world is most simply described as composed of *bodies:* bodies of water, bodies of land, bodies of plants and animals, and bodies of men. The subjective world of *mind*—of thought, will, desire, memory—is unextended and neither visible nor tangible. Descartes' separation of mind and body is a useful practical distinction; we make commonplace use of it still. But what bridges the gap between external facts and internal thoughts? Do the former create the latter; do the latter refer to the former? Or, with more specific reference to education, what shall we do about a series of practical questions which this view poses? Shall we simply exercise and develop minds and ignore manual skill? How much of the "whole child" do we educate? Is the child's bodily health any part of the school's concern? Different answers to these questions are important in the history of educational changes from the seventeenth century to the present.

Descartes added to this synthesis of Galilean physics and Augustinian psychology important discoveries of his own in mathematics and a general method of thinking that could be used by anyone willing to follow it carefully. This method was to provide for other fields of inquiry—physics, ethics, religion, and psychology—the kind of certainty so greatly admired in mathematics. The result was a philosophy that attacked the by then rather antiquated and distorted Aristotelianism taught at the Sorbonne. The University Doctors concentrated on qualities in things, virtues in man, and humors in the body. They reduced medicine, apparently, to something close to pure verbal manipulation: Molière, in one of his plays, makes fun of a medical examination which the candidate passes with honors by explaining that opium is a sleep-inducing drug because "it has a dormitive virtue." Descartes' attack was to prove in the long run decisive, though there were counterattacks by the opposition. Descartes' dislike of Aristotle, as he had encountered him, may have been important in leading him to look for both a non-Aristotelian psychology and a non-Aristotelian physics. He found such a physics, as we have seen, in the new astronomy; his psychology, in spite of some novel contributions, comes—as we noted above—from the Platonic tradition of Christianity, with its definitely non-Aristotelian stress on introspection as the way to inner illumination and certainty.[1]

The times were ripe for a new scientific view of man and the world. Galileo, having heard of Copernicus' telescope and having built one of his own, had published his *Message from the Stars* in 1610. Whereas Aristotle had taught that the sun and moon were perfect spheres, changeless save for their motion around the earth, the telescope showed craters on the moon and dark spots on the sun. Other data, such as the phases of Venus, suggested that Copernicus' heliocentric view was sound common sense, Greek philosophy and the Hebrew Old Testament notwithstanding. Galileo published his *Dialogues on the Two Principal World Systems,* defending Copernicus, in 1632. The Church reacted promptly: it condemned the work in 1633, brought

Galileo to trial before the Inquisition, and forced him to recant.[2]
When this news reached Descartes he abandoned work on a book
about astronomical theory, which he had planned to call *The World*,
and turned instead to a brief exposition of his new method, a draft of
which he had completed earlier. The *Discourse on Method* appeared,
along with the *Geometry* and two other works, in 1637.[3] The *Geometry* marked a brilliant advance in mathematics, the discovery of a
method by which geometry could be taken out of a realm of thinking
in pictures and subsumed under algebra. It was what we call analytic
geometry, and it underlies the calculus and the whole field of mathematical analysis.[4] The *Geometry* not only secured Descartes' lasting
fame but made it impossible to ignore his other work, the *Discourse*.
His aim in this was, in part, to show that natural reason, without recourse to revelation, can understand nature. With this idea Descartes
in effect struck a blow for a democracy of reason—since he thought
that anyone in his right mind could follow the procedure—as opposed
to the aristocracy of revelation.

Descartes' two methods were potent: one showed how to synthesize
two seemingly distinct mathematical fields, the other how to analyze
nature and man. He regarded his generalization of method from mathematics to other fields as the proper development of "philosophy," and
he proposed to use it to replace the decadent "school philosophy"
which he had studied as a youth.[5] Given such a foundation, the prospect seemed excellent that the new science could be justified, and its
application, particularly to medicine, would offer new human health
and new powers over nature.[6] And so the *Discourse* took the first
step: to explain the right philosophic method, given which anyone
could find out for himself what human certainty could be attained.[7]

There are just four rules to this method. The first rule is "to accept
nothing as true that I do not clearly know to be such."[8] Here we see a
mathematician's mind at work, as Descartes goes on to explain that to
know something clearly means to be unable to doubt it.[9] This is the
kind of certainty that attaches to mathematical proofs in a system:
while actually working out a proof, one cannot doubt that a properly
deduced conclusion follows. "Doubt" here, of course, does not mean
the mere verbal possibility of saying that I doubt something, but
rather the state of mind in which I "feel" that something is not necessarily so. Obviously, a good deal of critical work is going to be necessary before philosophy or ethics or politics can be grounded in ideas
that meet this demand for clarity, though Descartes believes that eventually they can.[10]

The second rule is "to divide each idea and problem into as .many
distinct parts as it is capable of."[11] Thus, the idea of space can be di-

vided into distinguishable points; the idea of matter into small units of extension; the idea of mind into memory, intellect, and will; and so on. (It will be important for later discussion of ideas to note here that for Descartes an idea does not mean a mental picture or memory image, but an abstract general concept: he is very clear that the idea of triangle is different, both in kind and clarity, from a memory file of snapshots of particular triangles.[12]) We take the analytic method so for granted that we may wonder why Descartes makes so much of it; actually, it was Descartes who by both precept and example showed the broad range of uses to which analysis can be put. The point of this second rule is that to understand methodically requires not only ideas that are clear, but also ideas that are sharply distinct. This again is characteristic of the mathematician's world, where there are no fuzzy or borderline cases. A positive integer, for example, is either prime or it is not. It can not be *somewhat* prime or *more* prime than another number is.

The third of the four rules of method is "to introduce an order even into those sequences that have no natural order."[13] This rule assumes that where there *is* a "natural order" of ideas, we will follow it. In a mathematical deduction, the steps have a logical natural order; in physics, causal sequences have a natural cause-to-effect order, though Descartes admits only what an Aristotelian would call "efficient causes" into scientific explanation.[14] This recognition of order as imposable is extremely important: our whole power to store and retrieve information rests on this third methodical procedure (which, of course, Descartes did not invent but simply formulated explicitly; the use of imposed order goes back at least as far as Hippias the Sophist and his "art of memory"). The device of alphabetical arrangement has proven the most obvious and useful way to order arbitrarily—from library card catalogue to telephone directory. The advances in geometry that Descartes himself made involved the successive application of his second rule (analyzing the plane into points) and his third (ordering the points to correspond with pairs of numbers standing for units on arbitrarily chosen coordinate lines). He was thus able to give algebraic equations for geometrical figures.[15]

The fourth rule of method is "to conduct reviews and enumerations to be sure nothing is omitted."[16] This rule—to be systematically complete—has long been a scientific ideal. As early as the thirteenth century Raymond Lull had devised an "art of combinations" that could generate all the possible sentences conceivable from a given list of subjects and predicates.[17] But a fairer example of the powers of systematic thought could hardly be found than in the "periodic chart of the elements" perfected by Mendelejeff. It may fairly be doubted whether this chart could have been conceived except in a scientific atmosphere of the sort that Descartes wanted to create. In accordance with Rule Two, Mendelejeff listed all the known chemical elements, the simplest stuffs of which the world is made up, and in accordance with Rule Three arranged them in an order of family resemblances; one column, for example, included all the inert gases, those which do not ordinarily combine with other elements. Mendelejeff's chart was incomplete; there were empty places in it for the elements that belonged there but had not been discovered. Nevertheless, so good was his arrangement that he successfully predicted the physical and chemical characteristics of three of these elements, merely by their location on the chart, *even before they had been isolated.* Eventually, the whole set of natural elements was discovered, and the theory was wholly confirmed.

During a winter in Germany, Descartes was able to advance with his method toward the project of putting philosophy on foundations that had absolute certainty. Was there any proposition he could think of that was so clear he could not doubt it?[18] If he found one, could he use his other rules of method to analyze it and go beyond it? Now, the propositions of mathematics certainly satisfied the condition of not being open to doubt, but they were all hypothetical. For example, *if* a figure is a triangle, *then* certain things follow necessarily; but that doesn't prove that any triangles exist. Philosophy and science, however, need to start with statements that say something about what actually exists; but is there any existence of which one can be certain?

The familiar facts of dreaming and illusion make it clear that any perception we have can be called into question. Suppose, to push the first rule of method with as full rigor as possible, that we assume some demon is bent on deceiving us. Could we be sure, beyond possible doubt, that certain ideas we hold—that we have bodies or that we are awake or that we live surrounded by an external world—are not illusions? No, but there still remains for me one absolute certainty. My own existence cannot be doubted, since every time I doubt, I assume my existence as a doubter. Further, the concept of deception, even by a malicious demon, assumes a thinker exists to be deceived. "I think; therefore I am," Descartes concludes. This is the starting point of his system. He must now move on to the second step of method —analyzing what this "I" is. It is a thing, a substance, that "affirms, denies, doubts, wills, and desires"; a subject with images before its mind which seem to refer to something external.[19] But the certainty of my own existence does not extend to the outer world, nor even to my belief that I have a material body; strictly, the "I" comes out as "a being, the essence of which is thought." Well, this is a beginning, though it leaves philosophy, physics, and theology a long way yet to go.

Why can I not doubt the *Cogito, ergo sum?* Because there is a "natural light" of reason which makes it evident to me beyond question. Perhaps there are other ideas of equal clarity?[20] Descartes finds another one: that "a cause is as real as or more real than its effect." If this were not so, then whatever was greater in the effect would be *something which had come from nothing,* an indubitably absurd supposition. Moreover, among his ideas, Descartes finds that he has an idea of a perfect being: a being who knows, who does not doubt or wish or feel passion. What can be the cause of this idea? Not Descartes himself, for he recognizes that he is not perfect: he would rather know than doubt, rather be immortal than mortal, and so on.[21] But not the outer world, either, for the ideas caused by that (assuming it does cause them) are all finite, changeable, capable of being illusions and their causes are at best material objects, no more perfect or real than the subject that thinks them. There remains only one possibility: God must exist as the cause of the idea in our minds of perfection.[22] But our idea of God is not a mental picture, nor is God an object of possible sense experience. Like the ideas of a self and of a cause-effect relationship, the idea of God must be innate in us, not something arising through some build-up of sense experience. This is the side of Descartes that leans heavily on subjectivity and inwardness; the foundations of all knowledge are to be found in the introspective search for indubitable ideas which are latent in our minds. This approach is quite distinct from the Thomistic one, which, being Aristotelian rather than Platonic, requires us to get knowledge by opening ourselves to external experience and generalizing from that.

The reader who is interested in innate ideas will find several considerations in their favor. Recent work in linguistics, for example, has come to the conclusion that a human child must already implicitly understand what language is in order to be able to learn it—a point that would have pleased but not surprised St. Augustine. Earlier in this century, Bertrand Russell came, at least temporarily, to believe that he needed Platonic forms and some innate ideas in his philosophy. For suppose my idea of "triangle" comes from seeing many particular triangles and grouping them together because they are "similar." Where do I get this idea of similarity, which I must use for this sorting? Russell concluded that ideas such as "similarity" and "difference" are not derivable from particular perceptions, but rather are the ways in which we group our sensations and ideas; they are Platonic forms.[23] In much the same spirit, Descartes insisted that the idea of a perfect being functions as a notion born into us; by using it we compare experiences and things as better or worse than one another. This youngster draws a "better" tree than another; that one's knowledge of arithmetic is "nearly perfect." The idea of a divine being is the criterion or limiting case—it is the notion of an absolutely perfect being.[24] Most people, not recognizing that this idea of God is innate, depend on imagination rather than reason and try to *picture* God. The result is likely to be either agnosticism or anthropomorphic superstition. But Descartes, by rigorous use of his method, claims to have clarified religious notions. What remains, given the self and God, is to find some way of establishing the existence of the physical world. Whether the step Descartes takes from his *idea* of God to the existence of God is or is not defensible remains a controversial question. But with some modifications, many contemporary process philosophers accept such an inference from the concept to the existence of a perfect being. Charles Hartshorne is perhaps the best known representative of this position.

The problem, however, of working from the subjective world of "ideas" to a genuine external world of physical reality—or even to having a genuine physical body—is not easily resolved. Ordinarily, philosophers who hold a mechanistic view of the world *begin* with the existence of a physical reality: their problem, if they recognize it, is rather to account for the subjective, introspective self that does the observations. It looks as if Descartes, working in the other direction, might find some bridge between his ideas and an outer world by using his method to discover the implications of God's existence as a perfect being. For example, unlike the demon we mentioned earlier, a perfect being would never deceive us: the only motives that lead to deceit are fear, envy, greed, or ill-will, and all of these are kinds of imperfection. And yet I seem to be constantly making mistakes: my senses show me a distant mountain as very small, though I know it is large; my imagination does not rebel at the vision of winged horses, though none exist; I can even misreason in so simple a matter as adding up a complicated tax return. Am I deceived, after all? Not if I analyze these cases and make the proper distinctions, for all of these mistakes are my own doing. Either they rest on the assumption that my senses give me reports on things as they really are, not as they appear, or on my assumption that a conclusion follows before I have a clear view of the evidence or proof. Actually, my senses seem designed for the survival value they have for my body; they picture the world in the way most useful for my physical adaptation in it. Thus, since things at a distance offer less of a threat or a promise than those near at hand, my sense of vision makes the vividness and scale inversely proportional to the distance squared. Since my will is capable of both belief and doubt and I have a "natural light" of understanding, I can learn to avoid precipitate judgments by preventing my will from leaping beyond what I clearly understand.

This reassures me concerning the possibility that I may be deceived by my clear and distinct ideas, and I can now return to the earlier question: What clear and distinct idea can I form of the outer physical world? Natural science had already shown, by Descartes' time, that a quantitative description of matter in motion conveys knowledge of a sort wholly unavailable in the "Aristotelian" qualitative tables, based on sensed properties. But what, then, is the physical reality that natural science studies? What properties does it have? Descartes takes the case of a piece of wax: its qualities—flavor, hardness, shape, odor—can all be changed if we heat it, but it still continues to exist as a physical thing and it is still called wax. So we must distinguish material existence, or matter, from flavor or color or shape. What, then, does it mean to say that the wax exists as a material substance? Not that it has certain unchanging and essential secondary qualities, nor even that all of its primary qualities, such as shape, are constant. There is something, however, which any existing material substance must clearly have: *extension*. It must have a space which it fills, and it must not permit any other material thing to occupy that space. This idea, that to exist as a material substance is to occupy space, is both clear and distinct; it is not just something I might choose to believe on inadequate consideration (as the idea that "the wax is really yellow" would be), but it is something I cannot choose to doubt.[25] For what would it mean for something to exist as a material object but to offer no resistance to and have no effect on any other object trying to pass through or occupy its place? I have so clear and distinct an idea of the existence of material things that—since God is not deceitful—I can be sure the external world exists. But external things fill up a uniform space, almost like pure volumes in solid geometry; they stick together or collide and transfer momentum to one another. Since something cannot come from nothing, Descartes feels that he can reason out the laws of conservation of matter and conservation of momentum. But it is certainly an unfamiliar "external world" that is thus discovered: nature so thought of is something we have *conceived* but never have encountered. As Whitehead says of nature in this Cartesian view, "Nature is a dull affair, soundless, scentless, colorless; merely the hurrying of material, endlessly, meaninglessly."[26] Such a nature was, however, precisely the neutral mathematical set of volumes that the new atomic-mathematical approach to the physical sciences required.[27]

Descartes claimed in the Dedication of his *Meditations* that his new method led to new and clearer "proofs of the existence of God and of the immortality of the Soul." He did not add, though he could have, that it also led to the new ideas of physics and astronomy that the Church authorities had disapproved of.[28] These two consequences of his use of the right method presented the West with a dualism at once so plausible and beset with puzzles that it has haunted us ever since. The dualism is a natural outcome of taking two very different models and using one to look for a self, the existence of which is certain, then using the other to describe an external world that is equally indubitable. It leaves us with the problem of the relation between a self, "a substance, the essence of which is thought," and its world, including its immediate body, which are "substances, the essence of which is extension." The two ideas are certainly distinct, so clearly so that the idea of a *physical* destruction of the conscious soul is an absurdity. (Hence Descartes' claim that his method proved—he should rather have said, offered support for—the doctrine of the soul's immortality.) But nonetheless, the body acts on its mind: the senses register events in the external world, and physical disturbances are registered as pain, pleasure, depression, and other passions of the soul. Conversely, ideas which I form in my mind—words to be written, for example—become executed as actual external fact. Though I have quite a *clear* idea that my mind and body interact, it is another matter to find any *distinct* idea of their interaction. Descartes hoped that somehow the application of physics to physiology could bridge the gap between mind and body by discovering "animal spirits" having kinship with both the physical and the mental realms. But this was a logically impossible task: "animal spirits" are an unclear and indistinct idea; on analysis they must be either physical or mental. "An organ moved by thought" —perhaps the pineal gland, suggested Descartes, since there is only one such gland as opposed to the other parts of the brain, which are paired—runs into the same difficulty.[29] This bumbling hypothesis is not Descartes at his best, but it shows how a purely postulational method, starting with a pair of apparently perfectly clear models, can bring itself to the despair of being unable to explain the obvious. For we *know* that mentality and physicality are intimately interconnected.[30] Yet an assumed unextended thinking self known by introspection and an assumed extended world and body surrounding it will stay distinct forever. So also will the laws of transfer of momentum, which catch the body in a physical determinism, and the laws of thought, which leave the mind and will free to design explanatory theories, remain distinct.

Descartes and the brilliant modern scientists who followed him gave to the world of learning a forward thrust that continues to the present day. And where learning went, education soon followed. Pope's "A

mighty maze, but not without a plan!" illustrates how scientific ideas
are reflected throughout human thought generally. The conception of
the physical world as a storehouse of resources that can be put to use
rests on an application of Descartes' methods. Also, since Descartes, the
study of scientific method has itself become an important part of science. Again, Descartes' work in mathematics gave further support to
the conviction that a logical order of *thought* can apply strictly and
exactly to the actual order of events. It is not just man who is rational
but the world also. The outcome is a line of scientific progress which
is still continuing and still accelerating. In this progress, Descartes'
dualism remains at work: human wonder expresses itself as curiosity
and excitement; the progress of our mastery of nature generates self-
lessness, patience, careful and precise thought. But other aspects of
human wonder—those which are manifested as awe, reverence, or aesthetic delight, and which have more to do with our attitude toward
nature than with our immediate actions on it—these aspects we tend
to treat as "purely subjective." [31] The "objective" order in the world
that science studies is the logical-mathematical order and the causal
order. The aesthetic order and the other value orders then become
treated as human inventions, having no basis in fact. The result is a
separation of man and nature which is the intellectual counterpart of
the Biblical story that man and nature are separate acts of creation.
Not until the theory of human evolution is there an effort to mend
this breach. It is hardly too strong to say that in Descartes there is almost nothing "wonderful," in the sense of awesome, left.

When we turn to man, not as a knower but as a moral agent, we
find that Descartes set up for himself a "provisional ethics" with four
rules which run parallel to his rules of philosophic method.[32] Here
again what he has to say anticipates many of our contemporary convictions. He is quite aware that his project of objective inquiry has ethical implications, that objectivity is not ethical neutrality. He is also
aware that in ethics most ideas are not clear and distinct, as they are
in mathematics and physics. The pursuit of "clarity" in practical affairs carries with it, as a first rule, the conservation of freedom: with
certainty seemingly impossible in ethics, the best alternative is to remain free always to analyze, doubt, and learn.[33] Still, in making
choices, one must recognize distinct possible courses of action, and
having made the distinction, aim at a course designed for minimum
error.[34] This rule, it seems to Descartes, means aiming always at actions that are moderate, between extremes; for an extreme will obviously be more disastrous if proved wrong than a moderate course.
Corresponding to the general rule of method that order should be introduced even when it is arbitrary is another ethical rule, namely to

act decisively even in situations where there is no objective basis for decision.[35] The fourth ethical rule, to review the customs and occupations of men, matches the review-and-enumeration fourth step of the general method; it recognizes a need for society and travel in pursuit of practical wisdom.

Descartes never took back or changed these four provisional rules, so presumably he found them satisfactory.[36] The vital difference between the two sets of rules, one theoretical, one practical, is that the determinism implied in the system of mechanical law governing nature is implicitly rejected in the ethical aim to conserve freedom through reflective action. Men can be free through the use of their minds. Thus in the realm of the theoretical, Descartes counsels clear foundations, rigorous deduction, and systematic order; in the realm of the practical, he counsels caution, expediency, and a shrewd attention to the ways of other men. This is still—in considerable measure—our contemporary temper.

The beautiful simplicity of the new method and its apparent ability to work with both the newest scientific models and the most traditional religious ones was counterbalanced by the complex problems its application presently raised. Are all animals merely machines, with no reason, intelligence, or freedom in any degree? Can I be theoretically certain that any thinking substances other than myself exist? Does it follow from the fact that I can imagine myself existing even though I am not thinking about *any given* idea or feeling from my senses that I could imagine myself existing without any such input *at all* as mental content? Is the inference from the idea of God to His existence really as "indubitable" as Descartes thought?

Most fascinating, because of its human interest, may be the question of how serious Descartes himself was. Were his theological arguments, based on respectable philosophic models, simply put in as life insurance against the attacks of hostile authorities? [37] This would be understandable; a decision on the point depends in part on *how good* these religious arguments are, and here opinion remains divided.[38] How should we fit together the modesty of Descartes' claim early in the *Discourse* that he is no wiser than anyone else with his claim toward the end that he uniquely deserves public support because he can give mankind complete control of health and nature? Is the initial modesty ironic? [39] Perhaps we will never know; but his critics and admirers alike took him seriously, with implications for education that we can readily see: scientific progress through careful study and enumeration and recording; mathematical proofs and structures as the framework of scientific understanding; personal freedom in the realm of ideas; caution tempered with moments of arbitrary incisiveness in the realm of action. Of all of his ideas, though, the most interesting and the most unendingly troublesome was the separation of body from mind.

Thus the elegant French mathematician set off a revolution in Western thought which is still reverberating today. He set his mark on modern education in many ways: (1) the study of facts as distinct from and more objective than values; (2) the possibility of intellectual certainty, without the intervention of authority, available to any man who will persist in his search for truth; (3) the intense devotion to mathematics as the very language of nature; (4) the separation in kind of mind and body, leading us to think of two patterns of education, rather than one; (5) finally, the search for a way to unify the insights and models of experimental physics and introspective psychology.

NOTES

1. For this Cartesian synthesis, see N. P. Stallknecht and R. S. Brumbaugh, *The Spirit of Western Philosophy*, New York, 1950, pp. 231–293.
2. See Giorgio de Santillana, *The Crime of Galileo*, Chicago, 1955.
3. René Descartes, *Discourse on Method*, trans. E. S. Haldane and G. R. T. Ross (vol. I of *Philosophical Works*, Cambridge, 1968; hereafter cited as *Works*). In section 5, Descartes explains how he had described the development of the world in his suppressed treatise.
4. For an account of the *Geometry*, see J. R. Newman, *The World of Mathematics*, New York, 1956, vol. I, pp. 238–253. The two other works published at the same time were the *Dioptrics* and *Meteors;* they and their place in science are described in L. Lafleur's introduction to his translation of the *Discourse*, New York, 1956.
5. In his earlier incomplete *Rules for the Direction of the Understanding*, we can see Descartes working toward the final simple version of method which he presents in the four rules of the *Discourse*.
6. This is the prospect that Descartes holds out in the final section of the *Discourse:* he expected at that point to solve all the remaining problems of medicine and technology within his own lifetime.
7. Note the very first sentence of the *Discourse:* "Good sense is of all things in the world the most equally distributed." The implication is clear enough, though Descartes frequently disclaims any intention of persuading others to follow him and suggests, perhaps disingenuously or ironically, that original inquiry may not be best for everyone.
8. *Discourse, Works* I, 92.
9. This notion of clarity is actually defined in the first rule: ". . . so clearly and distinctly that I could have no occasion to doubt it." In the *Meditations* we find Descartes testing his judgments for clarity by a method of systematic doubt: Can he think of any occasion where he might have any doubt of them?
10. On the other hand, Descartes himself seems to find one such clear idea in the notion of his *freedom*. And in reading the *Discourse*, one is struck by the constant use of illustrations drawn from city planning, civil administration, architecture, and military strategy, a use suggesting that these areas, too, may admit of *methodical* reconstruction. One may even wonder whether his insistence that he intends not to tear down and replan the intellectual foundations of the public world but only to redesign his own dwelling does not give us some insight into a real intention that he here disowns. See note 38.

11. *Discourse, Works* I, 92.

12. Again we see a mathematician's mind at work. The difference between concepts and images is treated in the *Meditations* where Descartes attributes most religious errors to mistaking an imagined picture for the concept of God.

13. *Discourse, Works* I, 92.

14. Quite possibly God has final causes in mind; but if so, they lie beyond human comprehension. See especially Descartes' *The Principles of Philosophy*, Part III, Principles I–II: *Works* I, 270–271.

15. This was the fundamental idea of analytic geometry. In the *Rules* we find Descartes working out various geometrical imaginative aids to this introduction of order.

16. *Discourse, Works* I, 92.

17. See Frances Yates, "The Art of Ramon Lull," *Journal of the Warburg Institute* XVII (1954): 115–173.

18. This is summarized in the *Discourse* and explained in detail in the *Meditations*.

19. *Meditations, Works* I, 150. Later philosophers sometimes claim that Descartes slipped in rigor here when he thought the "I think" clearly required an "I" that was a *substance*. Perhaps consciousness exists as a function or process? But note how well Descartes has analyzed the ideas involved in trying to doubt his argument: he is entitled to all of them.

20. *Discourse, Works* I, 101–102, summarizing a much longer discussion in the *Meditations*. The *Discourse* summary is important here, since the argument developed in this way avoids an immediate circularity that some critics read into the *Meditations*: (1) I have a clear idea of God; (2) God is a perfect being who therefore cannot deceive me; (3) if my clear ideas were false, God would be a deceiver: (4) therefore, my clear idea of God proves that He exists. But the actual argument follows another line: (1) I can be certain, by the natural light, that any judgment as clear as the *Cogito, ergo sum* is beyond doubt; (2) I can be equally certain of the judgment that "a cause must be equal to or greater than its effect"; (3) God exists as a perfect being; (4) hence, He cannot be a deceiver; (5) therefore, whatever I clearly and distinctly conceive must be true.

21. One's first impulse is to think that the idea of a perfect being *does* come, perhaps negatively, from introspection: I do not like doubting and so I imagine a consciousness without any doubts, etc. But Descartes has in mind a different notion, which recurs from Plato through Aquinas, that I cannot know that I am imperfect unless I have also some positive ideas of perfection. St. Augustine had argued that I cannot doubt unless I have some idea of certain truth (in *De Veritate* and elsewhere).

22. That is, given the clear idea of the relation of effects and causes, *there must exist a being equal in perfection to my idea and related to it as cause to effect.*

23. Bertrand Russell, *Problems of Philosophy*, London and New York, 1962 (reprint).

24. In *Works* II, we find *Objections* and his *Replies*. He summarizes these in the "Preface to the Reader," *Meditations, Works* I, 137–139. One of the two recurring objections that he believes important, though invalid, is to the step of inference—going from a concept to the existence of its object. The legitimacy of this in the particular case of a concept of God, The Good, or a perfect being, is a question with a long philosophical history. See, for example, the treatment of St. Anselm and his "ontological argument" in Stallknecht and Brumbaugh, pp. 222–227.

25. The reasoning here is worth following in detail; see the fifth *Meditation*.

26. A. N. Whitehead, *Science and the Modern World*, New York, 1948, p. 56.

27. On the other hand, Descartes' clear and distinct idea of matter only allows him to infer conservation of momentum (his "quantity of motion," which equals volume times velocity). The other ideas of "force," "gravitation," and "gravitational attraction" which modern physics needs—not to mention "energy" and its conservation—he rejects. Such ideas, he thinks, come from our own experience as

acting subjects with wills, and it is a foolish confusion to think they can describe mere extended neutral matter. But strangely enough, the idea of matter which modern common sense came to take for granted was Cartesian, not Newtonian.

28. "And in truth, I have noticed that you [the Faculty of Theology], along with all the theologians, did not only affirm that the existence of God may be proved by natural reason, but also that it may be inferred from the Holy Scriptures, that knowledge of Him is much clearer than that which we have of many created things, and, as a matter of fact, is so easy to acquire, that those who have it not are culpable in their ignorance." *Meditations,* "Dedication," *Works* I, 133–134.

29. See Descartes' various attempts to resolve this problem, running from the *Principles* through his later work *The Passions of the Soul.*

30. Descartes himself says that he has a *clear* idea of mind-body interaction, only there is no way to make the kind of causal relation involved *distinct.*

31. See, for example, Descartes' treatment of the passion of "wonder," *The Passions of the Soul, Works* I, 364–365: "Article LXXV. In what wonder particularity consists," "Article LXXVI. In what it may do harm, and how we may make good its deficiency and correct its errors. . . . But it much more frequently occurs that we wonder too much . . . than that we wonder too little. And this may entirely prevent or pervert the use of the reason."

32. *Discourse,* Part III. See Robert E. Cumming, "Descartes' Provisional Morality," *Review of Metaphysics* IX (1955): 207–235.

33. Thus, preserving freedom to doubt is the *ethical* counterpart of the *logical* rule to accept nothing as true that can be doubted.

34. And in making these distinctions—the second rule of method—I must distinguish clearly those things which are and those which are not within my power. Thus Descartes believes he can "succeed in mastering myself, rather than fortune," a kind of Stoic fatalism.

35. This is actually given as the second ethical maxim, though clearly it corresponds to the third rule of logical method.

36. See Cumming, *loc. cit.*

37. See Lafleur's introduction to the *Discourse* cited in note 4.

38. A recent dissertation by Hiram Caton argues that Descartes' responses to some of the objections to his *Meditations* are deliberate fumbles, responses set up in such a way that any alert reader would see that he did not believe his own case. "The Mastery of Nature and Wisdom: An Essay on the Means and End of Descartes' Design," Ph.D. thesis, Yale University, 1966; University of Michigan microfilm, 1966.

39. Here the student of philosophic literature needs the help of the literary critic to clarify the character of the speaker as the *Discourse* reveals it.

4

Knowledge as Understanding: Locke

If one had to name the one philosopher whose ideas were most influential in forming the pervasive common-sense ways of thought about education and society in the English speaking world, one would probably choose John Locke.[1] Modern as he was (and is), however, Locke's philosophic position can be located in relation to some major historical traditions. He seems to share with Hippias the Sophist and with contemporary information theory the convictions that thinking is reducible to storage, retrieval, and synthesis or analysis of a set of elementary items.[2] In Locke's vocabulary, these bits were called "simple ideas." [3] He shared with Aristotle the view that education is a psychophysical phenomenon; like Aristotle, Locke was trained as a doctor, and a constant awareness of the interpenetration of mind and body shows in his correspondence and his treatise on education.[4] Also like Aristotle, Locke believed that all knowledge originates in experience, conceived as either sense experience or awareness of our emotions and mental acts.[5] In an atmosphere permeated by popular Platonic theories and notions, which stressed intuitive recognition of objective form, Locke reacted as Aristotle had done earlier: he redirected attention to the need for educational content if educational "form" is to have any significance. Like Aristotle, Locke treated "abstraction" as a process of literal "drawing out," of using only parts of full experience to form a composite picture which will include characteristic elements of many individual cases and permit us to group the cases together.[6] We call the football field a "rectangle," for example, and use the same expression to refer to the dining-room ceiling, thus grouping diverse entities under a common abstract name. (The Platonic tradition, on the other hand, seemed to regard the movement of thought from particular to universal as a gain in insight, a closer approach to "seeing all things synoptically." [7] We have already noted in passing how some typical Platonists backed up this case with mathematical examples; Locke on the other hand, and again like Aristotle, substantiated his critique with examples from biology, anthropology, and child psychology.) Locke was a complex thinker and writer: he was not inclined to give up observation in the interest of symmetry or simplification. As a result, his essays are diffuse and contain many undeveloped strands and suggestions, not necessarily wholly consistent with one another but all invariably resting on some sort of relevant observation.

The basic change which Locke introduced into philosophy and psychology was his redefinition of the term "idea." An *idea* becomes a concrete item of mental content; it is like a photographic snapshot, filed in memory. The items in the file are images of simple or complex sense experiences, feelings, and compounds.[8] This is precisely the sort of thing Platonism rejected at the outset as "ideas" or "forms": Platonic or Cartesian essences (or concepts), whatever they may be, are *not* pictures and cannot be arrived at by looking at a picture gallery of particulars. Once Locke's redefinition of "idea" was accepted as ordinary English usage, no Platonic "theory of ideas" had much chance of sounding sensible in America or England. And Locke's views on education were so widely accepted that they carried his accompanying psychological analysis with them.

Locke's reflections on education were originally letters to various friends, which he collected and systematized. At the outset, he takes as given the idea that the aim of education is to produce an English gentleman able to manage his estates and affairs and to take part in a society that is a mixture of democracy and leisure-class aristocracy. What he thought about education for women, workmen, peasants, or foreigners must be determined by extrapolation, for his main concern was with the young man whose tutor and college must fit him for a gentleman's career.[9]

One theme that runs through the correspondence and the education essay is the interdependence of the physical and the mental, the medical and the pedagogical. Part of the responsibility of parents and tutors is to observe the physical characteristics of the individual pupil and to adopt a schedule which both observes certain general rules for fitness and adapts specific assignments to individual needs. As an alternative to a tradition of pedagogy which stressed the mental and the formal, with liberal use of physical punishment as motivation, and a tendency to set up inflexible criteria of "covering the material," Locke's ideas found an interested audience.[10] He seems to have been the sort of consultant on child development that Arnold Gesell and Benjamin Spock have been in the twentieth century.[11] By and large, our current educational practice meets Locke's ideas about halfway: we try to provide medical and psychiatric help for students who have serious problems and to annex physical education courses and school athletic activities to the curriculum to foster physical fitness. We try to design institutions in which physical conditions are favorable to mental activity: central heating, good ventilation, comfortable but not sleep-inducing classroom chairs and desks, and so on. We do not, as we probably should if Locke is right, include elementary medical work in the training of our teachers; and we have not been very eager to explore theories about the relation of physique to temperament and to learning.

Education must at every point be justified, according to Locke, by its usefulness in building character and intellectual skill. Its content, in addition, must be as far as possible grounded in firsthand experience. How far the tutorial system provides firsthand experience in social effectiveness before college is a question worth considering; Locke took it for granted that this could be done.[12] Further, how far the goal of "normality" should be preferred to excellence at the price of some eccentricity is a question he decided perhaps too abruptly in favor of normality. But the principles that come through are sound and welcome, and their applications are often original and illuminating. First, there is the matter of motivation. Obviously, a student who is caned for being "backward" transfers the negative quality of his punishment to the whole complex idea of school, learning, teacher, and subject matter. So Locke took a stand where other philosophers have stood, against harrassed and irate practicing pedagogues. Physical punishment should be avoided except in the very extreme cases, and extra school assignments should never be used as a form of punishment. If it can be done, a student who neglects his work should be treated in such a way that he will come to enjoy it. (Locke went as far as suggesting that the boy who prefers spinning a top to learning arithmetic should be *assigned* top-spinning and kept at it until he is thoroughly tired of it; or perhaps he should be given the opportunity to study his "Book" on completing his top-spinning assignment.[13]) Before backwardness is put down to perversity, one should consider possible physical and psychophysical explanations.[14]

Second, there is the matter of firsthand encounter. Locke's general principle was that it is a waste of time to memorize meaningless symbols that have no corresponding content in the student's experience. Modern languages can be taught better by the direct method than by textbook drill: send the young man to France for half a year and he will learn French better than he ever could in the classroom. In this respect language is like a sport; it can best be acquired through contact and action rather than by form and rote.[15] Locke advocated accounting and drawing as useful accomplishments, though they were not stylish in his time.[16] He introduced a conception of readiness into his curriculum which is worth noting: a child can to some extent understand himself and other people before he is ready for abstract notions of matter, motion, force, and so on. Reading, therefore, should be adapted to the level of mental content the child brings with him; at the same time the child's environment should be designed to provide a range of meaningful firsthand mental content.[17]

Third, in the matter of criteria, Locke had a clear notion of the kind of individual tolerance and autonomy he was aiming at: he wanted to fit the student for effectiveness in a liberal, predominantly middle-class, British society. The precise criteria were less important, particularly for admirers of Locke on the European continent, than his persistence in keeping them in mind.

The plausibility and attractiveness of Locke's thoughts on education are enhanced by the kind of inconsistency that is normal to common sense. Thus, although Locke found beatings usually a poor way to give children an enthusiasm for lessons or to develop character, he was not averse to severely beating boys who got too far out of hand.[18] Although physical causes or family tensions should be looked for as possible explanations of underachievement, a sheer perverse fondness for "sauntering" is wicked and should be nipped in the bud.[19] Although drawing is useful in developing powers of observation, too strong a commitment to fine art at the expense of more proper and genteel interests should be avoided.[20] And in this way each principle is put forward as a sort of generalization that admits of exceptions just where final exasperation sets in. The combination of a generally humane view, of the recognition that minds inhabit bodies, of the belief that firsthand encounters are more vivid than names, and the rider that some cases will not fit these principles but will require more traditional and drastic action made Locke's educational essay widely read. It was often reprinted, translated, and cited. And it carried with it into the mainstream of educational thought the more technical philosophy Locke developed in his investigation of human understanding, technical thought which justified the emphases on positive motivation and concrete content of his educational program. Locke's educational theory is part of a larger philosophy of thought, learning, and knowledge which is almost unparalleled in its capacity to meet the needs of common sense. In spite of many philosophical problems which this theory of knowledge generates, Locke's approach is still consistent with and contributes much to our modern views.

We can appreciate Locke's contribution because his emphasis on the organism offers insights that mediate between the apparently irreconcilable positions of materialism and idealism in both philosophy and educational theory. It seems true, however, that Locke's admiration for Newton's natural science led him to a certain shift of models, or at least to a compromise between them, when he turned from his thoughts on education to his project of designing a *science* of human understanding. The analytic sections of his psychological work seem to be trying to do for the mutual attraction and association of ideas what "force = mass × acceleration" does for the laws of motion in Newtonian physics. This is an attempt, then, to get laws of thought and a model of the mind which could be accurate only if it were like a mechanism, not an organism. There is an inconsistency between the idea as a simple, detachable item in the mind and the idea as a record of cumulative habit and experience. Unfortunately, perhaps, the attractiveness of the use of the organism model in the writings on education was submerged by a kind of external association of ideas in the more mechanistic model.

Locke began analyzing human understanding by sharply setting its limits. Our thinking proceeds by recognizing and combining ideas—recorded units of sense experience and feeling. The innate ideas which had been made much of on the continent and in England found no place in Locke's scheme: on analysis, he proved them to be nothing more than compound combinations of ideas that are acquired, in no sense innate. Take away experience, and what is left of supposed innate knowledge of theology or geometry or physics? Nothing, according to Locke; and there is no evidence at all to support the notion of human selves born with actual but unconscious knowledge of anything whatever. The mind is a "blank tablet" at birth, until experience has written on it.[21] This is the extreme position which underlies much modern associationism, including Skinner's.

From the axiom that thinking involves only arrangements of the discrete ideas in our minds it follows that we have no special way of knowing what the "real essences" as opposed to the "nominal essences" of things are. I can *define* matter or human nature or pigs by analyzing my complex ideas of them into those simple ideas I find combined. But I have no way of knowing whether all the stipulated components of the defined essence are in some sense *objectively* essential. Generally when we are dealing with natural kinds, our experience gives us similar combinations of qualities, assuming our perception to be normal. Only in rare cases do we find it hard to distinguish between a bush and a tree, a plant and an animal. But when we move from substances—objective things that act on us causally—to "modes" —properties that require definition in order to be understood—it becomes clear that what one individual considers an essential part of the meaning of a term is not essential to someone else's understanding of it.

Professor Charner Perry once used the example of a "parade" as such an idea. His idea of a parade may be at least four men marching in line and singing, but some of his students will be satisfied with a less grand or quieter spectacle and will disagree as to whether a silent, three-man picketing demonstration is "really" a parade or not. It is equally clear that even if there is somewhere in nature or heaven a Platonic form of the ideal parade, we, at least, have no way of telling when our ideas do and when they do not match it; all we know are particular processions of persons marching, singing, and so on.[22] Also, it is often quite important to distinguish a parade from a demonstration and a demonstration from a riot. But how do you draw the line? Is there a hard and fast rule?

It is interesting to notice and to question some of the underlying assumptions that Locke claimed to extract from his psychological observation and introspection. (1) Are "ideas in our minds" in fact mere representations in knowledge of things in the outer world? (2) If they are, can we make any sense of Locke's further assumption that these ideas correspond to qualities of external things? Or are we cut off altogether from comparing things as we encounter them with things as they are? (3) Are ideas in Locke's sense of stored definite memories the discrete, separate items he wants to make them? Don't they always get stored in a context? Locke's examples were of clearly defined ideas. Are all ideas of this sort? For example, where does jealousy leave off and hatred begin? Perhaps some ideas are in their nature only vaguely defined, while others depend on context, even though their symbols are distinct and can be manipulated as detachable.[23]

Keeping these questions in mind, let us follow Locke in the constructive inventory he took up after rejecting the claims (1) that we have actual innate ideas and (2) that we have some intuitive access to the real natures of substances. Ideas, said Locke, come from either (1) sensation caused by the external world, (2) inner states of feeling, or (3) combinations formed by joining simple ideas in different logical patterns of connection.

Although Locke believed that in principle we can never be as certain about matter in motion as we can about human nature and its feelings (since we have direct intuitive knowledge of ourselves, but only probable knowledge of material things), the elegance and predictive value of a Newtonian physics seemed so great that in practice no one could doubt it. The success of this mathematical physics also seemed to confirm a common-sense classification of the characteristics ("qualities") of things into three basic kinds. *Primary qualities* are the measurable, quantitative properties of things—size ("extension"), shape, impenetrability, motion. These stable characteristics are the same for every observer (under specified standard conditions) and their measurement leads to scientific laws that faithfully describe the physical universe. *Secondary qualities,* on the other hand—attributes like color, flavor, sound—vary so widely among individual observers and even among different observations by the same person that we cannot regard them as real properties of physical things themselves: they depend too much on who is observing. For example, there are people who see no distinction between what others discern as red or green. The colorblind man is all too aware that color in some strange way depends upon him. Similarly, the same lake feels warm on cold days, cold on warm days, though its temperature may remain the same. Locke concluded that the secondary qualities sensed in ourselves must be the outcome of the action of primary qualities—streams of fine particles, perhaps—on ourselves. In principle, therefore, the real world is quantitatively determinate but not qualitatively so; and science should be able to dispense with secondary qualities. The atom is such a particle. It is tasteless, colorless, etc., but it has quantitatively measurable properties which can be observationally tested. We hear a note, say F sharp. But that quality is in our response to molecules of air vibrating at a certain measurable rate. The vibrations are "out there," the sound "within us." [24]

Locke, however, with his medical background, his interest in nature, and his respect for what he observed, found in things still another kind of characteristic: their capacities or potentialities. He called these *tertiary qualities*. They are discernible through experience, but not necessarily through mere inspection. The combustibility of wood is a real property of it, but it is neither primary nor secondary. It can be discovered only by doing something to the wood to find out if it is combustible. Locke rightly discerned that there is a very considerable portion of our experience which results in knowledge of this tertiary sort. He lived at a time when experimentation was just beginning to reform scientific study, theretofore theorizing, and also beginning to change the most fundamental ideas of education.

Locke only partly realized the value of his own investigations, both for philosophy and for education. These ideas are destined to cause difficulty in the twentieth century to philosophers who try to equate meaning with passive observability: what do I actually observe in a handful of dry salt that shows me that it would dissolve in water? [25] On the other hand, Locke had freed himself from Descartes' rigid insistence that we can call nothing knowledge unless it is indubitable or is derived from what is indubitable. As a mathematician, Descartes wanted an utterly reliable structure of knowledge that would keep us from error and unprovable speculation. As a doctor, Locke knew that the knowledge that goes into medical cure and correction is not always theoretically clear, yet it is usually sound enough, being based on experience, to get results. Mathematicians *prove;* doctors *practice,* i.e. engage in activities with things, bodies, tissues, etc. Descartes rejected the notion that extended substance has force or power as being an illicit use of imagination.[26] But Locke was starting with a common-sense world, as well as with an analytic method for explaining it, and in this world, there *are* substances and there *are* powers that show themselves in causal patterns. How have we formed ideas of these?

On analysis, the idea of substance turns out to be a compound idea, one part of which—matter with extension—seems to come from sensation, but the other part from reflection, ideas that come from my inner awareness of my own feeling and thought. The ideas of existence and power, in their primary form, are based on our own self-consciousness and sense of effective effort in acting and are transferred to explain the unity of other things around us—spirits, animals, objects. By this transfer we can understand such concepts as gravitational force, causal power, or substantial self-identity holding together many properties in a kind of underlying field.[27] Locke did not question the legitimacy of this transfer. Most of his successors, admirers or critics, think that he should have. But if we were to draw so sharp a line between our intuitive insight into our own existence and the other beings we encounter, we would lose very basic concepts of common sense, ethics, and even physics. For example, where, except in our sense of action, do we get our idea of force? Locke was unwilling to deny that fundamental insights like this were genuine. If we insist on reducing "nature" to its primary qualities alone, it is explained (literally "flattened out") as mechanical; if we look at it with a sensitivity to its tertiary qualities, it is much more alive and vital. And physical science itself involves primitive ideas—force, acceleration, inertial mass—that cannot be built up out of the primary qualities of extension, shape, and momentum.

This complex analysis of ideas by Locke does preserve our common-sense world and still protects the use of power, force, and cause as meaningful terms in science. The suggestion is that other substances in nature are to be understood as not wholly alien but as being somewhat like a human self with its identity and diverse adventures. That we may have some direct awareness of such selflike qualities anticipates some very recent speculative thought—Whitehead, for example, claimed to have found in this aspect of Locke's work some of his own inspiration.[28] But the classification of ideas that comprised the second major part of Locke's investigation of understanding sets up inner logical tensions. Any attempt to simplify and tidy up the system (for example, by reducing tertiary to secondary qualities) brings these tensions into the open.[29]

Locke's educational views show a similar tension, resulting from the recognition of how important precision is and of how little precision can be actually attained in much of our working knowledge. This tension is clearly present in a letter that Locke wrote—before either the *Essay Concerning Human Understanding* and *Some Thoughts Concerning Education* were written—to William Molyneux, his friend and distinguished contemporary. Molyneux was educating his son on Lockean principles.[30] At this point Locke's ideas had been promulgated only as practical advice to friends and correspondents. The chatty, not too highly organized character of these remarks is still present in *Some Thoughts Concerning Education*. He said,

> Pray, let this be your chief care, to fill your son's head with clear and distinct ideas, and to teach him, on all occasions, both by practice and rule, how to get them, and the necessity of it [i.e. the necessity of getting such ideas]. This together with a mind active, and set upon the attaining of reputation and truth is the true principling of a young man.[31]

Locke used Descartes' phrase "clear and distinct ideas" but obviously meant something else by "ideas": he said they may be gained by practice. Again he shows the ambiguity of our notion then and now of an idea. If an idea is a genuinely mental thing, it is dangerous to regard it as even metaphorically lodged in a head, since the structure of mind is not the structure of the brain, however much the two are related. If these ideas are to be got into a head by practice as well as by rules, then sheer reasoning is only one side of knowledge; so also is the well-educated mind equally bent on reputation and truth. No lonely scholar following the operations of pure reason is adequate to the aims of education. Locke wanted men trained to be citizens and rational beings both, engaged with their fellowmen and possessed of common sense, curiosity, liveliness and a "clear head."

Rational action, participation, good habits both mental and moral —these are what are desirable. In these matters Locke was thoroughly modern, anticipating Rousseau, Kant, and Dewey. When it comes to toys for children, said Locke in section 130 of *Some Thoughts Concerning Education,* little children should not be diverted by "Toys from the Shops, which are presently put out of order, and broken." Their first toys should encourage their inventiveness: a pebble, a piece of paper, Mother's bunch of keys(!). Later they will make their own toys, or if these are "above their skill to make," then toys should be

bought with a view to physically vigorous exercise: tops, badminton
rackets, and so on. Children will play at almost anything; education
for the young child is the direction of healthy play "towards good and
useful Habits." [32]

What is true for the child is not special to his age, except insofar as
he is especially supple when he is young and can gain useful and self-
developing habits readily. Just as Locke was opposed to innate ideas
inborn in reason, he also was inclined to minimize the role of inborn
talent in the acquisition of skills both physical and mental. In the context of proposing this theme, he was led to larger themes in which it is
embedded.

> We are born with faculties and powers capable of almost anything
> . . . : but it is only the exercise of those powers which gives us abil-
> ity and skill in anything, and leads us towards perfection. . . . No-
> body is made any thing by hearing of rules, or laying them up in
> his memory [so much for Descartes!]; practice must settle the habit
> of doing, without reflecting on the rule. [33]

You might just as well try to make a good painter or musician by lectures, Locke continued, as to make a good reasoner by drumming into
him a set of rules for reasoning. It is more likely inadequate habits
than a "fault of nature" that make men defective in understanding.

In short, Locke does not fit neatly into the simple tradition that sees
ideas as items of information stored in a mind both passive and mechanical. He is more like Aristotle here, who viewed nature as made
up of individual centers of activity and attainment which are developed through good practice and good habituation, than like his predecessors and successors who see nature rather as a totality of facts, a
static actuality. Indeed Locke told us that there is no dearth of corpo-
real things which "fail not to fill our heads with lively and lasting
ideas of that kind." What we need, he continued, is to fill them with
moral and abstract ideas "which don't offer themselves to the
senses." [34] But even if "particular matters of fact are the undoubted
foundations on which our civil and natural knowledge is built: the
benefit the understanding makes of them, is to draw from these conclusions, which may be as standing rules of knowledge and consequently of practice." [35] Again, we notice the emphasis on abstraction
and putting abstraction to use. But even the deriving of practical abstractions and the development of the understanding are not ultimate
ends. The ultimate end is our old friend freedom. Locke gave us the
essential aim of the liberal education—that it teach men how to think
and hence to be free. So we study a variety of subjects not to become

walking encyclopedias like Hippias, but to exercise and develop our understanding.

> The business of education . . . is not . . . to make them ["the young"] perfect in any one of the sciences, but so to open and dispose their minds as may best make them capable of any, when they shall apply themselves to it. [Men who follow only one method for a long time tend to get narrow and inflexible.] It is, therefore, to give them this freedom, that I think they should be made to look into all sorts of knowledge and exercise their understandings in so wide a stock of knowledge. But I do not propose it as a variety and stock of knowledge, but a variety and freedom of thinking, as an increase of the powers and activities of the mind, not as an enlargement of its possessions.[36]

This is still the ideal of a liberal education, and it is under heavy fire from student critics who demand "relevance," direct connection between the problems which beset them and the world on the one hand and the materials they study in school on the other. The great question is, "How remote can general cultivation of mind and breadth of acquaintance with the world of learning be, in a time when problems of race, war, population, poverty, and social change are being neglected?" At the collegiate level and increasingly at the high school level the answer has been, "Present education is too remote. It is supposed to fit us for the world and for our self-realization, and it does neither."

The theme of the foregoing discussions which brought us to liberal education is that Locke's empiricism can be easily misunderstood. Locke's concern was that education be concrete, that it start with the world of experience and of common sense. He deplored a rigid formalism of rational rules which minimize experience and which propose to tell us in advance what experience must be like, and an intellectualism which separates emotions, manners, attitudes, and social sense from the educational development of men. In this emphasis on education of the whole man, he is thoroughly modern and the precurser not only of Dewey and Whitehead but of Bruner, Erikson, and Jones as well. And Locke undoubtedly exaggerated. At some points he told us that the mind is a *tabula rasa,* a blank tablet, on which the particulars of concrete experience write, whether they be moral, sensory, or even logical experience. Actually Locke was as committed to the *activity* of the mind as to its receptivity (a better word than "passivity"). The mind in its purely cognitive functions must compare similars, abstract universals, and compound new ideas in imagination. On the practical side and coordinately with its intellectual development the mind must learn self-motivation and a decent respect for other persons along with care for their welfare—this by being given examples to emulate, to be sure, but also through wishing to be like those whom it admires and respects. All of these things emphasize the activity of mind and are embodied in many themes which Locke repeatedly stated: The prime aim of education is "Vertue" (the excellence of the admirable *person*, not just the thinker, athlete, scholar, etc.). The teacher should be an example: "How prone we are all, especially Children, to Imitation. . . . You [the parent] must do nothing before him, which you would not have him imitate." [37] Development of motivation and mental activity from within also require not only the earlier mentioned virtual ban on corporal punishment ("The most unfit of any [form of punishment] to be used in education" [38]) but also recognition and acceptance of the unpredictability of moods and the need for allowing motivation the chance to spring up of itself. In this matter, Locke looked even beyond Rousseau to the controversial views of Neill.

Locke anticipated and maybe even guided both Rousseau and Neill. "None of the things [children] are to learn should ever be a Burthen to them, or imposed on them as a Task. Is it not so with grown Men?" [39] Even a good student, seriously inclined, "finds yet in himself certain Seasons wherein those things [which he is to learn] have no Relish to him. . . . This Change of Temper should be carefully observed in them, and the favorable *Seasons of Aptitude and Inclination* be heedfully laid hold of. . . ." [40] Locke summed up the point shortly in a thought that—save for its style—might have appeared in either Rousseau or Neill, especially the latter: "For a Child will learn three times as much when he is in *tune,* as he will with double the Time and Pains, when he goes awkwardly or is drag'd unwillingly to it." [41] Not only are there "seasons of aptitude and attention" alternating with their opposites, but the reasoning of a child is not that of an adult and should not be taxed beyond what is appropriate to the child's age. This emphasis on phasing seems close to self-evident to us, but was a needed warning to seventeenth-century tutors and schoolmasters oriented all too much toward education as a cure for immaturity. Better than half a century later Rousseau—and after him Kant—was to take up this point and elaborate it. These three were the early standard bearers of a theme which matures in Piaget—the conception of child development as passing through phases each prerequiring its predecessor and laying the groundwork for its successor. These phases are understood to have their own standards of imagination, insight, sensitivity, and rational control.

What then are we to say of this tension in Locke's writings between the mind as active and the mind as passive? Locke is often caricatured by philosophers as holding the latter view dominantly. Readers of his educational writings may well wonder how the same man would have written both these and his philosophical writings. Ironically, the difficulty lies in a mistake which Locke himself was concerned to eliminate from human understanding: rigid use of abstract terms.

When Locke described the mind as a *tabula rasa,* he meant that it is an informational blank. It does not even have explicit logical rules, he insisted, in the Introduction to the *Essay Concerning Human Understanding.* We may well want to disagree with Locke on the blankness of the mental endowment with which we are born. Some data seem to suggest that there is a latent structure at least to our thought which is more aroused, elicited, or actualized by our experience than it is created or stamped into our minds from the outside. And Locke even sounded a bit at odds with himself when he also talked of the reasoning appropriate to an age, as if there were at least latent *phases* of mind waiting for proper exposure to bring them out.[42] Nevertheless, nothing that Locke said about receptivity of mind should be taken to mean that it is inactive, save the unhappy phrase *tabula rasa* itself. Actually, the mind must be active to compare ideas and hence arrive at general ideas, to compound them and thus to extend human imagination and inventiveness beyond what is given or known. Furthermore, it is the self-activity of the child's mind which is to be encouraged, nourished, and developed in the name of freedom.

Nevertheless, Locke was obviously tempted by the precision of natural science to try for an equally precise analytic psychology. For that purpose, one might want to picture the mind as a kind of Newtonian "empty space," within which ideas combine or separate by some standard laws of association and attraction. And these ideas, like material objects in a Newtonian physics, would be "sharply located" rather than spread about; each would have its own "place," with no overlapping (at least the simple ideas; the complex ones would "include" their components). To Locke the theorist, as earlier with Descartes, alternative models which are not easily rendered consistent both proved attractive: it would fit the mechanistic model better if the ideas acted on each other in a passive mind, but it clearly fits the organic, medical approach better if the mind is more like a craftsman, sorting and associating its idea content.

The time for the richest concrete novelty of experience is childhood. It is harder for adults to learn.[43] In the maturer phases of education there is an increase in "general ideas." Here Locke took an extreme view that Aristotle could not have accepted, in spite of their agreement that our knowledge arises from sense experience and that habit is the aim and basis of educational development. For Locke, "universals," or "general ideas" (such as triangularity), are meaningless unless we supply concrete mental pictures: thus, when I think of triangle in general, I actually picture a particular triangle. Or so Locke claimed. Between the British philosophic tradition he initiated and the European philosophies developed by mathematicians, there is a radical difference as to a matter of fact: the mathematicians claim that the specific picture or figure is only a step toward a direct intellectual grasp of the general idea of triangle, which must be understood apart from such pictures. But in Locke's scheme, any general idea—of a triangle or whatever—turns out to be one of three things. It may be a completely specific mental picture but treated as replaceable by other similar pictures (so, in dealing with triangles, I picture a right isosceles triangle but try to see what remains the same if I replace it by an equilateral or scalene one). Or the general idea may be a sort of composite photographic image, derived by superimposing individual pictures and dropping out the specific peculiarities of each single image—in much the way that superimposing many snapshots will outline a composite photograph of a "typical" American girl or a diffraction pattern. Or the general idea may be a conventional symbol functioning as a variable. I may take the word "triangle" and manipulate this symbol as though it were itself an idea; but this gives no clue as to its meaning.

This third case is interesting because, since the name is a concrete sound or sign, one is tempted to mistake it for a concrete idea of what is meant, and various sorts of nonsense may result. It is a commonplace that children often learn early to manipulate quite abstract notions in a way that seems to indicate familiarity with meaning. They will speak of "justice," "the government," "happiness," and the like, generalizing from limited and highly personal acquaintance. This verbal facility, heavily motivated by the desire to break into the semiclosed world of the adult, is often misconstrued. Instead of regarding this kind of performance as a warning that a more concrete experience is needed as underpinning for verbal facility, the unwary parent may encourage the child toward rapid growth in reading "beyond his age level," thus intensifying the problem and possibly creating an emotional one as well. But as Locke knew, the development of knowledge cannot work from abstract principles down to special cases and instances. The learning process must be the reverse: the student must already be conversant with a considerable range of concrete instances before he can attach a meaning to a general or abstract notion. (Needless to say, Locke did not agree that there *exist* any such things as Platonic forms, which we can know directly and which are referred to by the terms and symbols of mathematics and science. The idea of *existence* is reserved for individual substances and the qualities or characteristics that belong to them.[44]) Sound educational practice must therefore begin through acquaintance with the wide variety of individual items that are the necessary base for a meaningful abstraction. It is a general rule that such items are more likely to be recalled and kept in mind if they are learned in connection with some proposed *use* and if they are encountered repeatedly. But beyond this, there are different ways of providing the needed experience as background, and there does not emerge any universal method of the sort Descartes claimed to have discovered.[45]

The tendencies to cognitive error that education must correct are the tendency to mistake symbols for things and the tendency to mistake complex ideas for unanalyzable simple ones. These errors may be of three types. (1) Words may be used with *no* ideas to correspond, or with eccentric and wrong ideas. (The blind man who used the word "scarlet" to mean "a sound like a trumpet" is cited by Locke as a case of such error.) (2) The same word may be used to name complex ideas by users who have different complexes in mind; the "parade" example cited earlier would apply here, or the much less harmless differences in the assumed content of "monarchy" or "democracy" or "property." (3) Even when words name complex or general ideas and two users agree on the elements that compose the ideas, they may disagree about the type of connection of the parts or about the range of instances an abstraction includes. (We might agree, for example, on the minimum abstract content of a "general idea of personal property," but differ as to whether the specific case of a composer who designs a new notation is a case of property rights.[46])

The avoidance of errors and controversies involves building systematically on firsthand experience so that a mind critically equipped with a wide range of ideas emerges. Such a mind avoids mistaking mere signs for things, is able to analyze presupposed definitions of complex ideas into their simple components, and habitually distrusts abstract generalization until it can be related to relevant concrete examples.

The resulting prescriptions for educational practice have an appealing simplicity. We must "cover material" in such a way that our students will "have in mind" all the requisite simple ideas. We can test this phase by the number of items a student can identify and respond to correctly. (Locke's idea here is echoed by some students of "cultural deprivation": they think of that problem as a lack of some normal items of experience, and the proposed remedies take the form of "enrichment" programs to add needed but omitted ideas.) Then the ability to combine these single ideas into general, complex, and causal sets gives meaning to the words we use as a technical shorthand for extended ranges of experience. The analysis of complex into simple ideas is a corrective for logical error and for mistaken judgments of what exists and what does not, and so also a method for resolving controversy. The whole set of mental operations, on this theory, can be represented mechanically and atomically. (Locke did not deny that there is a dimension of insight and recognition of symbols as such that the student supplies; but he presupposed this in the analysis he used.) The content of a well-informed mind can be selected and fed into this mind item by item and tested in the same way. Simple types of connection can be used as input to build simple ideas into complex ones, separate ideas into judgments, concrete experiences into highly abstract sciences.[47]

The main heritage from Locke that has shaped our common sense is a double one. His writings on education offer a program of humane and practical interpretation of the educational enterprise, a recognition of the interdependence of mind, will, and body that rests on sound medical insights and cultural sensitivity. His philosophic treatment of human understanding, carried into popularity by his political writings on the one hand and his educational essays on the other, has issued in four main attitudes or notions:

1. The distrust of general ideas detached from specific individual cases reinforced a tendency that for some reason was already typical of English (and later of American) culture. (As late as World War II, English courses in some New York City high schools were devoting themselves to teaching students to distrust all "glittering generalities," in a sound—if overaustere—Lockean fashion.)

2. The notion of reducing complex and general ideas to sets of simple ones had great influence; it reinforced the metaphor of a "well-stocked" mind and stressed the role of factual information. Since Hippias, we have all admired the omniscient expert who knows all the facts; and we have all noticed the relative ease of recording, imparting, and measuring such information—as contrasted, say, to grading answers to Socrates' question "Can human excellence be taught?" Here is a theoretical justification for practices of testing that a desire for efficiency and objectivity make tempting in any case.

3. The insistence on a range of firsthand experience became diffused and was influential in many ways. From backing up the importance of laboratory work in science to justifying foreign travel as an intrinsically worthwhile part of education through the sort of reading of travel and psychological books that Locke himself enjoyed, this theme reverberated. (Furthermore, Locke's voyages were to be in the real

world, not in some inner sea of thought where the mind found unexpected discoveries—the Continental rationalists were rather in favor of this latter sort of travel.)

4. Locke's notion that what is called "thinking" in the several educational philosophies we have discussed was reducible even in its most complex forms to many repeated simple combinatorial operations involving associations of ideas opened the way for a closer integration of biology, neurology, and psychology than did other current theories; the total chasm between man and other animals that Descartes defended and that was part of the Christian Augustinian tradition could be viewed merely as a difference in degree.[48] The mental faculty known from classical times as "intelligence," if it was simply the power of repeated elementary operations, could perhaps be measured or tested by seeing how quickly sets of these basic operations were performed. Subject matters, consisting of multiple items of information arranged in patterns of association, could presumably be programed for maximum coverage and efficiency.[49] While the loss of confidence in real essences which were recognized by "insight" led to greater pessimism regarding the possibility of absolutely reliable knowledge, it led also to an attitude of tolerance for diverse opinion and to a new technique for arriving at agreement in discussion, by appeal to clear definitions of what each party meant rather than by invoking objective standards about which only one party could be right while the other must be perverse.

Locke's successors in England in philosophy and psychology (like David Hume) emphasized and sharpened the skeptical, analytic side of his theory. With the passage of time they became increasingly rigorous in limiting "understanding" to ideas capable of direct encounter through the senses or immediate subjective feelings. As this critical aspect was pressed, many of the distinctions Locke had accepted were rejected: sharp consistency led to a denial of any difference in principle between ideas of primary and secondary qualities, as Bishop Berkeley was to demonstrate. It led also to dismissing notions of power and cause as subjective and hence not corresponding to anything directly observable, to calling the idea of a "self" into question by treating introspection as another case of detached observation, and so on. In particular, Locke's idea of matter as a something, "I know not what," was thrown out of court—a philosopher who insists on experience as the test of meaning is not entitled to such a vague, unexperienceable entity!

On the other hand, Locke's own work began with a common-sense view of man immersed in a world of nature, a dynamic world of substances, dispositions, powers, and other selves. By stressing this side of Locke we can see why Whitehead claimed that he had been strongly influenced by themes in Locke's *Essay* in forming his own philosophy, which he characterized as a "philosophy of organism." [50] Evidently, other lines of interpretation could be found leading out of Locke's position. If we follow his stress on the crucial role that *using* ideas plays in motivation and learning, the result lies somewhere in the direction of Dewey's pragmatism. [51] But if we emphasize the crucial role of language in thought and the danger of being misled by misuse of words, we can see Locke, along with Augustine, as still another predecessor of modern linguistic and analytic philosophy. [52]

NOTES

1. For evidence of his impact on education, see James L. Axtell, ed., *The Educational Writings of John Locke,* Cambridge, Mass., 1968 (hereafter cited as *Educational Writings*), pp. 98 ff. (A Checklist of Printings of Locke on Education). F. S. C. Northrop has argued the case for calling our modern political common sense "Lockean," e.g. in his *The Meeting of East and West,* New York, 1946. In the history of philosophy Locke occupies a rather transitional position: his ideas do not fit together with the tight systematic architecture of the rationalists, and his analytic work stops short of the critical precision of later empiricists. Even at the expense of some inconsistency, he stays close to ordinary experience, avoiding both systematization of a Cartesian sort and "critical precision" of the kind we will find in Hume.

2. This, with the further thesis that the elements of thought all originate in sense experience or introspective "feeling," is the theme of the *Essay Concerning Human Understanding* (hereafter cited as *Essay*), 5th ed., London, 1706. But this is only one of the themes we meet in the writings on education and politics; Locke is not single-minded in applying his model.

3. This, of course, amounts to a drastic redefinition of "ideas" away from the Platonic tradition. Compare Descartes' not entirely clear claim that the most important philosophic ideas are known by an act of intuition wholly distinct from sense experience and imagination. See the account of the relation of Locke's position to Descartes' in N. P. Stallknecht and R. S. Brumbaugh, *The Spirit of Western Philosophy,* New York, 1950, pp. 294 ff.

4. This is one of the central themes of this chapter. Axtell makes the same point in *Educational Writings.* As evidence of Locke's medical competence and interest, see the article by Jerry Stannard, "Materia Medica in the Locke-Clarke Correspondence," *Bulletin of the History of Medicine* XXXVII (1963): 201–225. An interesting suggestion that Locke's advice concerning the education of Edward Clarke, Jr., is tailored to a very specific case and by no means intended as a general program or theory was put forward in 1967 by Janice Gorn, "The Strange 'Case' of Edward Clarke, Jr.: Attending Physician—John Locke, Gent.," *Educational Theory* XVII (1967): 298–316. Perhaps the main difference in emphasis between the project of training in a craft for Clarke and the general curricular plan in *Some Thoughts Concerning Education* (*Works* III, 1–96; hereafter cited as *Education*) can be explained in this way. At least the point deserves further investigation.

5. He is very precise about this in the *Essay*, which opens with the classification of ideas as simple or complex and as derived from sensation or "reflection."

6. Locke develops this in the *Essay*, Book III, where he treats the role of words in making generalizations possible and communicable. Aristotle seems to presuppose rather than to argue for the distinction between "abstraction" and "intuition."

7. In Whitehead's version of Platonism, however, there is a strong awareness of the incompleteness of an education that deals only in abstractions. See R. S. Brumbaugh and N. M. Lawrence, *Philosophers on Education*, Boston, 1963, Chapter 7.

8. *Essay*, Book II, Chapter 1, secs. 1–8 sets up the crucial definitions for Locke's analysis. "Sec. 1. 1. Idea is the object of thinking. 2. All ideas come from sensation or reflection. 3. The objects of sensation one source of ideas. 4. The operations of our minds the other source of them. 5. All our ideas are of the one or the other of these. 6. Observable in children. 7. Men are differently furnished with these, according to the different objects they converse with. 8. Ideas of reflection later because they need attention."

9. A gentleman is understood to have a business or a profession, however, and to be an integral rather than a parasitic part of society.

10. On the status of children, Axtell finds Philippe Ariès, *Centuries of Childhood: A Social History of Family Life* (trans. R. Balsick, New York, 1965) important documentation. Axtell argues in *Educational Writings* that Locke's importance in altering ideas about children—seeing them as persons rather than objects or bits of property or pets—stands out far more clearly when Ariès' history is kept in mind.

11. On Locke as a doctor, in addition to the citations above see Kenneth Dewhurst, *John Locke (1632–1704) Physician and Philosopher: A Medical Biography with an Edition of the Medical Notes in His Journals*, London, 1963. See also James Axtell, "Education and Status in Stuart England: The London Physician," *History of Education Quarterly* X (1970): 141–159.

12. See *Education*, *Educational Writings*, pp. 165–167. On the disadvantages of school, see Axtell, *Educational Writings*, pp. 21–23.

13. *Educational Writings*, p. 236.

14. This Locke considers his revolutionary contribution of "a new method" for education.

15. Direct method in language, *Educational Writings*, p. 266.

16. "I am not for painting," *Educational Writings*, p. 315.

17. Readiness used as principle, *Educational Writings*, pp. 289 ff.

18. *Educational Writings*, pp. 177 ff. "*Stubbornness* and an obstinate Disobedience, must be master'd with Force and Blows . . ."

19. "Sauntring," *Educational Writings*, p. 233.

20. Compare note 14 and *Educational Writings*, p. 289.

21. *Essay*, Book I, "Of Innate Notions" contends that there are none. Here Locke clearly sides with Aristotle against the Platonic tradition and Descartes.

22. *Essay*, Book III, Chapter 3, sec. 15: "Real and Nominal Essences . . ."; sec. 17: "Supposition, that species are distinguished by their real essences, useless. . . ." This rejects an important part of both the Platonic and the Aristotelian positions, in which we do know real essences as forms (Platonic) or species (Aristotelian).

23. All three of these assumptions are recognized and rejected for example by Leibniz in his *New Essays Concerning Human Understanding*, trans. Alfred G. Langley, New York, 1896. In fact, as Leibniz saw the case, all three of these assumptions should be replaced by their opposites!

24. The distinction between primary and secondary qualities, although denied by Berkeley, found its way into general common-sense acceptance. The problems this raises and a proposed alternative are treated in a twentieth-century context by A. N. Whitehead, *Science and the Modern World*, New York, 1925.

25. Dispositions or potentialities are concepts that are indispensable in any philosophic system that takes the notion of organism as fundamental. On the other

hand, they create a puzzle for formalist and mechanist systems since they are not observable or recognizable until they become actual (and so are actual properties rather than dispositions). A recent treatment of this subject is David Weissman, *Dispositional Properties*, Carbondale, Ill., 1965.

26. See Chapter 3, note 27 for this Cartesian rejection. But, as Leibniz showed in his *Discourse on Metaphysics*, the laws of motion and the acceleration of freely falling bodies *do* require a concept of force distinct from Descartes' "quantity of motion" (i.e. momentum).

27. *Essay*, Book II, Chapter 23, secs. 1–37.

28. A. N. Whitehead, *Process and Reality*, New York, 1929, p. v: "The writer who most fully anticipated the main positions of the philosophy of organism is John Locke in his *Essay*, especially in its later books." (In a footnote, Whitehead refers here to Book IV, Chapter 6, sec. 11.)

29. The two main developments in British Empiricism after Locke were critiques rigorously using his analytic-experiential method. First, Berkeley showed that we cannot have clear ideas of what Locke calls matter or material substance. Then Hume denied the existence of a clear idea (as opposed to a feeling) of causality and further found that one could not discover a clear idea of the self. Locke himself did not push the analytic strand of his philsophy to the limit.

30. See H. R. Fox Bourne, *The Life of John Locke*, London, 1876, vol. II, p. 254.

31. Cited in *Educational Writings*, p. 59.

32. *Ibid.*, p. 238.

33. *Of the Conduct of the Understanding* (hereafter cited as *Conduct*), *Works* III, 371–409; especially sec. 4, pp. 375–376.

34. *Conduct*, sec. 9: *Works* III, 381.

35. *Conduct*, sec. 13: *Works* III, 384–385.

36. *Conduct*, sec. 18: *Works* III, 387.

37. *Education*, sec. 71: *Works* III, 26; *Educational Writings*, pp. 171–172. Also see secs. 70, 135.

38. *Education*, sec. 47: *Works* III, 15; *Educational Writings*, pp. 148–149. Compare sec. 84.

39. *Education*, sec. 73: *Works* III, 27; *Educational Writings*, pp. 172–173.

40. *Education*, sec. 74: *Works* III, 27; *Educational Writings*, p. 173.

41. *Education*, secs. 74–75: *Works* III, 27; *Educational Writings*, pp. 173–175.

42. It should be noticed here (*Education*, sec. 8) that the reasonableness Locke recommends in the correction of children is just as much characterized by composure and calmness as it is by any precise intellectual correctness—the reasonableness of behavior, that is, fully as much as the rationale of thought. Thus Rousseau's protest against Locke's "reasoning" with children is wide of the mark and even suggests hasty acquaintance with what Locke said.

43. *Conduct*, sec. 6. Pretty hard for Americans also, thinks Locke.

44. *Essay*, Book III, Chapter 3: "Of General Terms," secs. 1–20.

45. *Education* constantly refers to the "usefulness" and "putting to use" of what is to be studied, from accounting to letter writing. It is certainly not his only criterion, but just as certainly it is a break with the traditional conception of a liberal education.

46. This example of "property rights" rests on the actual case of a composer trying to protect his invention of a new musical notation. He could not patent it, but he could get a "design copyright" on it

47. It is interesting to compare Locke's account of our operations with Hume's ideas (see Chapter 5); Locke uses the metaphor of a craftsman, where Hume comes closer to taking a mechanism as his paradigm. On the formation of complex concepts, see also the recent work of Piaget (discussed in Chapter 9).

48. *Essay*, Book II, Chapters 9, 10.

49. Axtell discusses Locke's actual teaching career (*Educational Writings*, pp. 18–48). Particularly interesting is the herbarium (p. 40) consisting of pressed plants

mounted on student letters and essays, dating from his early teaching years at Oxford.

50. See note 28.
51. See note 27.
52. Compare *Philosophers on Education*, Chapter 6.

5

An Appendix on Understanding Through Analysis: Hume

Locke's firm attachment to common sense involved him in logical tensions both in his more technical psychology and in his educational theory. On the one hand, like Aristotle in the classical period and St. Thomas in the medieval, Locke took an everyday world of substances, causes, persons, and powers as a starting point. But on the other hand, he introduced a critical, analytic method into his technical investigations of the mind's inventory of simple ideas, their combinations, and the words we use to designate them. The two standpoints fit together only if we recognize that for Locke—in opposition to Descartes and to the whole Platonic tradition—the sharp analysis is to be trusted just so far as it is sensible; Cartesian certainty and precision are not to be expected in the diverse natural world we inhabit.[1]

The philosophy of David Hume, to put the matter very simply, recognized that the realm of the practical and the realm of the theoretical may not be *capable* of being brought under one set of overarching principles. Theory wants certainty, clarity, completeness of the sort aimed at by Descartes. Practical action, however, may rest on quite different considerations. Hume undertook, for example, to show that the notion that everything that happened had to have a cause could not be either proven by logic or witnessed by experience. No sane person would, in the domain of action, doubt it for a moment. Hume's point is simply that a belief strong enough to live by is still much less than logically certain and hence of limited use in philosophical theory. By sharply distinguishing the theoretical from the practical, Hume in effect stifled a whole domain of possible criticism—that which comes from practical belief—and was thus able to pursue Locke's analytic procedures with less restraint and greater persistence.

Hume inherited from Locke still another problem: the nature of perception and the relation between feeling and fact. Locke shared with Descartes a critical doctrine *not* in line with common sense, the doctrine of representative perception. This is the thesis that what I perceive are ideas or images *in my own mind,* which thus becomes a kind of picture gallery. Strictly speaking, I do not perceive things outside my mind; these, I feel, *cause* many of my ideas, but there is no way for me to inspect such outside things directly.[2] Now, if we take it seriously, this notion leads to skepticism—the doctrine that everything is dubious—and solipsism—the doctrine that one's consciousness is the only consciousness, all others being merely assumed to exist through the appearance of what are, after all, only images. For the most part, extreme skepticism and extreme solipsism are philosophers' toys. We can bring ourselves to our practical senses by noticing that the doctrine that everything is dubious excludes itself, and we may ask the man who wishes to persuade us of solipsism why he bothers to argue with beings that exist only as figments of his consciousness. Yet the notions of a world which is knowable to us only as that which stimulates our senses and of consciousness isolated in its privacy have had penetrating effects on educational theory and practice. For example, the desks in most classrooms face the teacher so that the windows of the child's consciousness open primarily toward the teacher. Much testing is arranged so that students who assist one another are cheating. Other work is arranged so that if the students talk to one another they are disturbing the isolated thoughts of others as they plow through the problem, the review, the memorization, or the essay to be written. But from these classrooms we have hoped to bring forth men and women who assist one another in the life beyond the school and who have learned to share the thoughts and emotions without which life is barren.

We do not mean to say that there is no place in education for independent, solitary work, nor that the individual should never be challenged to study and to use his knowledge on his own. Nonetheless, the concept of a mind locked up in the head away from the common real world, whose identity can be guessed at only as it causes the same effects inside isolated minds, lends itself well to the concept of education as factual, rational, schematic, and instructional. There are serious byproducts of these notions. It is easy to think that men mentally isolated also have their sense of value turned primarily toward themselves. Indeed Locke's predecessor, Thomas Hobbes, held that men were naturally antisocial; their benevolence, their concern for others, and their sense of sociality are all acquired feelings, not natural to them at all, but forced on them because they were forced to depend upon one another for livelihood and protection. Society is thus an artifact—a great Leviathan, a giant machine—created by men to house and to inhibit their natural self-centeredness, to calm it and restrain it, thus making life tolerable—a life, said Hobbes, which in a state of nature was solitary, nasty, brutish, and short. Solipsistic minds, solitary interests—by nature; this is Hobbes's picture. Locke, it is true, also thought that the political condition of man is an artifact but that it arises from a natural fellow-feeling among men—so that implicit kinship naturally underlies the political society of men. If a government is not natural, at least it arises from natural inclinations. Hobbes's state is built on fear. However, even Locke bases his fellow-feeling on our "being all the workmanship of one omnipotent and infinitely wise master . . . [from whom we ultimately derive] . . . [t]he law of nature . . . which wills the peace and preservation of all mankind. . . .³ And ultimately we are faced with somewhat the same situation. As the classroom is held together by the teacher of all the class, so is mankind bound together by the same God. Locke's own humane interests in the learning process led him to invoke the assistance of tutor and father. Thus Locke embeds his *learning* theory in a doctrine of education which does not rely exclusively or even largely on the notion of classroom study.

Like Locke, Hume was committed to a doctrine of feeling, which he more frequently refered to as sentiment or moral sentiment. In Hume's thought, then, "understanding" and "sentiment" are relatively distinct faculties. The faculty of understanding can be analyzed along quite didactic, intellectual lines. The faculty of sentiment is "a feeling for the happiness of mankind." ⁴ He goes on to say,

> This partition between the faculties of understanding and senti-
> ment, in all moral decisions, seems clear from the preceding
> hypothesis (that it is feeling, not reason, which decides right and
> wrong and does so on the basis of utility). . . .
>   When it is affirmed that two and three are equal to the half of
> ten, this relation of equality I understand perfectly. . . . But when
> you draw thence a comparison to moral relations, I own that I am
> at a loss to understand you.⁵

What Hume does is to distinguish between "fact" and "right," explicitly and sharply.⁶ The usefulness of this distinction, like Locke's between the world as it is in itself and the world as it is presented to our limited, particular, sensory organs, can hardly be denied. For example as a *fact,* the Hiroshima bomb was a public occasion, its physical nature, death toll, radioactive aftermath, etc.,⁷ agreed upon by all. As to its moral and political value, any degree of feeling—"sentiment" —exists, from its being unequivocally morally heinous to its being a moral necessity.

Once the distinction between fact and right is made, several things happen. Hume plainly rests the case for education of the sentiments

upon *custom, tradition,* and *the decency of civilized man*—what came
to be called "the done thing" in nineteenth- and twentieth-century
Britain. "It isn't done" was a firmer and a less arguable reproof than
"It's wrong." The total weight of society, its relatively homogeneous
pressure from a relatively homogeneous culture (for all its diversity),
served England's small continent well. And it left the way open for a
rational study of fact, the problems of knowledge, and the faculty of
understanding itself. The transition from Locke to Hume is the transition from human understanding as concerned with feelings and fact to
human understanding as concerned dominantly with fact, feeling
being left to the educative powers of an immediate society—the family
and so on. The goal on the side of feeling and sentiment, depending
on whether you give it its objective status or its personal quality, is
utility or pleasure—including the gratification of serving another
man's happiness or well-being. The goal on the side of understanding
is truth—either that of logical certainty or empirical probability.
Hume's distinction between fact and right made it easy to sever learning in the intellectual sense from education in the broad sense that
Locke had intended.

The analytical side of Locke's work was sharpened and carried to its
logical conclusion by Hume; and Hume's theory of meaning has been
influential ever since his philosophic work gained recognition.[8]
Hume's influence has been transmitted through many channels: Kant
began his revolution in philosophy as an attempt to go beyond
Hume's skepticism; in religion, Hume's posthumously published criti-
cisms stirred up a great controversy; his essays became a model of clarity and analysis for later British analytic philosophy; and the logical
positivists carried forward his examination and condemnation of
"meaningless discourse." Hume was a diplomat, essayist, and historian,
not a physician like Locke nor a mathematician like Descartes. Perhaps some of the differences among these men reflect the difference between handling proof and evidence in mathematics, in medicine, and
in history.[9]

In his philosophy Hume took over the project of constructing a "science of the mind" by observing and describing our ideas and the "laws
governing their patterns of association." (This project would get
around the mind-body chasm in Descartes by applying to thinking
substance exactly the same method that physics had used for extended
substance.[10]) Knowledge, according to Hume, consists of the ideas in
our minds which are memories of firsthand impressions (either
through our senses or of our inner feelings).[11] The analogy of mind to
a modern camera will fit very well here. Suppose our memory is a sen-
sitized film, moving frame by frame, and suppose the impressions from

our senses reach this film through a variable lens called imagination. The developed snapshots are the ideas we store in a filing system of understanding, and thinking, which consists in grasping associations of ideas, is a method of retrieval of information from this file. Although Hume, like Locke, recognized two sorts of impressions, those coming through the senses and those representing our inner feeling, he concentrated, as we have seen, on the former.[12] For any judgment about existence we must look to those impressions that come to us from outside.[13]

We have said that the imagination is like a lens that comes between our firsthand impressions and our ideas that copy the impressions and file them. In a brief, incisive analysis that would take all mystery out of creativity and imagination if it were right, Hume reduced the operations of imagination (in inventing new ideas and in modifying impressions as we form ideas of them) into exactly four. Imagination can (1) diminish or (2) augment or (3) separate or (4) superimpose impressions.[14] It may do any one or more of these in creating a new idea or in modifying an impression as it gets filed. A stranger jumping out at me at night in a dark forest may be only five feet tall, but my memory of this sudden apparition may be of a seven-foot giant, for example. It is worth noting that operation 4, the superimposing of ideas, accounts for the fact that we seem to perceive flow and continuity, not successive static snapshots: here the motion-picture film, whose static frames create the illusion of motion, is a good analogue to Hume's imagination.[15]

Once ideas are "in" the mind, they are stored and recalled by rules of association. On first glance, Hume finds the same set of such laws that Aristotle had recognized much earlier in his treatise *On Memory:* we associate ideas that are *similar* or *opposite;* ideas that represent impressions close together in *space;* ideas of impressions that follow closely in *time;* and ideas that stand in a *"cause-and-effect"* relation.[16] But before he is done, Hume modifies this in a way that completely rules out the causal explanation of Aristotle and even the weaker notions of Descartes and Locke.[17]

To make our ideas clear and meaningful, according to Hume, we must trace them back to the impressions they arose from, and by checking the context or repeating similar impressions, we must correct for possible distortions of imagination. In the course of such checking, it turns out that we use a good many words that we *feel* mean something yet to which no idea, let alone any sense impression, corresponds. These words are "meaningless" in the technical sense that we cannot connect them with any experience outside of a feeling of significance that comes with them.[18]

This new precision in analysis required a drastic limitation of Locke. For example, the powers and dispositions of things cannot be the source of our impressions until they become actual properties. (I cannot see the characteristic solubility of sugar, though I can see sugar dissolving when it is actually put into water. If I expect sugar to dissolve, that is because I have seen it dissolve in the past, not because any power or tendency is part of my impression of this sugar in the present. Thus the certainty that I feel about the sugar's dissolving is in me, as the result of past experience, and not in the sugar.) [19] Nor is the idea of a material substance meaningful in this new, strict sense. How can there be an impression or idea of such a thing, which Locke himself finally characterized as a "something, I know not what"? [20] And throughout the work of Hume there are similar restrictions on the range and relations of ideas that are meaningful.

Hume's model of the mind, and of reasoning as an association of ideas by rules reflecting the order of elements in our experience, has a beautiful, if oversimple, precision. On first glance it seems to describe the way my understanding actually works. I think of "heat" (of a hot particular something), and my next idea may be "cold"—association by resemblance and opposition. I think of my office, and my next idea is a picture of the courtyard outside it—association by contiguity in space. I think of yesterday's boat ride and then of the town where we got off—contiguity in time. [21] If this were indeed the whole analysis of the laws of operation of understanding, it could be exactly the theory of knowledge that education needs as the connecting link between its general goals and specific tactics. But a second look—a second look that Hume himself took—shows that some very strange consequences follow from this very plausible analysis. [22]

In the first place, the analysis gives us no way of telling whether there exists an external world, let alone whether such a world is at all like our ideas. My idea of an external world is only my memory of the *feeling* that sense impressions come from outside me and are independent of my own wishes. [23] But there is no way to get beyond the ideas of these qualities that impress me—the blueness of the sea, noisiness of a siren, hardness of a bench—to discover their causes and to see whether the impression and the cause of it are alike. (And, unlike Locke, Hume saw that the same account applies to primary qualities as to secondary; the ideas of primary qualities depend just as much on the sensory equipment of the perceiver as secondary ones do; they are merely a bit more reliable. If Locke, with his fondness for abnormal psychology, had read some modern studies of the effects of hallucinogenic drugs, he too might have given up this distinction. [24])

Hume showed that if we stick to the analytic method of breaking things down into their least parts, even causal relationships become nothing but familiar sequences of events occurring always in the same order.[25] What Descartes had taken for a clear innate conception and Locke for an idea derived from experience (with a dash of intuition) reduces in Hume to a complex of three simpler parts. When I say that *A* caused *B,* what I *mean* is that events which are like one another are followed by others which are also like one another, which adjoin one another in space and are successive in time, and that they are related by a feeling of necessary or probable connection.[26] If the first event is a thrown rock, book, or log, and the second is a characteristic noise issuing from far off—say the breaking of a window—we say the first caused the second. If one of these sequences occurs and, at the time the window breaks, the sun comes out from behind the clouds and I feel a pain in my arm, I may look for glass in my arm, but I won't wonder what the window's breaking had to do with the sun. The reason is that a sequence of the latter sort is too unfamiliar in my previous experience and its parts are too remote in space; whereas the former experience, though not invariable, has enough similarities to past sequences to make me want to check. On *analysis,* then, it is the mind itself which supplies the causal chains that "bind the universe together." [27] This is an unwelcome conclusion and an odd one. It makes natural science rest on irrational acts of faith, and—as we will see—it rules out religious attempts to discover God as either cause of our world or cause of our idea of Him.[28]

Another surprise comes when Hume analyzes the idea of a self: all he can find, as he objectively itemizes the ideas in his understanding, is a "bundle of impressions," internal and external, but with no separate impression of some single strand or element, an ego, self, or subject, holding them together.[29] This again is unwelcome and seems extreme, but the student is advised, before rejecting it out of hand, to try to meet Hume's demand for meaning by producing the single impression that is the source of the ideas which the word "self" names! [30]

When we are dealing with existence, not with fictions, we reason by probabilities: we expect *B* to follow *A,* and our expectation grows stronger the more often *B* has in fact followed *A* in the past. We do not expect all eggs to be fresh, but we do expect all cannonballs to be heavy, and so on.[31] We will return presently to the impact of Hume's theory on religion (and, though he did not anticipate this point, to its impact on our contemporary cosmology), a skeptical impact that results from our inability to know what to expect in an unprecedented situation. What is the probability that our universe has a divine creator—or a definite beginning in time? [32] There is no way to tell;

since there is only one case, experience gives us no ground for thinking there is a cause of a given type any more than for thinking there is
not. And so on.[33]

Now, it should be clear that Hume's development of the analytic
side of Locke in the direction of clarity and consistency would lend itself beautifully to educational application if it were not bought at so
high a price. For by tracing ideas back to the impressions from which
they arise we could do away with meaningless and vague words. By
using the laws of association, we could program and reinforce the learning of matters of fact—A/B sets of ideas in causal sequences. By applying the rules that govern imagination, we might be able to develop
public taste and almost certainly could work out a science of aesthetics
and art criticism.[34] Philosophy and science, stripped of ambiguous jar-
gon, could be written in clear and simple language (Hume's own style
is a model of this), and all pretenses of religion, pseudoscience, or psychology to go *beyond* experience could be given healthy correction.[35]

For two purposes, Hume's account was particularly admirable. As a
way of weighting historical evidence, it works well.[36] And in a day
when Christian authors were claiming that purely secular *historical*
evidence—reports of miracles, for example—established the truth of
their religion, Hume's criticism quickly pointed out their mistake.[37]
The probability that a true miracle—an exception to all the past regu-
larities of nature—really took place is far less than the probability of
deceit, misobservation, and misreporting. These are frequent enough,
whereas by definition the miracle has a probability of almost zero:
strictly, $1/$no. past observations of connection of A and B.[38]

Many aspects of Hume's program to establish his new science of the
mind have had twentieth-century attempts at application. The idea of
recasting all science (both that dealing with thinking and that dealing
with material things) in a clear, uniform language was one goal of the
Encyclopedia of Unified Science organized by Charles Morris and Rudolph Carnap in the 1930's.[39] The distrust of "glittering generalities"
and "meaningless discourse" which Hume shared with Locke was re-
iterated both in the general semantics of Korzybski and Hayakawa, and
in the strict logical positivist approach to meaning of Carnap, Feigl,
Hempel, and others. A needed reinterpretation of the sense in which
Christianity *can* be understood as history has been developed by
Barth, Bultmann, Tillich, and others.[40] The mechanism of creativity,
seemingly a weak point in the theory, has been applied to tone-row
musical composition by computer and by random combinatorial patterns.[41] Philosophy in England, from G. E. Moore through Russell,
Ayer, and Austin, has pursued a program of recasting philosophy

within clear ordinary language, a program in good part admittedly following Hume's example.[42]

And yet this incisive development of the critical side of Locke is *not* philosophically or educationally satisfactory. Useful as it may be for the writer of history, it does not do justice to aesthetics, mathematics, natural science, or even psychology. It applies beautifully—as we will see when we discuss B. F. Skinner—to the memorization of related patterns of information already known, but offers no clues as to methods of creativity or discovery. It does not explain where we get the *patterns* that we use to order the atomic items of experience ("similarity," for example, is not a simple quality like "blueness," yet Hume presupposes in his account of the mind at work that we have such an idea [43]). In short, we have here a limited tool, excellent for certain historical and critical uses, but fatal when extended to a general method of teaching and learning, since neither learning nor knowledge can be reduced to the retrospective memory and sorting of atomic ideas or bits of information already discovered in the past. The limitation of Hume's examination of thought and understanding is built in at the ground level. It lies in his restricted idea of experience as arising exclusively from impressions and as reducible without loss back to those impressions. This view, in spite of its usefulness, obviously construes experience too narrowly. For example, the whole thrust of creativity, imagination, insight, and inquiry which are part of our experience of learning have been left out of the present account.[44] Admirers as well as critics of the machine-scored tests and small-step learning programs that follow Humean principles have agreed that a machine can only live in the past, to speak metaphorically. It can score right and wrong responses by comparing each response with its memory; it lacks a Cartesian self or a Freudian ego or a Whiteheadian appetite for novelty; it lacks a body (some implications of this are drawn in a provocative recent article [45]): but it also clearly falls short of the living teacher who works with the learner and subject matter in present and future, as well as in past, time.[46]

Though his analysis is not, as Hume had hoped, either a complete or an ultimate philosophic answer, it is an extremely suggestive and useful approach for certain types of critical and pedagogical purposes. We will discuss these in more detail in Chapter 8 in connection with the contemporary psychological and educational ideas of B. F. Skinner.

NOTES

1. See Chapter 2 and the contrast of Aristotle and Plato in R. S. Brumbaugh and N. M. Lawrence, *Philosophers on Education*, Boston, 1963, Chapter 3.

2. Stallknecht offers an excellent account of this in N. P. Stallknecht and R. S. Brumbaugh, *The Spirit of Western Philosophy*, New York, 1950, pp. 326–341. Compare Hume's investigation of our idea of the external world in *Treatise*, Book I, Part 2, sec. 6.

3. John Locke, *Second Treatise*, sec. 6: *Works*, 5th ed., London, 1706, vol. II, p. 7.

4. David Hume, *An Inquiry Concerning the Principles of Morals*, ed. C. W. Hendel, New York, 1957, p. 105.

5. *Ibid.*, p. 107.

6. *Ibid.*, pp. 109 ff.

7. As we write, the AEC is—ironically—denying an establishable relationship between its tests and the sextupling of leukemia statistics in communities located near the testing grounds.

8. The Open Court edition of Hume's *Enquiry Concerning Human Understanding* (LaSalle, Ill., 1907,, pp. v–xvi; hereafter cited as *Enquiry*) contains a brief autobiography. See also C. W. Hendel, *Studies in the Philosophy of David Hume*, Indianapolis, 1963.

9. This repeats the point made in the introduction to Part One about the many and very different kinds of phenomena which are grouped together under the term "learning" (page 11).

10. Hume thus resolves Cartesian dualism by extending the methods of science to cover psychology as well as physics and by rejecting Descartes' intuition of some outer extended world distinct from thinking substance. In fact, as we will see, he can find no clear meaning in the Cartesian idea of "thinking substance."

11. *Enquiry*, sec. 2.

12. Thus Hume keeps Locke's split of sensation and reflection as distinct sources of ideas. Nevertheless, Hume himself considered his study of feeling, sentiment, and ethics (*An Inquiry Concerning the Principles of Morals*) his best book.

13. Compare note 2. The point is made even more sharply in the conclusion of Hume's *Abstract of a Treatise of Human Nature*, ed. J. M. Keynes and P. Sraffa, Cambridge, 1938.

14. *Enquiry*, pp. 16–17. "But though our thought seems to possess this unbounded liberty, we shall find, upon a nearer examination, that it is really confined *within very narrow limits,* and that all this creative power of the mind amounts to no more than the faculty of compounding, transposing, augmenting, or diminishing the materials afforded us by the senses and experience" (p. 16; emphasis ours).

15. "Continuity" seems always to be a construction of the imagination and indeed wholly fictitious and unrelated to real existence. Hence Hume's careful use of "contiguity" rather than "continuity." For Hume's view of the status of continuity in geometry and of geometry itself as a field that studies this imaginary quality, see *Enquiry*, p. 168, especially note 1.

16. *Enquiry*, sec. 3.

17. Aristotle's scheme of four causes is discussed in Chapter 3 of *Philosophers on Education*, Descartes' weakened version in Chapter 3 of this volume, and Locke's in Chapter 4 in connection with the ideas of substance and power.

18. There may be some interesting technical problems in defining "meaningless" as distinct from "internally inconsistent" or "nonsensical." Hume does it this way: "All ideas, especially abstract ones, are naturally faint and obscure: the mind has but a slender hold of them: they are apt to be confounded with other resembling ideas; and when we have often employed any term, though without a distinct meaning, we are apt to imagine it has a determinate idea annexed to it" (*Enquiry*, p. 19). For a more recent look at the nature of nonsense, see S. Jack Odell, "Nonsense" (abstract), *Journal of Philosophy* LXVII (1970): p. 830.

19. Compare Locke's ideas of powers and tertiary qualities in Chapter 4.

20. George Berkeley maintains the empiricist approach but uses it to show that "material reality" is either a derivative rather than a basic notion, or nonsense.

21. On the ways in which Western philosophers and authors have treated the question of whether distinct impressions are or are not continuous, see Georges Poulet, *Studies in Human Time*, trans. Elliott Coleman, Baltimore, 1956, introduction and chapter on Proust.

22. Hume's honesty about his own difficulties is very engaging, for example, in his discussion of one special case in which he can imagine an idea might be supplied without the corresponding impression (*Enquiry*, p. 18). His conclusion there, however, is "though this instance is so singular, that it is scarcely worth our observing, and does not merit that for it alone we should alter our general maxim" (p. 19).

23. See notes 2 and 9.

24. In particular, of course, hallucinations of walking through extended substances without encountering resistance would count strongly against the thesis that shape and resistance are radically different from color and other secondary qualities.

25. We do have an idea, but on analysis it turns out to be a strong subjective *feeling* of expectation, not a memory of some *sense impression* of causality. When Hume's *Treatise on Human Nature* failed to attract attention, he wrote (in 1740) an anonymous review concentrating on this theme (identified as Hume's and edited by J. M. Keynes and P. Sraffa; see note 13).

26. *Enquiry*, sec. 7.

27. In the *Abstract* Hume explicitly draws the conclusion from his analysis that since causality is a mental or subjective association of ideas it is the mind that holds the universe (understood as a nexus of facts connected by causal relations) together.

28. Hume touches on this in the *Enquiry* and gives a much fuller statement in his *Dialogues on Natural Religion*, a work which—unlike the *Treatise*—attracted immediate and widespread public attention. The dialogues are modeled on Cicero rather than on Plato: positions and objections are stated on an equal footing, and there is no positive conclusion. If our judgment that *B* was caused by *A* depends on the past frequency with which *A* has preceded *B* compared to the frequency of *B* alone, there is simply no way to reason from a *unique* case, *B*, to any one cause rather than another. See notes 33, 35, 36.

29. *Treatise*, Book I, Part 4, sec. 6. Here in particular the reader will find Hendel's *Studies* incisive and interesting.

30. Some of the most basic issues of Western philosophy (and issues with important implications for educational theory) could be traced in a history or anthology of the search for the self, a search begun by Socrates; in Sartre, it still goes on.

31. This is fatal, of course, to any attempt to go beyond a history of past experiences and equally so to any attempt to assign probabilities to unique, one-time, *A-B* connections. The modern computer, stuffed with historical information, is in good shape so long as it is asked to recall the past but useless in appraising new ideas and unprecedented situations. The same computer, programed to permute familiar words, tunes, or phrases, can turn out wretched English sentences and mediocre tunes for nursery rhymes, but unless some circuit shorts, it does not exhibit much creativity. See *Computers for the Humanities?* (a symposium), New Haven, Conn., 1965; H. L. Dreyfuss, "Why Computers Must Have Bodies in Order to Be Intelligent," *Review of Metaphysics* XXI (1967): 13–32. One issue this raises—one touched on in *Philosophers on Education*—is the difference between creativity and simple eccentricity.

32. Hume, of course, has a strong point here. For if we assume that every event has a previous cause, so must God's creation of the world; but if we accept the orthodox *creatio ex nihilo* doctrine, we accept the idea that something can come from sheer nothing, an idea that, for scientific or psychological contexts, Descartes found he could no more accept than he could doubt his own existence. The issue is

still debated in modern cosmology, with alternative theories of sudden cosmic creation, a steady state, and alternating phases of contraction and expansion.

33. "Probability" for Hume, as we have seen, equals "strength of expectation."
This in turn is based on a mental review of the number of times *A* has been observed as a cause of *B* and the number of times *A* has been observed without *B* as
its effect. Hume's own example, in which he imagines the different effects of throwing dice, seems to confuse this with another (a priori) meaning of probability. But
it brings out the point that a *correct* expectation requires a review of all the *A*'s
and *B*'s, e.g. all women drivers and all observed cases of bad driving.

34. In his edition of the *Enquiry*, Hendel includes an addition to sec. 3 ("On the
Association of Ideas") which Hume provided for a later edition of the work. In this
section Hume tries to show how an epic, for example, gets an intensified impact by
the close texture and heightened resemblance of the impressions it presents to the
reader. But Hume does not take back or modify his earlier restriction of imagination to the four operations cited in note 14.

35. Far from thinking, as have many philosophers—skeptical or otherwise—that
philosophy is not of much practical importance, Hume is incredibly optimistic in
his hopes for the effect of philosophical analysis. "And though a philosopher may
live remote from business, the genius of philosophy, if carefully cultivated by several, must gradually diffuse itself throughout the whole society, and bestow a similar correctness on every art and calling" (*Enquiry*, p. 9).

36. A testimony to this is the success and excellence of Hume's *History of England*. But, as noted on page 54, the application to mathematics seems either an
irrelevance or a total disaster. As a basis for aesthetics, as Hume's *Essay on Taste*
shows, it seems to reduce the field to individual differences in sensitivity of perception, which lie outside the range of argument or discussion. How well the method
would have worked for zoology, ethology, medicine, etc., had it been tried there, is
not clear.

37. Surprisingly enough, this was really widely claimed and accepted as a defense
of the truth of Christianity.

38. The plus 1 in the numerator is included (by us but totally in accord with
Hume's discussion) particularly to cover singular cases of observed sequence where
evidence is not on hand to lead us to expect either repetition or failure the next
time. This, by the rule, gives the totally indeterminate (suspended judgment) probability of $\frac{1}{2}$ for either outcome.

39. *International Encyclopedia of Unified Science*, vols. I and II: Foundations of
the Unity of Science; Chicago, 1938.

40. The ideas of meaning in A. Korzybski, *Science and Sanity* (2d ed., Lancaster,
Pa., 1941) and S. Hayakawa, *Language in Action* (New York, 1941) were translated
into "semantic approach" high school materials by the Institute for Propaganda
Analysis. The first sections used a radically empirical notion of meaning to teach
students to distrust all the glittering generalities of propaganda and advertising.
But it turned out that the criticism also applied to such documents as the Constitution of the United States, and it was discontinued. Perhaps the strongest statement of the logical positivist theory of meaning, an extension of Hume plus new
formal logic, was Rudolph Carnap, *Philosophy and Logical Syntax*, London, 1935.

41. See for example, Edmund A. Bowles, "Computers in Musicology" (*Computers
for the Humanities?* pp. 103–107) and Ercolino Ferretti, "The Computer as a Tool
for the Creative Musician" (*ibid.*, pp. 107–113).

42. See "A Short History of Analytic Philosophy," the prefatory essay to *Classics
of Analytic Philosophy*, ed. Robert R. Ammerman, New York, 1965. See also G. E.
Moore, "A Defence of Common Sense," *ibid.*, Chapter 4.

43. What kind of an idea is "similarity"? The question proves hard to answer.
Russell, in one of his early works, *The Problems of Philosophy* (London, 1929),
thought that this notion could not be traced back to sensations but was presupposed by experience; and at that time he gave it the status of a Platonic form.

44. The reader who wants a fuller discussion of the experiences that Hume does not (and cannot) account for is referred to our *Philosophers on Education,* especially Chapter 7.

45. See Dreyfuss' article, cited in note 31.

46. Compare, for example, the theoretical role of the "teacher" in the Augustinian tradition (Chapter 2).

PART TWO

THEORIES OF HUMAN NATURE
AND PERSONALITY

In the second part of this book we examine the thought of four men who have profoundly influenced—often without their names being more than barely known—our contemporary views of education, and we conclude with a brief look at their influence on three educational theorists working today. Only the first of the seven, Sigmund Freud, was not a wholly twentieth-century phenomenon. But even his known work is distinctively of our time. It was not until World War I that he had an opportunity to explain his still budding and growing views to a large and attentive audience.

With Freud came a recognition of two features of human life which much educational practice appears even now to ignore or deny. These features are the depths of consciousness, much of it darkened by a kind of primeval obscurity, and the essentiality of emotional life to the whole inner life. Freud never wrote a sustained treatise directed to educational theory. However his effect on educational theory in broad terms has even now not been fully assessed. The most recent substantial and balanced evidence of this fact is in the work of Dr. Richard Jones, whose recognition that therapy cannot be substituted for education is complemented by an eloquent and forceful plea that educators avail themselves of the vital knowledge of the emotional needs and development of the child *in the process of his education*.

In A. S. Neill we discover a Freudian whose life and even in some cases attitudes seem quite contrary to Freud's. Freud was never a working educator; Neill was. Freud took a rather remote authoritarian approach to his patients; Neill's attitude toward his pupils was warm, egalitarian, antiauthoritarian. Freud was pessimistic about man's future and his relation to his society; Neill was cautiously optimistic, hopeful—in a secular sense, full of faith. Neill disliked prestige; Freud fought for it with all the fury of ignored genius. Where Freud was always neurotic, worried about personal relationships, deeply self-examining, and a scholar, Neill was easy, little demanding of friends or family, open to the suggestion of error, but with perfect confidence that his attitude and the basic features of his method would, with patience, succeed; and as Neill said himself, he did not care much for books but spent much time with his tools. Yet Neill took several themes from Freud and cast them in his own straightforward and hopeful mold. He was convinced that much of the world's ill arises from repression—in his view needless. Further, the deformation of the sexual instincts and related drives and feelings struck him as perhaps the most significant element in the malformation of personality, unless it was the arbitrary and unnecessary imposition of authority. Like Freud he subscribed, although with different emphasis, to an antireligious view of the world, but like some men of religion as well as like Freud, he held that it is Love (Freud preferred "Eros") alone that can save the world and that can combat the persistence of despair and death. (Here Neill preferred to refer to certain attitudes as "anti life.")

B. F. Skinner has one simple, straightforward foundation idea. If there is a natural kinship between men and animals, it follows that men and animals can be trained by the same basic method. The training of animals is ancient; dancing bears are pre-Christian. The techniques are familiar; any child who has trained a pup or domesticated a wild animal knows the method. Skinner thinks that we not only can be so trained/taught but that we should be. He uses pigeon training as the model for human teaching machines. In his method a skill is acquired in a series of steps small enough to avoid failure and frustration, with rewards at each step as a kind of glue cementing the new training to the old. Skinner has little interest in the sociology of teaching and not much use for the unconscious. His aim is to interpret education as a set of skills and to devise the most successful engineering he can for the acquisition of these skills.

Finally, in Piaget we discover a confluence of several old themes. One is suggested faintly in Locke's talk of "seasons" through which a youngster passes and which, if allowed to run their own course, will create pulses of motivation permitting the child to learn faster. He will also discover the infinitely greater value of operating on inwardly given motivation as opposed to outwardly created coercion. This conception of an inner rhythm, a shade unpredictable and maybe even irritating to the adult tutor with his idea of a smooth chain of daily achievements, leads to a dominating theory of "natural" growth, in which the *intellectual* growth of the child is regarded as a late phase in his total education.

It is not Locke, however, who has directly influenced Piaget's thought, but Piaget's countryman Rousseau, who extended and modified Locke's insight in this fashion.[1] Certainly Rousseau is the coping stone of the idea of phased development. For Rousseau these phases lead to adult life, but are not therefore just faint or imperfect copies of that life and its world. Rather, they constitute a series of worlds gradually mutating into one another which at any stage are quite different from the world of the adult. For Rousseau the outcome is that these phases are of irreplaceable and autonomous value; they ought to be recognized, encouraged, and treated with respect. For Piaget, who would certainly not deny Rousseau's conclusions, they constitute a challenge to empirical study, for they contain a view of the core of intellect and meaning as well as the central features of personality which give us a window on the educational process that can be gained in no other way. Where Freud saw these phases in terms of inner struggle at the level of emotion, instinct, and feeling—in a word, *conation*—Piaget exhibits the developing child in dominantly *cognitive* terms, constantly reorganizing the world and himself in terms of the reorganized world. Piaget works dominantly with the healthy and joyfully, Freud with the ill and broodingly, watchfully.

The work of Piaget is vast and varied. His insights and descriptions are directed more toward illumination than toward systematic clarity. Even less is he concerned with systematic conditions. Piaget's views permeate his practice and are diffused by the writings of those who have worked with him and under him. For this reason, it is hard to summarize his achievements briefly, but impossible to ignore him.

Freud's most creative disciple is Erik Erikson. Deeply devoted to the great pioneer, he passes respectfully into finer analysis, more humanely oriented and less blunderingly applied. Where Freud wrote of a half-mythical Moses, Erikson writes of a very real Luther. Where Freud speculated about the tribal horde, Erikson writes brilliantly about the Sioux and his values. Where Freud postulated full genitality as the fulfillment of adult sexuality, Erikson sees it as the beginning.

As Erikson is to Freud, so is Bruner to Piaget. Bruner is perhaps the outstanding educational thinker writing in English. Where Piaget does much of his work intimately, often with his own children, Bruner goes to the world of the public school child. Where Piaget carefully documents the emergent groping of individuals, Bruner asks himself hard questions about curricula and administration. Yet Bruner's admiration for and dependence upon Piaget are as manifest as that of Erikson upon Freud.

The contrast between these two approaches, conative and cognitive, is the modern descendant of the struggle between values and facts, although in a very sophisticated form. It is—and maybe always was—the central issue, as we find again and again that we cannot go far with one while ignoring the other. Our last chapter closes with a brief discussion of Richard Jones, who makes an eloquent plea for the recognition by each side of the worth of the other.

Where the first part of this study provides a context of what might be called philosophical aspects of theories of learning and knowledge, this second part concentrates on man as the subject of knowledge and is therefore concerned with theories of human nature and personality.

NOTE

1. Rousseau, one of the giant figures in the history of educational philosophy, is treated in detail in R.S. Brumbaugh and N. M. Lawrence, *Philosophers on Education*, Boston, 1963, Chapter 4.

6

The Depths of Mental Life:
Freud

For sheer revolutionary insight into the vague conception of mental life, backed up by powerful theory, Freud has few if any peers. Freud is at once a product of his time and a reformer of it. His own consciousness is embedded in a complex of European life and civilization which at the time was strongly reflected in American culture. We must begin briefly with the culture in order to get to the theory of human nature to which it gives rise.

BACKGROUND

Sigmund Freud was born in 1856. His development as a doctor and as the first psychoanalyst took place in a period of great changes. The earlier years of his life were spent in a hard, upward struggle for recognition of himself and his new science.

The broadest social influence on Freud was the coordinate rise of a prosperous middle class and an industrial economy. The economy and the class may be said to have created one another. From this class and nearly related classes—doctors, lawyers, and professors—came the largest group of Freud's patients. Unlike the nobility, the small farmers, and laborers, this group had relatively little tradition. They were for the most part educated, ambitious, nominally (often nothing more) religious, and financially well off. Speaking generally and in broad caricature, the pressure of their professional employment often led to personal problems for the men. The women—frequently cultivated, sensitive, intelligent, and above all, unemployed—found themselves wives, perhaps, in a marital and social but not in a domestic sense. A Vermont farmer, speaking of the unpleasantness of city women, once re-

The authors wish to thank Richard Rouse for a detailed reading, with many helpful comments, of this chapter.

marked, "They don't have anythin' to do." It applies to Freud's Vienna.

This perhaps too simple portrait of the middle class must be kept in mind as we assess Freud's view of human nature. The question of how seriously we take Freud is partly a question of how far a theory of human nature can be generalized from the mental illness of a particular class of persons in a particular phase of history. Clearly, anyone who undertakes a general theory of human nature should get beyond pure case-history study. And the literacy of Freud's writings shows that he was not completely culture bound nor case-history bound. Thus, while his cases are for the most part contemporary, his techniques of reflection on the cases have a somewhat broader scope.

Closely linked with the social influences on Freud are the political influences. In 1856 France was once again, after 1848, in the hands of a powerful central government under Napoleon III. Germany was experiencing both the desire for and the pains of unification. The United States was not yet eighty years old, and full universal male suffrage—regardless of property—had only just come into being. In Vienna the Austro-Hungarian Empire had survived the revolt which toppled Metternich and had placed the new young emperor, Franz Josef, firmly on the throne. A century before, Rousseau had opened his great treatise on political freedom, *The Social Contract,* with the remark that "Men are born free, but everywhere they are in chains." And in 1848 Marx had closed the *Communist Manifesto* with the exhortation: "The proletarians have nothing to lose but their chains. . . . Working men of all countries, unite!" Freud, fired with the idea of the power of science and the betterment of men, was to discover chains in the human psyche that had only been guessed at before. But he was also to come to somewhat gloomy convictions about the needs for restraint, if social man and individual man were not to be at odds with one another, and indeed if individual men were not to be divided among themselves.

The latter half of the nineteenth century in Europe and America saw a continuation of the surge toward freedom. Perhaps it would be better to call the period one of a surge toward the idea of liberation rather than liberty. For the idea was often only a negative conception, a freedom *from:* freedom from economic domination, freedom from church rule, political and spiritual. Commonly if you inquire of this period, "Freedom *for* what?" the answer comes back, "Pleasure." So answered John Stuart Mill, who grew up in a circle of men who brought about the passage of the great Reform Bills in England. And so Freud answered also. "Pleasure" does not necessarily mean indulgence or sensuality for either man, but the satisfaction that arises from fulfilled wants. The "pleasure principle" is for Freud a major factor, perhaps the major positive factor, in motivation.

The intellectual climate of the time was extremely exciting. In 1859 appeared Darwin's *Origin of Species*. Up till then, though there were already some signs of the drive toward "unified science," the scientific disciplines had been pretty well recognized and fairly clearly separated: mechanics, physics, chemistry, mathematics, biology, natural history, and medicine. It was largely accepted that the human psyche, the human spirit, was not a proper object of scientific study.

Not that the Biblical account of creation, including the creation of man, was uniformly accepted. There was atheism aplenty before Darwin's time, though no large-scale systematic alternative for the origins of men had been developed. But a growing doubt about the deducible age of the earth—something less than six thousand years, according to the Old Testament—had not necessarily eroded the conviction as to the nature of the origins of things. Darwin himself remarked in his autobiography that the teleological argument for the existence of a supreme being always seemed to him very persuasive.[1] Nevertheless, as he grew older, this proof—the argument that the intricate machinery of the course of nature is necessarily the created product of a superhuman designer, a Creator God—relaxed its hold on his convictions somewhat. The effect of Darwin's theory, in the hands of his friends and followers, was even more revolutionary. (1) The conception of the distinctness between animal kind and human kind received, naturally, a heavy blow from Darwin's work. According to the book of Genesis, the creation of man was separate from that of animals; it even took place on a different day. The new theory proposed at least to find the stirrings of humanity in more primitive apelike forms, relatives of which continue to survive today. (2) Closely related to this idea of separate creation was another: that the inner workings of human nature are inaccessible to scientists. But if science could give an account of the descent of man, the task of investigating his nature already lay open and at hand. (3) The notion that nature as a whole is God's handiwork suffered a staggering, if not mortal, blow. The doctrine of the survival of the fittest is implicit in Darwin's theory. The term actually comes from his great contemporary Russell Wallace, himself a brilliant naturalist and champion of the new doctrine. And Darwin was well aware of the struggle to survive emphasized in the Malthusian doctrine: the food supply increases at a slower rate than the animal population expands, and conflict for the limited food must come, unless the competing species be reduced by some disaster that thins their rank—flood, disease, fire, and so on. But the new vision of nature as "red in tooth and claw" places a good God in apparent competition with an omnipotent God. If God is both all good and all powerful, why the bloody cruelty in nature, the meaningless deaths, the terrible natural holocausts of famine, flood, pestilence, earthquake? John Stuart Mill gracefully gave up God's all-powerfulness, saving His goodness as an object of worship. Biblical literalists fell back on the Psalm that says, "How unsearchable are His judgments and His ways past finding out." But this doctrine was cold comfort for reformers who knew that the improvement of life depended on human effort guided by human reason. The Old Testament had said the beasts were put on the earth for man's use. Their suffering thus mattered little. It also interpreted the varying fortunes of the Jewish people as the result of the rise and fall in the index of piety and worship of Jehovah. When Israel did "that which was right in the sight of the Lord," Israel prospered, and the converse was true also. But now it began to be evident to some that the ways of nature were not at all past finding out, that men are but animals, however complex and superior, and that Providence was not so good a friend of human progress as was knowledge of facts and exercise of reason.

Of these three major consequences of the promulgation of Darwin's theory, the first, the release from commitment to Biblical literalism, received ideologically powerful help from Friedrich Nietzsche. Nietzsche wanted no part of the mere shelving of Christianity on grounds that it was founded upon outworn and unscientific myth. Honorable retirement was not enough. Nietzsche undertook to show that Christianity was positively vicious. The principal charge was that Christianity is dedicated to the weak, the humble, the average—in short, to the survival of the unfittest. Nietzsche's watchwords were "the will to power." His ideal is that of the *Übermensch,* a term often misleadingly translated as "superman." What Nietzsche dreamed of was a heroic figure incarnating the best in humanity—in vision, power, achievement—rid of all pettiness, including what he regarded as a maudlin Christian sentimentality. Nietzsche had little patience with Darwin and his theory; for him the whole thing smacked of an unbecoming materialism. But he actively undertook what evolution passively (in most proponents) achieved—the setting aside of religious guidance as a help in the understanding of human beings. And like the evolutionist, he saw life as a struggle for power. Nietzsche thus contributed his share of momentum to the third of the points mentioned above, also—even though he did not approach the struggle for power by way of natural history. Nietzsche's main influence came about twenty years after the publication of *The Origin of Species.*

Other seminal minds were at work asking themselves what the basic considerations of power are that bring men into conflict, and whether this conflict is inescapable. Principal among these questioners were Marx and Engels. In their view also, human life is a struggle for power. But this is a feature of the evolution of society and no necessary constant for all time. The basic drives in human existence are economic. Human nature is shaped, in a sense, by itself; its method of production makes it what it is. And this means material production, the goods of life. Thus, medieval peasant and nobleman were related to one another by the way in which they produced for their needs and in their society. After them, in the rise of commerce, other classes— merchant, seller, worker, farmer—arose as the product of their mode of production. According to Marx, the final stage in this evolution arises in the tension between worker and bourgeois owner, the capitalist. The middle class, said Marx and Engels, have served their purpose, bringing the instruments of production to a peak of technical and administrative efficiency. The final stage will come as a revolution, in which the real producers, the workers, take over the instruments of production, crush the parasitic administration, the owning but non-producing middle class, and inaugurate a new era in a classless society composed exclusively of workers. In this way, and in this way alone, can the struggle of men against men be abolished, by removing the very existence of the classes which underlie class conflict.

Moreover, Marx added his fire to the flames that surrounded Christianity. For him Christianity was but another instrument in the more or less vast network of institutions—law, government, bourgeois morality, custom, social stratification, etc.—by which the entrenched bourgeoisie sought to stabilize their hold on the basic power, economic power, against the inevitable revolution. Christianity's other-worldliness was a master deceit. "Render unto Caesar," if believed by the poor, gave the bourgeoisie *carte blanche* to be Caesar. Hope of a future reward would keep the workers docile in this brief life. Humility, patience, turning the other cheek were exactly what the bourgeoisie wanted. Meanwhile, churches piled up treasure; churchmen lived well, if not dissolutely; church buildings became more and more magnificent; religious authority wielded enormous political power. All this, combined with the dread spiritual authority over their flock, made the churchman and his religion an ideal target for Marx's criticism. Marx wanted to dedicate his masterpiece, *Das Kapital,* to Darwin, but Darwin politely declined, saying he knew nothing of economics.

The great lure of the time for the mind of young Dr. Freud, however, was in the second theme: the opportunity for the scientific study of man. Involved in this interest was the passion of every true reformer: the betterment of man. Freud, too, had his charges to make against religion, especially the Judeo-Christian religion. And they were relatively distinct from those of Nietzsche and Marx. (He was, among other things, one of the more penetrating critics of Marx; his last systematic treatise on psychoanalysis concluded with a final chapter assailing both religion and Marx.) Like Nietzsche he saw the volitional element in humanity as its major feature, but like John Stuart Mill, he believed it was primarily directed toward pleasure. Like Marx, he saw the conflict between man and society as fundamental; unlike Marx, he came to the conclusion that the situation was not likely to change much, except insofar as men, through their improved understanding of themselves, learned how to avoid the major pitfalls in a contest which he at one point calls "immortal." But like all these men he was filled with the spirit of reform, and like some of them he was convinced that reform came through science.

In our investigation of Freud's philosophy of human nature we must recognize that his systematic analysis of the psyche went through many changes. Whether or not psychoanalysis is a science depends on how narrow a definition of "science" we hold to. One feature of a science is that it be open to change under the impact of inquiry. Continued research should always admit, if not foresee, the possibility of revised views. Science should be open to facts that challenge convictions. In this respect, psychoanalysis in Freud's hands was a science.

In explication of Freud's theories we will concentrate on two important works of Freud, *A General Introduction to Psycho-Analysis* and the *New Introductory Lectures on Psychoanalysis,*[2] with relevant detail from other works. The first of these works is a revision of three courses of lectures given in 1915–1917, during World War I, at the University of Vienna. Although Freud's first memorable work, *The Interpretation of Dreams,*[3] had appeared in 1900, recognition came slowly, and it was not till the Vienna lectures that he undertook to present a rounded view of the whole scope of psychoanalysis. Moreover, this work began with an assumption of no previous acquaintance with psychoanalysis and—although it was addressed by a doctor to a medical faculty and students—virtually no medical knowledge. It is thus a book that the interested reader of the present sketch can consult for further understanding.

The *New Introductory Lectures* appeared fifteen years later. Freud was then seventy-six years of age; he was of sound mind and if anything writing even more simply, although dealing with problems of a larger scope. In this work he summarized the achievements of the previous decade and a half and specifically—in the introduction—referred to the new lectures as "continuations . . . supplements . . . [and] fresh treatments of subjects which were already dealt with fifteen years ago but which, as a result of a deepening of our knowledge and an alteration in our views, call for . . . critical revisions." [4] He under-scored the continuity by giving the first lecture in the new series the number 29; there had been twenty-eight lectures in the first series. The new lectures were actually not given to an audience; Freud had had a disfiguring operation for cancer of the palate. But they are true lectures and are comparatively easy reading, and Freud made it clear that he was writing for the interested and intelligent but nonprofessional audience.

OUTLINES OF THE THEORY

For all its modifications and reversals, Freud's view of human nature displayed certain constant themes grounded in extensive case study and in professional contact. Our first task is to examine these themes in simple outline.

The value of a science does not lie simply in its ability to explain satisfactorily. If convincing explanation were the only test, then we should not be able to choose between the angry-earth-God and the fault-structure accounts of volcanic action. What is most satisfactory in a science is not even its ability to control—most astrophysics, for example, deals with data that are not very manipulable, and evolutionary theory may be wholly beyond any general experimental confirmation. The prime requisite of a science is that the account it gives of its data is systematically explainable, but only as *cohering* with other data and with other theories. Geology as a science is not directly concerned with appeasing or quieting volcanoes. It is, however, interested in bringing together the data of volcanic action, fault-block lifts, lava fields, basaltic cliffs, earthquakes, and theories of the origins of our planet into one consistent systematic view.

In this respect, too, Freud obeyed the traditions of scientific study. His Vienna lectures divided psychic phenomena into three fields: the psychology of error, the interpretation of dreams, and the analysis of neuroses and psychoses. In none of these fields was he the first inquirer. Consider the psychology of error. Aristotle regarded all material being as —in the nature of the case—fallible. In his ethical theory in particular, he speaks of *hamartia,* failure to "hit the mark." We aim and sometimes we miss; this is a fact of life, improvable but not eliminable. Outside of philosophy and science other kinds of slips and errors—especially those with dire consequences—have been treated by witchcraft, magic, and the black arts. They have been regarded as the results of unseen forces, known only to the initiate. Freud's theory was somewhat like the latter account, except that he regarded the forces as wholly within nature and scientifically accountable. Also in the realm of the occult, the interpretation of dreams has fascinated men, evidently from earliest times. Joseph rose to favor in Pharaoh's palace by the cogent interpretation of Pharaoh's dreams. In the area of the black arts, the world long had an account of the seizures and psychic distortions of her unhappier citizens. They were victims, especially in the severe cases, of diabolic investment. Evil spirits possessed them, or they were under some permanent "hex" directed by masters of occult forces. Even before Freud some advance had been made in discovering the physiological bases of psychic disorder—brain damage, for example. But such material analysis was largely in its infancy as compared with the modern study of the chemical aspects of physiology.

Freud's unique contribution was not wholly in conceiving of these three fields in terms of their interconnection, for the vague conception of "magic" and its associated demonology were often written over all three of them. Freud's discovery was the revival, renovation, and analysis of the ancient idea of the unconscious.

THE UNCONSCIOUS

The first systematic statement of the unconscious in Western thought occurred in Plato. In the *Meno* Plato developed a theory of learning as being a kind of revival of forgotten understanding acqired by the soul or psyche in a previous life.[5] Plato thought of the psyche as by nature immortal and passing through a series of reincarnations punctuated by loss of personal identity. The continuity of this series of reincarnations lay in what we would call dispositions and character traits. Like the philosophies of the East—Hinduism and Buddhism—the Platonic view regarded the actions of men as primary causes which necessarily must have effects of a moral nature; and while individual memories of men might come to an abrupt end with death, their deeds did not merely vanish like a river petering out in the desert. Rather, the water runs underground, only to reappear later in another form. Plato evidently held that genuine understanding also continued and was arousable in the new life by appropriate experience and guidance. This view seems strange to us who take our individuality for granted and who are inclined to regard our lives as beginning somewhat arbitrarily and simply evaporating at our death. But the Greek felt himself part of a general life force present in all things that live and move. Plato unhesitatingly spoke of a "world soul" or "world psyche" in the *Timaeus*. There is no myth of the gradual emergence of life from nonlife, as in the modern ideology, and the Greek saw himself in sharp distinction from other life only through his sharing with other men of the faculty of reason. Moreover, for Plato the faculty of reason was closely akin to the divine, and the divine was part of nature, not above it. This general sharing of life with one's contemporaries, along with the divine in the world and the continuity of the past and the future, is the enemy of extreme individualism, the doctrine of each person as a separate and distinct individual.

From Plato to Freud, in spite of the Christian emphasis on *individual* responsibility and the increasing political emphasis on individual liberty, there was always a background recognition of the nonconscious elements in human life, broader than individual attention and longer lived than a single person's.[6] In the same century as Freud, Hegel revived the classical conception of a world soul. For Hegel the whole course of human history could be understood vitally in terms of a "world spirit," manifesting itself in many realms—art, religion, etc. —and in many cultures—Germanic, for example—as men evolve toward greater and greater self-consciousness. Freud's theory of the unconscious was different from Hegel's world spirit, deeper and more obscure. It fell into two relatively distinct parts.

The individual unconscious   Freud divided this individual mental life into three parts: the conscious, the preconscious, and the unconscious. The conscious life is the public part of man's psychic life, known to himself and to a great extent to his fellows. It is that which is acceptable and under immediate attention: the writing I am doing at the moment, my sense of its importance, the effort to be clear and simple, and so on. The preconscious is also acceptable; it is what I am capable of becoming conscious of. Of course it is not preconscious when I spell it out, but the preconscious would be such things as the later points to be made, the faint crackle of the fire and my latent pleasure in the sound, the memory of a funny occurrence to be told my family when they come home. However, the great part of my mental life, in Freud's view, is not in present focus nor can it safely be permitted to be. This is the unconscious conceived as the lower six-sevenths of the iceberg. Between it and the preconscious there stands a "doorkeeper," the *censor*.

This censor has a single complex task: to be sure that all the person knows of himself and all that he seems to be to the world is publicly acceptable. It does not always perform its task well, of course, nor conform to all demands made upon it. We all know boors, oafs, antisocial misanthropes, ruthless exploiters, and so on. The censor is not at fault here. Its function is *not* to keep things nice and pretty. There is a broad range of manners or the lack of them, of decency and the opposite, of human warmth or its opposite, all possible on the conscious side of the censor. The primary task of the censor is concerned with much more profound problems than social and personal amenities. Its task is to hold in check the antisocially wild, irrational, contradictory, and potentially destructive impulses which lie at the heart of the human psyche.

This part of the psyche Freud called the *libido*. The more conscious part of our existence Freud called the *ego*. Ego instincts and libidinous instincts are alike influenced by the pleasure principle, which bids us seek pleasure and avoid pain.[7] The libido, blind and unreasoning, a mere fountain of energy, is wholly ruled by this principle; and since "pleasure in the performance of the sexual act" is "the most intense pleasure of which man is capable," the libido's primary disposition is sexual.[8] It will stick at nothing—incest, rape, murder—to obtain gratification. The ego on the other hand is confronted with the reality principle and has the aim of self-preservation. The libido has no contact with reality and seeks none. The ego has eyes, so to speak; it sees not only a real physical world about it but also a world of men in the society, which needs it and which it needs. Thus it happens that "sexual instincts and self-preservative instincts do not behave alike when confronted with the necessity of real life." [9] Man is by nature divided.

The theme of human personality as composite is an old one. One of the most consistent products of man's reflection on himself is his internal tendencies toward multiplicity, with the ideal of unity always evading his grasp. The ancient Egyptian even invested mankind with two souls, a *ba* and a *kha*. One stayed in the body and the other adventured abroad during sleep. Hence men dream. So also Freud claimed that the censor is at work in the formation of dream symbols, as we shall see. Plato had divided the soul into three parts: rational, volitional, appetitive. His student Aristotle accomplished a somewhat similar division.[10] Stevenson's Dr. Jekyll was also Mr. Hyde. Goethe's Faust cries in torment, "Two natures struggle within my breast!" But Freud's treatment of this familiar intuition was unique in several respects. For one thing he came perilously close to saying that all instincts are basically sexual. Not directly sexual, of course, but disguised. Part of the task of the censor is to admit to consciousness those sexual impulses which have been sublimated into other pursuits and aims. The elaborated pursuits include, indeed, our various arts and professions. Moreover, Freud used the term "sexual" to cover much more than is usually meant by the term. He reserved the term "genital" for much of what we should ordinarily call "sexual." His "genital" was but one part of sexuality.[11] Freud stated flatly, however, that "An overwhelming majority of symbols in dreams are sexual symbols." [12] And he repeatedly made self-preservation and sexual instincts the fundamental ones.[13] Nonetheless, the capitulation to the idea that all instincts other than self-preservation are basically sexual was never complete, in spite of such remarks as that, in dreams, "all objects capable of elongation are symbols of the male organ." [14]

One exception to the rule that sexuality lies at the base of all of our nonconscious instincts is the death instinct. Even in 1917 Freud mentioned the presence of symbols for death in dreams.[15] His thought in this period must be taken with his late work, though, if it is to be properly understood. The subject of the death instinct opens up several aspects of Freud's thought: dreams, regression, the impact of evolutionary thought on him, and the collective unconscious. We have been dealing with the individual unconscious. Let us look at the collective unconscious.

The collective unconscious One of the doctrines which grew out of the advent of evolution is by now a commonplace in biology. In its briefest form this doctrine states that "Ontogeny follows phylogeny." "Ontogeny" refers to the genesis of the individual; "phylogeny" refers to the genesis of the kind, the species. The rule is not borne out in total detail, but it applies in a rough general way too well to be ignored. Many rather complicated animals, men and insects to name two, seem to touch the highlights of their presumed evolution as a kind in coming into being as individuals. Thus, men have tails at one embryonic stage—a few never lose them—and all human embryos have gill slits in a crude form at another stage, exactly where their presumed ancestral fish did. Again, many insects, descended from prearticulate worms, go through a worm phase first—grub or caterpillar. Other more subtle recapitulations of phylogeny are equally suggestive to a trained naturalist. And there are many examples among plants as well.

One theme from biological science imported into Freud's effort at a science of human nature is the struggle for survival. This he saw embodied not merely among men, but *within* the individual. The potentially destructive libido, bound only to the pleasure principle, has to be held in check by the survival-oriented ego, which equally has an eye on the reality principle. If the ego relaxes its aim, or is not strong enough, anything from a mild neurosis to the total withdrawal called "dementia praecox" can ensue.

In short, to the extent that the libido is in charge, the fundamental commitment of an individual to society and the actual world diminishes. What occurs then is *regression*. Often the regression is toward childhood, the particular childhood of the person in question. So-called "traumatic" experiences, vitally important to the child, perhaps unnoticed by others, may be relived again and again in some symbolic form. Or some undernourished aspect of childhood development is sought out in an effort to obtain satisfaction. Thumb sucking, to take a mild and familiar example, is an effort to return to the security, dependence, and possessiveness of a child at its mother's breast. Not all regressions are sinister, nor more than occasionally periodic. They may turn up only under stress. They may also become *fixations* or *obsessions*. Or the person may finally enter a total fantasy world. The brilliant young Jew (or Gentile, for that matter), out of whack with himself and his immediate human and physical reality, may come to the conclusion that he is a reincarnated Moses, aloof, remote, visionary, a leader—not of the mob. Regressions thus unhesitatingly may jump backwards beyond the individual's life. In this case the fixation fastens upon a fairly historical person. Regressions are not abnormal in the sense of being exceptional.

Freud, in his general works, dealt with three domains of psychically significant behavior: (1) everyday slips and errors, (2) dreams, and (3) mental illness—neurotic and psychotic. For the most part the familiar *slips* of speaking, reading, writing, and hearing are only minor safety valves. Many of these slips are simply releases of some small internal pressure to express something which the person felt he could not say or write, often on grounds of decency or courtesy. Freud related many amusing incidents of slips in his own life and those of others. The neurotic and psychotic *regressions* are exceptional and constitute the primary aim of Freud's analysis. It is *dreams* that lead most clearly from the individual unconscious to the collective unconscious. The "dream work"—what the dream accomplishes in the way of symbolic release of all those memories, impulses, wants, desires, and motivations which the prevailing social mode will not (and cannot) acknowledge or accept—is itself primarily "archaic or regressive." Freud said,

> The era to which the dream-work takes us back is "primitive" in a two-fold sense: in the first place, it means the early days of the individual—his childhood—and, secondly, in so far as each individual repeats in some abbreviated fashion during childhood the whole course of the development of the human race, the reference is phylogenetic. . . . It seems to me, for instance, that symbolism, a mode of expression which has never been individually acquired, may claim to be regarded as a racial heritage.[16]

Elsewhere Freud used the vocabulary of an ancient controversy. The question stated too simply to be answerable is "Given that some characteristics are inherited from generation to generation and other characteristics are acquired, are the new characteristics then inherited in the subsequent generations?" Everything hinged here, of course, on what was intended by "acquired." The leather-headed German investigator who chopped off the tails of a great number of sequent generations of mice, winding up at the end with mice whose tails were just as long as their ancestors', probably did not disprove anything that very many men have seriously held. Freud, however, clearly believed in one kind of inheritance of acquired characteristics: "Contributional predispositions are undoubtedly the after-effects of the experiences of an earlier ancestry; they have also been at one time acquired; without such acquired characters there would be no heredity." [17]

Midway between the symbolism of dreams, which may be regarded as a language insofar as it is expressive and articulate, and "constitutional predispositions," which are the residue of the collective race experience, lies language. Freud enlisted the assistance of H. Sperber of Upsala, who held that "all words had originally meanings based on the calling of a sexual partner and the consummation of the sexual act." Later the words were made as rhythmic utterances accompanying work, helping "to transfer a sexual intent to the work." [18] This theory pleased Freud, for symbols would survive the old words for them; even though the names for things changed, the things themselves would still appear in dreams as symbols of the genitalia. It would be hard to claim that we had here discovered Freud doing some of his best and most well-grounded thinking, but it does help us to round out the theory of the collective unconscious. This unconscious, prehistorically formed, lies at the base of all dreams, speaking its own language of sexual symbolism, regardless of the individuals in which it manifests itself, and surviving, like other race characteristics, in the sublimated form of actual language and disposition. In this collective unconscious, existing beneath the individual consciousness and even before the individual unconscious, we see Freud's reaction against the tide of individualism in his own time.

If we begin with the survival instinct, embodied in the ego, and ask where the struggle comes from within the person, we are led from one biological datum to another: from survival of the fittest to the recapitulation theory of development. Here we find Freud regarding each individual as an accumulation of factors, many of which are "repressed" by the censor and driven either down or back into the unconscious. If the person cannot "sublimate" these instincts and occurrences into publicly acceptable form, then he may "regress" to some earlier stage of his development where his unconscious seeks and demands satisfaction, either by slips of the tongue and pen, or by dreams, or by a variety of eccentric behavioral symptoms. These symptoms of repression show that the former stages have not been surpassed, perfectly or imperfectly, and normally play a hidden role in the constitution of the adult. Freud said that "in fact a particular determinant of anxiety (that is, situation of danger) is allotted to every age of development as being appropriate to it." [19] Contemporary Freudians are willing to think of the child who seeks the dark closet or withdraws under a bed as symbolically returning to the womb. Freud himself thought of the womb fantasy as symbolic of coitus. A biological analogy would be the development of a tail by someone who was forced into an arboreal existence—or perhaps the delusion of the development of a tail. But regression stretches even farther back, according to Freud in his late years. Not only does regression to earlier stages of our individual and collective existence lie potentially in all of us, it even extends to the preliving stage of our existence! He said of the death instinct:

> What earlier state of things does an instinct such as this want to restore? Well, the answer is not far to seek and opens wide perspectives. If it is true that—at some immeasurably remote time and in a manner we cannot conceive—life once proceeded out of inorganic matter, then, according to our presumption, an instinct must have arisen which sought to do away with life once more and to reestablish the inorganic state. If we recognize in this instinct the self-destructiveness of our hypothesis, we may regard the self-destructiveness as an expression of a "death instinct" which cannot fail to be present in every vital process.[20]

THE THREE FIELDS OF THE UNCONSCIOUS

We remarked earlier that the test of science is not merely its capacity to answer questions satisfactorily. Most systematic thought does that, from theology to radio repair manuals. The force of science lies in its capacity to state in general terms reasons which have a wide application to a variety of related fields. It lies, therefore, in the very nature of a science to demand coherence with other sciences. We have seen that three major areas of human mentality, according to Freud, are linked together: (1) inadvertencies—slips of tongue, pen, and communication generally, (2) dreams, (3) psychic diseases, neuroses and psychoses. Although superficially distinct, these three realms are really connected, below the phenomenal surface, by the unconscious. Each of them includes instances of a direct overwhelming of the censor or a sublimation into transmuted forms or symbolic disguise which gets by the censor because of its disguise.

If we keep this underground continuity of the unconscious in mind, a number of features appear concerning both the Freudian account of human nature and the closely associated therapy that goes with it.

THE CONTINUITY OF MENTAL LIFE

The plain fact is that conscious mental life is spotty. It is broken by sleep and coma. It also may be so chaotic that although there are no blanks in it, as in sleep or coma, the lack of order produced by distractions, fantasies, moods, and so on, amount to qualitative discontinuity. Freud's theory of the unconscious postulated a base line, a kind of steady undercurrent of existence, of which the more specific features of consciousness are partial revelations. Moreover, this continuity joins the mental life of persons with prior consciousness as well.[21]

FREE ASSOCIATION

The technique of free association, in which the patient (classically prone and in a darkened room) is asked to repeat whatever comes to his mind, by whatever means he wishes, but without inhibition or prejudgment, thus has several aims. First, it opens a door into the underground stream of unconscious life. Secondly, it bleeds off some of the pressure that has built up there. Thirdly, it puts the patient in some active and "voluntary" role in his own analysis. Fourthly, and most important for therapy, disconnected, mysterious, and oppressive manifest symptoms fall into a pattern with other pieces of the jigsaw puzzle which have lain buried alive in the unconscious. Both analyst and patient can then begin the painfully slow effort to assemble a fuller view of the patient's personality. Light may come from above, but the data come from below.

THE PSYCHOPATHOLOGY OF EVERYDAY LIFE

This is the title of a book published by Freud sixteen years before the Vienna lectures.[22] The same material is dubbed "The Psychology of Errors" in the Vienna lectures. Through this portal, Freud conducted the novice to the more exotic realms of dreams and mental illness. It is the area with which everyone is familiar, perhaps too familiar to be curious as to why. In general, the elements which make it up —commonly nothing more than inconveniences in themselves—are passed over with irritation and momentary discomfort. They fall into three classes:

Slips These are misreadings, miswritings, mishearings, misspeakings—errors in the practice of normal communication. Here suppressed wishes, hopes, fears, and even intents, that the prim ego cannot abide or admit, slip past the censor and seize on convenient similarities in words of sometimes quite different and even contradictory meanings. English is susceptible to such errors, German apparently even more so. The envious or competitive lady says to another, "You must have *thrown* this delightful hat together." She said "thrown," but she meant to say "sewn" (in German, "aufgepatzt" instead of "aufgeputzt"). Stories of this sort are legion. There is, for example, the famous story of the superintendent of the Harvard College

Library who regaled a group of students with exploits of his adventurous youth, touring the streets of Cambridge, picking up girls. "But they always got into the car of their own violation," he said.

Temporary forgetfulness We "mislay" names, important dates, appointments; we forget tasks and chores which have only duty to recommend them (the pleasure principle is working in its negative capacity here). Then later we remember, often when it is "too late."

Permanent forgetfulness This third kind of forgetfulness includes permanently putting something where one cannot get at it, forgetting its location entirely or for a while, or resisting the truth of something that one has earlier accepted and may well again. Of course people who are tired, under great pressure, distracted, or worried are more susceptible than they would be in average circumstances. Why did he forget his doctor's appointment? "He was worried about his work, his son," etc. Freud did not doubt these explanations for a moment. What is needed is a kind of two-level explanation. Fatigue may indeed increase the incidence of error. But this only generally explains why errors are more common at certain times. Why *this* error rather than another, in this particular form, in regard to this situation and/or person? This is the theme that engaged Freud's attention. Of course it is of little use to pursue these matters indefinitely. But they *can* be part of a syndrome, a set of coordinated symptoms each pointing to and cohering with the rest, which is of towering significance. Usually one cannot see the significance of a particular symptom of this sort without having other data that go with it.

The basic rule here is the determinism of all occurrences. Freud was explicit on this point. Challenging the explanation of slips as mere accidents, he asked sharply: "Does he [such an explainer] mean to maintain that there are any occurrences so small that they might fail to come within the causal sequence of things, that they might as well be other than they are? Anyone thus breaking away from the determinism of natural phenomena, at any single point, has thrown over the whole scientific outlook on the world." [23] There could be no clearer statement of the conception of scientific study in the time when Freud was writing; without saddling Newton himself with this view, we may call the development of science in the eighteenth and nineteenth century Newtonian. This view of the world regarded each event as explainable on principle in terms of prior events—completely explainable. To ask "Why?" is to ask for reasons, to ask for prior conditions. Such prior conditions are, however, only occurrences themselves and are subject to the same question. Determinism—total, complete, inflexible—seems to be absolutely required by any objective inquiry that seeks facts. Science cannot just shrug its shoulders at some events and say, "No reason; it just happened."

We will return to this determinism in more detail, especially as it bears on the educational process, but a few things may be noted here. Freud assumed all that is thinkable—everything of which we are aware or may be aware—is susceptible to the objectification which science requires. Further, Freud breached another important barrier. He brought inferential objects—ego, libido, complex, neurosis, etc.—under the rule of observed objects. It is by this tactic that the common-sense distinction between the mental and the physical was perforated. A hundred years and more before Freud's writings Kant had held in effect that men know their own motives better than others can. What we observe through the senses, objectively, comes under the rigid rule of determinism, in Kant's view. In this way alone is science possible. But actions are not mere physically observable things; they are grounded in motives, the reasons for which rather than from which the action is undertaken.[24] This does not mean that *free* action, which has to be assumed to make any behavior praiseworthy or blamable, is nonlawlike. It does mean that physical law is supreme over only what we can observe. The ethical law, which men administer to themselves, is therefore not imposed by nature, but is just as universal over its domain as scientific law is over the physical domain. This *noumenal*—potentially free—side of the world is known to us directly only in the depths of our consciousness. What the senses yield is a world of absolute determinism of *phenomena,* the sheer appearance of objects, not subjects. "Phenomenal" and "noumenal" mean "what manifestly appears" and "what exists primarily as spirit," respectively. It is highly significant that Kant's moral imperatives were rules that men address to themselves as fundamental tests for the ethicality of their intentions. Only by a kind of admittedly fallible inference can I reason backwards from a man's actions to his intent. And every moral judgment on him runs the risk of being mistaken, vain, and presumptuous. As a sheerly observed object, considered coldly under the flat light of "just the facts," any man might as well be a machine, explainable wholly in terms of the prior conditions that govern his actions. That he is more complex would be beside the point.

How did Freud dare to assault so popular a view, yet one so grounded in expert philosophical reflection (we have exposed the argument in its barest outline)? The answer is relatively simple; we have exposed it already, en route. Freud had acquired abundant evidence that men did *not* know their own motives. It may be questioned whether the tricky word "know" is being used unequivocally in this context. But in one clear sense Freud's patients did not know why they did the things they did. Beginning with their own confession of ignorance and continuing to their helplessness before mental disease, the patients in Freud's case books were all massed around one central point—overwhelming ignorance of themselves. What was needed Freud supplied: (1) personal courage to face the unpleasant and unpleasantness in general; (2) boldness in accepting the causal pattern which made it possible for him to understand his patients better. But, in brief, Kant's assumption that the datum of motivation was best known to the subject himself was refuted by the mental illness that Freud wished to cure. That the determinism of all occurrences extends to even the most trivial aspects of behavior is not only a good introduction to the Freudian analysis but a necessary one. As the quotation above shows, Freud feared that any exception to the rule of universal causation would constitute a breach which would bring the whole "scientific outlook" tumbling down. The psychopathology of everyday life thus supported the universal rule of cause—in Freud's view—and rendered possible the task of explaining more resistant ailments on principle. The sick man is of course a stronger case—but not different in kind—of what happens in small degree to all of us.

DREAMS

Armed with the rule of determinism, we must now enter a strange territory where magic, superstition, and mysticism have long held sway. In some ways, the dream is the strongest direct evidence of a mental life which is at least superficially divorced from consciousness. To be sure, we say, "In the dream I was conscious of . . ." but it might be wiser not to. Consciousness guarantees a roughly understandable order of things, with continuities and coherencies that are difficult to define exactly yet seem manifest. Perhaps the difficulty lies in the fact that we must bring our dream into consciousness in order to distinguish it from consciousness. Thus of an experience that is exceptional, beyond ordinary experience, we say, "It was like a bad (or beautiful) dream."

In the slips of everyday life we say, "Why did he blunder?" "He was tired." And Freud adds, "Yes, but what particular factors influenced *this* blunder?" So also Freud distinguished two levels of explanation of dreams. Analogous to the conditions of fatigue, worry, and distraction, which are the general conditions of common slips, there is in the dream a *general* reason for all dreams. "We have learnt that the function of dreams is to protect sleep; that they arise out of two conflicting tendencies, of which the one, the desire for sleep, remains constant, whilst the other endeavors to satisfy some mental stimulus; that dreams are proved to be mental acts, rich in meaning; that they have two characteristics, i.e. they are wish fulfillments and hallucinatory experiences." [25] Freud said that any psychologist could point out that wishes are fulfilled in dreams and that the world of dreams is in some sense an hallucination. The difficulty is that dreams of adults do not play as simple and direct a role as those of children. As human beings grow older, their lives make greater and greater demands upon them. The purview of their actions and their understanding extends further. With these greater demands come greater inhibitions.[26] The wishes of dreams can be expected accordingly to be more complex and less acceptable. The result is a greater and greater separation between what the dream is after, so to speak, and what it seems to be saying or presenting.

The function of dreams   The general function of dreams is that they "protect sleep" by providing an outlet and expression for modes of consciousness which have no place in the constricted world of public life and conduct, nor even in the intimacies in the personal lives of the most intimate friends, family members, and loved ones. But the specific dreams, especially by reason of their recourse to a varied symbolism, must be thought of in terms of the "dream work," the particular *how* in terms of this particular person and his unique circumstances. Dreams protect sleep by permitting a kind of quasi consciousness during sleep, which if it attained to full consciousness would destroy sleep. But the threats to rest come from different quarters for different people. How does the dream do its job? This is the analysis of the "dream work."

The dream work   This is how the dream accomplishes its function of "protecting sleep." It is "the process by which the latent dream is transformed into the manifest dream. . . ." [27] Freud's analysis of further divisions and aspects of this major distinction was intricate. It was based on a lifelong preoccupation with dreams and an extensive professional acquaintance with them. We give here only a minimal outline.

The dream work is the method by which the forbidden elements of the latent dream are assembled into a presentation in the actual dream (the "manifest dream"; sometimes the "manifest dream content"). The path followed in this transformation is the exact opposite from the path taken by the interpreter, who must begin with the dream as reported. From the dream as reported he must try to reconstruct the actual dream. Consciously or unconsciously the patient may have misled him. If this is discovered, then it constitutes separate and significant evidence of its own. But even where there seems to be no reason why the report should not be accepted as valid, a barrier appears. This bar-

rier lies in what is often the great gap between the forbidden elements
of the latent dream thoughts and the manifest dream content. To get
beyond this barrier the analyst must assemble all the other data about
the patient that he can. The analysis is intended primarily to relieve or
cure mental disease; the analysis of the dream is secondary. But the
lengthiness of the normal analysis is based on the difficulty of making
this backward journey into the hidden rationale of the unconscious.
Dreams must be analyzed with other dreams, family history, slips of
the tongue, neurotic symptoms, prevailing phobias—all under the patient stimulation of free association. Slowly a pattern begins to emerge.
When it does, we find the unconscious is perhaps blind and willful, but
not without cunning. The censor is also at work in the dream; it has
to be got around if there is to be a satisfactory discharge of the buried
wish or desire. The dream work is the route taken in this process.

The latent dream thought is centered in some wish.[28] The wish may
be directly represented with little or no modification. An analysis of
children's dreams shows a very high incidence of such dreams.[29] Adults
also may have such "infantile dreams," involving cleverness neither on
the part of the unconscious nor, therefore, on the part of the analyst.
But there is still a translation which occurs, for a wish is a thought,
and a dream is a collection of sensory images. The usual dominant
sense here is vision, but other senses are often represented, and almost
invariably some emotional feeling appears as well. Often emotion is
the dominant residual impression of a dream. The dream guards sleep
by giving expression to the wish: "the truth is that without the help of
the dream we should not have slept at all." [30] The youngster who
wants to rifle a box of candy does so in his dream. But in the case of
the adult dream, the deception may be double. Not only does the
dream present an unreal satisfaction, as all dreams do, but it also may
provide a symbolic satisfaction, *within the framework of the dream.*
Adults have experienced more inhibition (from what Freud later came
to call the "superego") than children and are subject to more diversified wishes. There is more demand for expression in the unconscious
life and a deeper distaste for direct expression. A number of devices
arise to meet this double problem: (1) *Condensation,* the elimination,
selection, and blending of various wish elements. Some of the nonco-
herence of dreams arises here. (2) *Displacement,* the tactic whereby the
real emphasis of the dream is either replaced by or shifted to something trivial. (3) *Transformation,* the importation of allowable symbols for unallowable wishes. Here the final work of distortion is accomplished. It is here that the elaborate symbolism occurs which
Freud not only regarded as universal, but universal by reason of going
back to a kind of primal language of thought, and perhaps even a pri-

mal language of words, as claimed by Sperber. "An overwhelming majority of symbols in dreams are sexual symbols," said Freud and dream distortions "mainly (but here again not exclusively) give expression to sexual desires." [31] The list of the actual symbols given does not concern us here. The reader should consult Freud himself for these dream interpretations. Some of them will strike the reader as fantastic. The impulsive critic should be reminded, however, of the broad experience that underlies bizarre claims such as that the so-called "toothache dreams" always refer to onanism and the fear of punishment for onanism.

The manifest dream content, or the actual dream, is the practical outcome of all these processes. A single problem remains: where does this content come from? What stockpile of memory supplies us with the garments or symbols by which our unconscious wishes are translated into (for the most part) acceptable and perceptible dream images? Freud's answer brings up one final distinction. The term "unconscious" refers, we recall, to two fairly distinct elements; the division holds in the case of the dream. (1) The dream wish "has its roots in the infantile period." [32] The dream work in reaching back to this infantile period is "archaic" and "regressive" insofar as the individual's personal life and the early period of human history are archaic and regressive.[33] (2) The other factor is called the "residue from the previous day." The generic and primal wishes do not account for the specific images. These must come from the person himself, from his "residue from the great interests of waking life," [34] and from interests of the day before which have not yet abated.[35] Though these lingering interests clearly may arouse memories that provide a bridge between the conscious life of the patient and the archaic and regressive elements which bind him to his species, it is the latter which Freud unswervingly regarded as giving the motivating push in the dream whose content is always wish fulfillment.[36]

Anxiety dreams A serious objection now appears. Let us place the objection in the context of a summary. Dreams represent the fulfillment of wishes. The conscious life never can include more than a selection of our wishes. Conscious life is taken up with this "economy" of the "distribution of quantities of mental excitation." [37] But the demand outruns the supply, and there is a surfeit of wish which somehow must find expression; this it does in dreams. The "residue" is a surplus, a surplus of demand. The particular residue is then fused with a primal wish. There may be, of course, many particular wishes, for even if there are dominant sexual wishes, not all pleasure is subtended under sexual pleasure, and one instinctual wish—the death wish—cannot properly be said to be included under the pleasure principle at all. The fusion, however, draws its main power from the primal nature of the archaic preindividual elements in consciousness. Perhaps one may think of the auxiliary energy of the residue as like that of a human pilot on a great ship. The difficulty with this picture is that it seems incapable of explaining all those arresting and painful dreams, nightmares, and tension dreams which are the very opposite of anything that men could wish for, allowed or not. Dreams of this sort Freud called "anxiety dreams."

Anxiety dreams do not constitute an exception to the pattern of wish fulfillment; they complete it. Infantile dreams are straightforward. Ordinary dreams are disguised fulfillments. Anxiety dreams are straightforward. One represses wishes. He has to, both because of the censor and for reason of sheer "economy." Freud said, "The formula for the anxiety dream is that it is the open fulfillment [within the framework of the dream, of course] of a repressed wish." [38] These dreams often wake us and so the dream has stopped shy of its purpose, which is to guard sleep. How does this happen? Freud said that in the night it is very likely the censor is somewhat weakened; it shows "diminished vigilance." [39] It is also possible to think of the wish in such cases as becoming extremely strong. Freud generally preferred blaming a weakened censor to a strengthened wish, as the explanation for the overt character of the anxiety dream.

But what is wished for in such dreams? These horrors? Exactly, said Freud. There are powerful "punishment tendencies" in the human mind. The wishes to punish oneself or others, which in neuroses and psychoses are called *masochistic* and *sadistic* wishes respectively, occur in dreams as well. Freud continued throughout his life to be fascinated by these tendencies toward punishment. His research in anxiety showed him that either he must abandon the idea that all dreams are wish fulfillments or else there must be wishes whose relation to pleasure is somewhat perverse. To take pleasure in hurting someone else seems deformed; to take pleasure in causing pain to oneself seems almost contradictory. Freud's last overarching work on psychoanalysis brings into sharper focus the relation between the instinct of aggression and the superego in the "punishment tendencies." This "unconscious need for punishment . . . behaves like a piece of conscience, like a prolongation of our conscience into the unconscious; and it must have the same origin as conscience and correspond, therefore, to a piece of aggressiveness that has been internalized and taken over by the super-ego." He goes on to say, "If only the words went together better, we should be justified for all practical purposes in calling it an 'unconscious sense of guilt'." [40]

Speaking roughly, the superego and what is normally called "conscience" are the same in this passage. The term "superego" never appeared in the Vienna lectures; it is a late development in Freud's thought, one which was brought about by his speculative extension of personal psychology into the psychology of society and civilization. More and more, between 1917 and 1932, Freud saw in the phenomenon of anxiety not merely a "tendency" toward punishment issuing in a wish for punishment which the anxiety dream releases; he began to recognize as well that powerful forces of a quite external but unavoidable nature were at work. In these years he published *The Ego and the Id, The Future of an Illusion,* and *Civilization and Its Discontents.*[41] Then came the *New Introductory Lectures on Psychoanalysis,* incorporating salient features of all three of these books and a revised theory of dreams.

THE TRIPARTITE PERSONALITY

The new structure of the psyche, as Freud saw it, has three principal parts: id, ego, and superego. None of these is closed to the other. Relations shift among them, and psychic functions depend upon their joint functioning.

THE ID

This is the subterranean part of the psyche, embracing the unconscious, and it is therefore the prison house of the repressions. But it is also more than this. It includes the libidinous drives and interrelates with both the ego and the superego. Freud at one point identified the id with the whole personality, but this was plainly not his usual doctrine.[42] The main contact between id and ego is the familiar one: the censor.

The word "id" Freud took from Georg Groddeck, who in turn got it from Nietzsche. Freud specifically used the word to replace the term "unconscious," and it is one of the three realms, regions, or provinces into which he divided "the provinces of the mental apparatus." [43] It is "a chaos, a cauldron full of seething excitations." [44] Freud went on to spell out the dimensions of disorder in the id. (1) It does not know negation; hence (2) it is not bothered by the laws of logic. (3) It is a stranger to the passage of time. Both native drives and repressed wishes, when they break forth, seem to be as fresh as if they were brand new. (4) It knows no values except that of the pleasure principle. "Instinctual cathexes seeking discharge—that in our view is all there is in the id."[45]

THE EGO

The evolutionary doctrine of ontogeny-phylogeny, mentioned earlier, is indirectly involved in the revised account of the unconscious. Just as life emerged from nonlife, so the conscious emerged from the nonconscious. This historical priority of the id Freud evidently regarded as a constant threat to the independence of the ego, which is derived from it. Thus, as we saw, he sometimes went so far as to speak of the id as the whole personality. But elsewhere Freud said that the ego should be regarded as a part of the id which has come into being through its contact with the external world.[46] The mediation that the ego provides is by way of perception and reflection upon memory—in a word, thought. It thus presents the id with the reality principle and undertakes to install this principle in the place of the pleasure principle. The replacement is not wholly successful. The vision belongs to the ego, but the power lies in the hands of the id, and Freud seemed to think that normality and balance are relatively fragile achievements which are never entirely secure. The ego is like a rider on a horse— the id—he says. The ego may or may not be successful in guiding the energies of the horse to its proper goal.[47]

The struggle is even more complicated, however. The ego must not deal merely with the id, but with the external world and the superego as well. Each of these "tyrants" is a source of possible danger and hence a taproot of some kind of anxiety. Freud's earlier position insisted on the theme that anxiety in general is the outcome, not surprisingly, of some surmised threat, a blend of a sense of danger and a perverse wish. The further analysis of anxiety among other researchers led him to restructure the shape of the psyche in the form we are now considering.

Each struggle gives rise to a kind of anxiety.[48] The relation of the id with the perceptually revealed external world gives rise to the reality anxiety. Goaded by the id, which it must restrain, the ego may fall into neurotic anxiety. Faced with the demands of the superego it may fall into normal anxiety.

There is no indication that the id, the ego, or the superego occurs in a pure distilled form. On the contrary, it is likely they will be mixed: Freud gave us a diagram exhibiting all the parts of the psyche as open by one channel or another to every other.[49] To complete the picture we turn to the superego. This late Freudian conception, which has caught the popular fancy, and which clarified certain problems for Freud, is the outcome of reflection on man in relation to society.

THE SUPEREGO

The notion of a superego lay close to the surface in the Vienna lectures. There Freud discerned a faculty within the ego which he called the "ego-ideal." [50] It is the same as the ego censor, which turns up in every kind of conflict from the most trivial slip of the tongue to the most profound psychic disturbance. Freud also called it "conscience," putting the word in quotation marks. In certain kinds of degeneracy of the ego—where conscience dissolves into the delusion that one is constantly being watched and criticized—one finds "the origin of the ego-ideal in the influence of parents and those who trained the child, together with his social surroundings, by a process of identification with certain of these persons who were taken as a model." [51] We shall return to this highly useful passage in an effort to examine some Freudian notions critically. At the moment our interest in the statement is that it leads directly to the conception of the superego.

The superego, as developed in the *New Introductory Lectures,* is a structural enlargement of the ego ideal mentioned above. It is also—at least potentially—a faculty of greater distinctness from the ego than the ego ideal. Hence its functions, being less dependent, are likely to be more complex. Its origins are in society. In the social works—*The Future of an Illusion, Civilization and Its Discontents*—the point was stressed that society is like the individual organism. It must survive and it takes steps to do so. It generates, on grounds which at the outset are pure expediency, rules and laws, customs and traditions, mores and morals. Social structure is the social organism's defense against collapse from internal disharmony. There is necessarily a multifaceted clash between individual and society, therefore, insofar as the individual is grounded in the id. The aim of social institutions of all sorts is harmony, the economy of energies in the social whole. To this end there arise values and ideals, aims, principles, and so on. But the id does not know these exist. It does not even bother to deny them, so to speak. We recall that, beyond pleasure in the form of consummation, the id has no values, just as it recognizes no negation, no logic, and no passage of time. The collision is not external to the person. For the adult, at least, the superego and the id are both internal to him, the former by nature, the latter by acquisition.

The situation is different for the child. He does not come into immediate contact with the great social world. That world is represented to him through the medium of his family, particularly through his father as head of the family.[52] Although the mother may play a substantial role, especially for the male child, she is not the representative of the outside world of business, professional life, politics, and so on. As the child matures, he gradually incorporates his understanding of the demands of the social world into his own psyche. Impulsive, he is taught by punishment, by restraint, and by rebuff to discipline himself, just as physical accidents, pains, and hurts teach him to have a high perceptual regard for the physical world and his relations to it. But this incorporation of the superego, the making of society's rules his own rules, is not a smooth and certain process. It is bound to present some difficulties. The conflict between the child's id and the social demand now becomes a conflict within himself. It is at this point that straightforward, realistic, wish-fulfilling dreams may give way to transformations of a complex and puzzling sort. It is at this same point—and the two facts are but aspects of the same maturation process—that the "conscience" of the child is born.

The superego now takes up a critical role. It censures, forbids, and punishes. What started out as external restraint becomes internal. The restraint is not only judicial and policelike, it is penal as well. Freud said we may call this superego the "conscience"—but "quietly." [53] The difference lies, according to Freud, in the fact that the superego is a "genuine structural entity" and not "an abstraction such as conscience." [54] Presumably he wanted to divorce the superego from any necessary dependence on absolute moral laws or religious authority. As superego it stems straight from society and the developing child's need to take his place in that society. [55]

The id is not composed exclusively of sexual instinct or even *basically* grounded in sexuality. The superego must deal with the instincts of aggression as well. To be sure, these aggressive instincts are never isolated from the erotic ones, but they are distinct. [56] We thus come full circle to what introduced the theory of the tripartite psyche in the first place, the further probing of anxiety. Anxiety is now differentiated into three kinds: "Neurotic anxiety is only one of these, arising from the force of the passions of the id." The destructive passion of aggressiveness which the ego "would have been glad to employ itself against others" is assimilated to the superego, which enlarges its role as critic to that of punisher. [57] Thereby, there arises an "unconscious sense of guilt." [58] We recall that the desire for self-punishment is at the root of the anxiety dream, understood as wish fulfilling. In the late lectures, Freud differentiated dreams into wish dreams, anxiety dreams, and punishment dreams, but still regarded the wish element as fundamental to all of them, submitting to modifications from erotic and destructive instincts in the id.

THE EDUCATION OF CHILDREN

Freud's influence on education has probably been more marked than that of any man who did not write a treatise on the subject. The reason is clear. He accomplished a revolution in the very mode of thinking about human nature and how it develops. For society at large—in however popular a way—to take Freud seriously is to accept a quite new way of regarding children, what they are, why they are, what they can be, and how they come to adulthood. Let us summarize some general points from the foregoing analysis and examine some pertinent features of the doctrine.

THE DISPENSABILITY OF RELIGION

First, the child is looked at in a wholly secular light. Freud's life-long antireligious attitude matured late in his life into attacks upon religion. For him, in *Civilization and its Discontents* and in *The Future of an Illusion,* religion was nothing but an institutionalizing of the superego, coupled with occult and supernatural trappings. The need of men for father worship, for a persistent ego ideal, coupled with dread of death and love of life, issues in the generation of an eternal "Father God," giving immortality to those who are obedient to His will. The religious ideal is embodied in a precise set of rules, moral and legal (more true of the Judaism of the Old Testament, with its rich emphasis on performance, than of the Christianity of the New Testament, which emphasizes inwardness). It arose as a necessary help in the socialization of men, but now—as the prime source of the sense of guilt, the cause of so much tragic suffering—it has outlived its time and should be replaced by reason. Freud clearly regarded his own work as an introduction to the replacement. Men equipped with a sound understanding of themselves and of society should have no need of supernatural threats and promises. Mature men are those who have passed beyond the restrictions of the Oedipal complex, the child's early dependence upon and competition with his father.

TOTAL EXPERIENCE AS EDUCATION

Second, education in the institutional sense is but a small part of the total process which is necessary to human development. Freud did not hesitate to speak of the "struggle for life" as educative, of the "educative influence of real necessity." [59] And the psychoanalytic process itself is said to be a kind of education or reeducation.[60] One is reminded of the Socratic dictum, "Know thyself."

THE DEVELOPMENTAL VIEW OF CHILDHOOD

Third, Freud continued and extended a view of childhood found in both Rousseau and Kant. Each of these philosophers in his own way made much of the fact that the child is too often regarded as an imperfect—or at least incomplete—adult.[61] Education is administered by adults; the partisan outcome is that education is exclusively pointed toward attaining the ideal state of adulthood. Routine drills, the orderly acquirement of systematic knowledge, conformity to the truths that the world has struggled so long to obtain, the regarding of play as an impediment to serious study, and a careful attention to the distinct areas of recognized human knowledge—these are some of the results of the conviction that education is the cure of the incompleteness of being a child. Both Kant and Rousseau, on the other hand, emphasized that stages of development in childhood do and must have at least intrinsic interest for the child, as well as being instrumental in pointing toward the goal of adulthood. Whitehead also emphasized the importance of objectives in study which are not too far over the horizon to be seen or at least felt. There must be a satisfaction of now-interest and of now-ways of thinking and living, regardless of what longer-term objectives guide the structure of education as a whole.

The upshot of this new mode of thought, beginning even with Locke, is to treat child development as a series of transitional phases characterized by positive needs and horizons, rather than as a series of fillings-in of gaps in the adult-to-be. This mode of thought was developed by both Dewey and Whitehead, writing in English. In Switzerland, Piaget's life work has been an elaboration of the same approach.[62] Out of it flowers the nursery school and the kindergarten movement, with approaches to education adapted as much to what the child is as to what he is going to be. From it stems the work of Gesell and Ilg, so influential as almost to be canonical in the understanding of the early phases of child development.

In a sense, Freud's place in this movement was radical. We may say that Kant and Rousseau and their followers sought a balanced perspective between adult states and childhood needs and aims. Freud went further. In his view the primary problems of education were conative—desiring, willing, wishing—rather than intellectual. Even more radically, Freud thought that a child accomplishes his primary educational developments no later than his fifth year. These two points are closely interconnected, according to Freud. He said, "Educability practically ceases with the full onset of the sexual instinct." [63] Education, accordingly, must begin vastly earlier than anyone might have supposed, for society has need of the work that is accomplished by the diversion of sexual energies into useful channels. Moreover, it is necessary that sexual development be postponed until it can be accompanied by some intellectual maturity. To this end, early natural sexual curiosity and activities are prohibited and restrained, for the safety and security of the next generation. Freud thought that the conflict thus necessarily engendered is responsible for the curious phenomenon of childhood amnesia which is all but universal.[64] He wanted us to understand that we are not to think of the term "sexual" as meaning activities concerned with procreation or reproduction, but rather be willing "to extend the designation 'sexual' to include those activities of early infancy which aim at organ-pleasure." [65] After the third year a rapid period of sexual maturation occurs. The child learns to select particular persons for affection, a certain amount of genital curiosity arises, and the polymorphous tendencies toward perversion appear. By eight at the latest, a "latency period" sets in and the sexual concerns largely dive underground. The period preceding the onset of the latency period is then commonly characterized by infantile amnesia. But these influences are nevertheless there. "The little human being is frequently a finished product in his fourth or fifth year, and only gradually reveals in later years what lies buried in him." [66]

THE NATURE AND AIM OF EDUCATION

Sexual constitution and development being what they are, the task of education is clear. If most of the crucial job is done in the first five years, it is largely nonintellectual in the ordinary sense of the term. The evolution of the race has produced a complex culture which is the child's social inheritance, but the time for inheriting is short. Here again we face the doctrine of phylogenetic recapitulation, not on a biological scale but on a cultural one. The cultural development "has extended over tens of thousands of years," only part of which a person can achieve "through his own development; a great deal must be *imposed* on him by education." [67] Accordingly,

> education must inhibit, forbid, and suppress, and this it has abundantly seen to in all periods of history. . . . [This involves the risk of neurotic illness.] Thus education has to find its way between the Scylla of non-interference and the Charybdis of frustration.[68]

PSYCHOANALYSIS AND EDUCATION

Freud regarded the "refractory instinctual constitution as incapable of being got rid of by education." This means that the task of finding the safe channel between Scylla and Charybdis requires the greatest skill in balancing *love* and *authority*. Consequently, "the only appropriate preparation for the profession of educator is a thorough psychoanalytic training. It would be best that he should have been analysed himself, for, when all is said and done, it is impossible to assimilate analysis without experiencing it personally." [69] This is more practical than analyzing the children. Also, any child would benefit, Freud thought, from the analysis of his parents; for the insight gained by parents would enable them to avoid difficulties with their children that they suffered from their parents before them.

Finally, Freud pointed out that since the individual makeup of each child is so different from the rest, and his past history so specific to him alone, one cannot expect different children to profit equally from the same educational procedure. He criticized education up to the present (1932) for its failure to recognize this fact.[70]

CRITICAL EVALUATION

Our principal interest in Freud has been to expose in outline the views of a man whose influence on modern thought is almost inestimable. By and large, his services (and disservices) to education are those, consequently, which derive from his influence on our general understanding of ourselves. Some of these gains and disadvantages will have more immediate pungency in their educational context, however.

CONTRIBUTIONS

The unconscious   We began this essay by pointing to Freud's theories of the unconscious. No future development in the human understanding of human beings will be uninfluenced by these theories and the facts which back them up. In the future Freud may be found to be crude and even credulous. But no one will ever again identify conscious life with mental life. In a time of excitable and somewhat irresponsible individualism and libertarianism, induced primarily by the great advances in political liberty, Freud is a cautionary figure, showing us how interdependent upon one another we are for our psychic constitution, and how much we are children of the past. In a way, this feature of Freud's view of human nature includes all the rest.

The analysis of human failure   Before Freud, human weakness often was referred to by a number of terms which, especially if they were not spelled out, were somewhat unilluminating. Men in trouble were regarded as being of "degenerate type." The implication was that of the presence of a congenital or hereditary flaw. Or they were said to be "weaklings." Or they were understood as showing "original sin." And the old medieval demonism was not entirely wanting, at least among ordinary people.[71]

As a result, those who are fortunate in their upbringing and environment often do not understand how important early childhood conditioning and environment are. Freud spoke of the application of his views to delinquency and criminology.[72] The differences in penal practice between 1860 and 1960, for example, reflect the great reform in the understanding of the determinative influences in people's lives. No figure stands out more clearly in this revised view of what makes men behave as they do than does Sigmund Freud.

The effects in education are far reaching. Teachers are profound shapers of the environment of children. In the early nineteenth century they regarded themselves, for the most part, as primarily having a duty to adult society to provide children with the means of growing up for that society. In the twentieth century, both the duty to children and the complexity of the task have become much more evident.

Closely related to this revised view of human behavior is the dawn of a new understanding of the relation between body and psyche. The field of psychosomatic medicine received its strongest impetus from the work of Freud and his associates. Medicine in general was thus released from a narrowing influence which treated only the observable as medically analyzable or respectable. Vast progress has taken place between Freud's first work on hysteria and the modern man-in-the-street's understanding that worry can cause ulcers and worse. The modern teacher can be expected to suspect trouble at home, poor upbringing, and related difficulties in the cranky child, the so-called "bored" or "rebellious" student, the "underperformer," and others like him. Locke's straightforward, empirically founded rejection of the cane as a major teaching aid now receives not merely humane support but confirmation from the study of motivation.

In short, Freud's analysis advanced the cause of humaneness in teaching by exposing the determining factors that push the plastic psyches of children and youth in or out of line. For the reflective teacher this knowledge cannot help but mean a heightened sense of obligation, responsibility, and opportunity.

The enlightened view of sexuality   In Freud's time, the subject of sex was fit talk only for intimate friends and learned men. The resulting inhibition ranged from the tragic to the comic. Sexual illiteracy was widespread among men, even more so among women. Women jumped out of hotel rooms on their wedding nights. Men shot themselves for impotency, or from motives made up of personal honor and wifely frigidity. But perhaps the most debilitating thing of all, from our modern view, was the widespread hypocrisy which made lying the normal mode of discussion of sex. Ignorance and inhibition—to Freud's way of thinking both quite unnecessary—drove hundreds of desperate men and women to seek Freud's help and later that of his followers. In an area where religion might have been of the greatest help, since its practitioners were traditionally trusted as spiritual guides, the common religious attitude was more unbending and more uninformed than that of the ordinary person. The psychoanalyst, then and now, fills the place of the reliable counselor, a place vacated by priests and parsons who have unwittingly ignored the duties of their profession.

Summary   The overall gain is in tolerance and enlightenment. Any school of any size which does not have at least the part-time help of a psychologist may be asked, "Why don't you?" Failing that, we expect trained counselors, part of whose task is not immediately academic, and we expect them to know how to look below the surface of what they see when they talk to their students. In the history of education, there are certain seminal minds that ask questions and give answers which were hardly dreamed of before. Even if we ultimately change, modify, or reject the answers, the questions remain as permanent contributions. Freud was such a mind.

PROBLEMS AND WEAKNESSES

The negative criticism of Freud has to be incomplete. A thorough probing of Freud's views and a thorough defense of them are equally beyond what an essay can accomplish. The effect of Freud's teaching, resting at least in part on what he has said, is not wholly sound or advantageous, however. It is not hard to show that Freud differed with himself to the point of contradiction, as well. Technical psychology has much to quarrel with him about. Few modern psychologists or doctors could agree, for example, to the proposition that neurotic conditions cannot be helped through physical treatment.[73] Freud's retort to most protest from orthodox therapy, medicine, and psychology was that his work was supplementary, exploring neglected areas of an infinitely rich subject. Freud's general opinion of philosophers was not high: he coupled them with poets and mystics.[74] He quoted with some pleasure Heine's lines about the philosopher: "With his nightcap and his nightshirt tatters, he botches up the loop holes in the structure of the world!"[75] He certainly had read some philosophers, how extensively it is hard to say. One can not adduce overwhelming philosophical literacy, on his part, from his writings.

Freud undertook to be hard headed, to deal with facts, and to allow facts to revise his theories. To a very considerable degree he accomplished these aims. However, he made speculative flights into the realm of the "archaic language" and guessed that the death wish arises from the urge of living matter to return, archaically, to a preorganic condition. Both of these speculations were magnificently grounded on virtually no facts at all. But he undertook to make no dogma of these guesses, and they are products of a rich imagination which gave us more valid notions. So imaginative a mind, however, should be tolerant of the guesses of others as well. One of Freud's limitations was that he confined his major suppositions about the superego to its representation in a family dominated by the father. The modern family may be different in two ways. First, modern parents are, in many ways, nearly coequal. Secondly, the modern family itself does not necessarily play the only important role in bringing social demands into the developing child's life. To this extent we may want to reassess the means of a child's acquiring a superego without necessarily challenging its source. If the source is to be challenged, this is a separate problem.

There are crucial subjects, however, in which Freud's posture or his doctrine or both ought to be investigated with some care. We examine four:

Religion Freud's work did not give him a very balanced view of religion. He is one of the great trio—the other two are Marx and Nietzsche—of the nineteenth century who regarded religion as not merely mistaken and false, but positively vicious. The common charge from all three men was that religion directed the wills of men away from the human solution of human problems. But Freud saw more evils of a very specific sort. Guilt-ridden patients often suffer from an excessive sense of being watched and judged; these symptoms may well seize on religious doctrines for expression. And the abundant cases of needless inhibition and ignorance about sex and sexuality Freud traced to an absolutistic morality founded in puritanical and tyrannical religion. These charges are not properly understood except in a larger context.

Religion, as Freud saw it, pretends to three main functions: [76] (1) it satisfies the thirst for knowledge by giving an account of the origin of the universe; (2) it holds out a future reward for good behavior, regardless of the miseries of the present life (this point is also much stressed by Marx and Nietzsche); and (3) it provides a moral law. These three distinguishable themes in religion are tied together by one basic human relation, that of fatherhood. It is the father status that engenders the famous Oedipal complex—the almost structural competition between the young male and the father, whose authority and command he must displace in order to achieve his own manhood. Unconsciously (as a rule) this complex manifests itself in the boy's desire to kill his father and sleep with his mother, as did Oedipus. Our religious feeling is to be understood as a regressive and therefore infantile wish to stabilize a lost childhood dream, the overwhelming majesty of the father before we grew up and saw him as he really was.

Thus, the origin of the universe through God's creation is an extension of the child's awareness of his father having created him. God as protector and guarantor of happiness derives from the child's dependence upon his father for well-being and love, a dependence he cannot entirely quell as an adult. God as lawgiver and restrainer is a patent projection of the father's role vis-à-vis the child. Religion takes over these wishes when reality has all but quashed them. Of the adult Freud said,

> Even now, therefore, he cannot do without the protection which he
> enjoyed as a child. But he has long since recognized, too, that his

father is a being of narrowly restricted power, and not equipped
with every excellence. He therefore harks back to the mnemic
image of the father whom in his childhood he so greatly overvalued.
He exalts the image into a deity and makes it into something contemporary and real. The effective strength of this mnemic image
and the persistence of his need for protection jointly sustain his
belief in God.[77]

But all this is quite wrong, said Freud. The primitive account of the
origins of the world crumples under our advancing knowledge of natural law; the wicked unjustly prosper; and the true origins of ethics lie
in the principle of survival and pleasure. Thus, while religion has
partly delivered us from the demonology of animism, the truth of religion is that it

is an attempt to master the sensory world in which we are situated
by means of the wishful world which we have developed within us
as a result of biological and psychological necessities. But religion
cannot achieve this. . . . If we attempt to assign the place of religion in the evolution of mankind, it appears not as a permanent
acquisition but as a counterpart to the neurosis which individual
civilized men have to go through in their passage from childhood
to maturity.[78]

Here again we see the imprint of evolution on areas of thought
larger than sheer biology. The evolution of the various purposes to
which religion has been put and the functions it has served are hardly
contestable. No doubt it is often the vanished childhood dream that
draws men and holds them to religious doctrine. The course of the argument, however, has two serious flaws. First, it omits too much.
Freud had little cause in his analytic practice to encounter or to comprehend the lives enriched, stabilized, and made serene by profound
religious commitment. These were precisely the people who would not
have turned up on Freud's couch. As a rule such persons are not
overly concerned with the intellectual aspects of religions, nor even
with its bad habit of incorporating creation stories, rigid religious
practice, and intransigeant moral codes. In any case, the heart of religion does not lie in any of these areas. These aspects of religion proceed from the act of personal faith; they do not govern or create religion. It is bad science to put aside relevant facts that might damage
one's theory. Freud praised Darwin for making special note of counter-
evidence, for example. William James, who also began life as a doctor
and a psychologist, regarded himself as an "outsider" to much of what
could be called "religious faith." Nonetheless in *The Varieties of Religious Experience,* he points out that not only the value but the truth
of held beliefs is partly to be found in their fruitfulness and enlarge-

ment of character.[79] As a doctor himself, he remarked that those who associate religious experience with medical pathology and then condemn the worth of religion because of the medical pathology are engaged in a rudimentary fallacy. He called it "medical materialism." It is a special form of the genetic fallacy. Our minds are not working well when we estimate the truth or falsity of a claim we are examining in terms of where it came from. For example, only in very restricted issues—e.g. perjury, slander, libel, and divorce—will the law allow the source of the evidence to be entered as a test of its truth. Suppose we could establish that Karl Marx was the author of the modern practice of social security. Would a distaste for Marxism be grounds for condemning social security? Einstein, a superb physicist, believed in God. Is this to be brought forward as an argument for God's existence?

We have come to the second major weakness in Freud's account of religion, namely: he confused the origins and stages of our ideas about religion and some of the functions these have served (even if his analysis is completely sound) with their value and their truth. To take a modern example: if laws and public criticism coerce the segregationist into supporting desegregation does that mean that it is wrong? Or right? "Consider the source" and "Consider why he believes or does as he does" often have little to do with honest opinions. They smack more of propaganda.

We should, of course, have no trouble in piecing together a Freudian account of the lives enriched by religious faith, and of serenity gained. It would be a final self-hypnosis in which reality was totally glossed over and the wish world had accomplished a complete infantile regression, held in balance with the normal conduct of one's public existence. But the problem thus only begins all over again. We know of religious men whose maturity is indubitable and beside whom the panting, hard-riding, compulsive atheist appears as a rebellious youth. Having thrown off the paternal authority, he is now looking for new worlds to conquer. Indeed, it is not too much to raise a question about Freud himself. If it be legitimate to ask about motives of men as bearing on the worth of their beliefs—and we have indicated the difficulties of this view—then what of Freud himself? Does his war with religion not seem a bit Oedipal itself? The competition with the oppressive authority, the rebellion against the age-old taboos, the desire to kill the father? This much can be said: Freud, who claimed that he once had a phonographic memory, fell into interesting amnesias of his own when he quoted religious scripture.[80]

The critical points must not be smeared over by more detailed critique, however. Freud did not collect all the kinds of facts he could. Other psychoanalysts, even those strongly influenced by and indebted to Freud—for example Medard Boss, a past president of the International Federation for Medical Psychotherapy [81]—have felt no need to approach the data of religious feeling with a predisposition to change it into something else. This second fallacy, the abuse of the important but limited method of tracing the origins of our institutions and beliefs, is part of a widespread weakness in Freud which we discuss on pages 148–157 under the heading "Reductionism and determinism."

Love and sexuality Already, in 1917, Freud found it necessary to defend himself on the subject of sex. On the one hand, sex was a forbidden topic in many kinds of company. Even in his medical lectures Freud had to warn women students that they came to learn and would have to take the consequences. But the real scandal—if there was one —lay not in speaking of sex but in using the term too sweepingly. Such overemphasis on one motivation is not unique, of course to Freud. Calvin treated sin as the constant factor in all human motivation; for Marx all human activity was determined by the mode of production; Nietzsche saw all life as the "will to power." Any other kind of life, then, had to be called not genuine, diseased, and so on.

The tendency toward a single-minded account of motivation is a peculiarly nineteenth-century ailment. Freud did not wholly escape it. He defended the earliest childhood tendencies toward pleasure seeking as sexual "because in the course of analyzing symptoms we reach them by way of material which is undeniably sexual." [82] He granted that this would not make them "undeniably sexual," but as an analogy he bade us consider two seeds, an apple and a bean. Each belongs to that group of plants whose seeds have two food storage parts (dicotyledonous). Suppose we could not see their different developments from seed to plant but could only trace them back to their seeds. The seed's cotyledons are undistinguishable. Should we suppose that the differences came later, asked Freud, or that the difference exists already? We must pass over the unhappy facts that bean seeds are quite distinguishable from apple seeds and that the difference doesn't lie in the cotyledons. Stating the point less vulnerably, the stuff of the cotyledons and the germ—the third part that happens to bear the chromosomes which will determine the plant's life—give us little or no clue to the differences to come. But the differences must have been there all along. However he nominally agreed to leave the matter suspended and remarked that from there on, in any case, the sexuality is clear. [83]

We have already seen that Freud found basic instincts other than the pleasure principle, even in the id—aggression and the curious retrograde death wish that seeks the inorganic for itself. But these are in a sense both negative; their object is some kind of destruction. In spite of a few qualifications, the pleasure principle is the most positive urge, sex is its commonest basic manifestation, and the task of learning to adapt to society is the task of diverting and transforming this basic energy—the exchange of a sexual aim for a social one.[84] Similar transformations take place in the transition from the oral pleasure of an infant to the genital pleasure of the adult, but the aim in both cases is sexual gratification. The means changes with physical maturation. The "look of perfect content" on the child sated with nursing "will come back again later in life after the experience of orgasm." [85] The logic of this remark cannot in charity stand much scrutiny. Such a look may also appear on the face of a man who has discovered a fine wine or swindled the opposition out of a grand slam.

Heterosexual adult love has a complex history, in Freud's view. Motivationally, the tendency to love is an extension of egoism; it has no independent status at the outset. The child loves himself first, and then others only because he needs them. "Only later does the impulse of love detach itself from egoism: it is a literal fact that the child learns how to love through his own egoism." [86] The instinct of giving begins with bowel movements: "Faeces were the first gift that an infant could make, something he could part with out of love for whoever was looking after him. After this, corresponding exactly to analogous changes of meaning that occur in linguistic development, this ancient interest in faeces is transformed into the high valuation of *gold* and *money*." [87] The child's earliest stage is thus oral-anal, and the hazards of the anal-sadistic and phallic phases lie between it and the mature genital phase. In this area lie the perversions and other forms of neurotic immaturity, where the developing person may be caught in an endless eddy or to which he may regress under adult strain. They cannot here be considered in detail.

If one takes the Freudian view seriously, it is a near miracle that mature love occurs at all. Physically it must go through a series of transformations from the love of nipples and the giving of excrement to adult reciprocal fulfillment. Motivationally it must develop from an interest in others as they may serve you to a willingness to sacrifice one's selfhood for another. Yet that these stages occur seems undeniable. The disagreement with Freud must lie in how he saw what he saw.

The genetic fallacy which we saw in Freud's treatment of religion is even more evident in his account of sex and love: (1) the emphasis in Freud's account is on roots, the fruits being merely the outcome; (2) Freud hybridized infant and child behavior with adult vocabulary in describing the behavior. No doubt he got assistance in this weakness from the general public, but a scientist must have standards of precision.

Let us postpone this difficulty for a moment and consider the roots. First, consider Freud's support of the proposition that a child is primarily interested in himself and others only as they serve him. It is, so far as we can discover, entirely without experimental confirmation. And indeed, it is hard even to envisage how such experiments would be possible. Moreover, there is very little evidence that Freud spent a great deal of time even observing children, outside of analytic contact with them. Such contact constitutes an exception to the normal, not its index. The want of data does not make his conclusions wrong, but it deprives them of force and permits lay observers to ask questions. For instance, in defending egoism Freud said that those whom the child seems to love are loved because he needs them, hence from motives of egoism. What is there about the "them" that makes this necessary? Nothing biological, surely. Foster children exist in loving relationship with their families. Warmth, tenderness, nourishment, care, affection, creature comfort—these are what the child needs. In short, he needs love in the only form he can use it and assimilate it. He offers love for love, if indeed the word "love" is right for this primitive impulse. Whatever it is, it lies side by side with primitive and impulsive self-centeredness, if *that* term is deserved.

But perhaps we should abandon the terms ego, love, self-love, and so on, for a very good reason. There isn't enough of a self or an ego present to be object or subject of gratification. Some subjective element, in a general sense, is present. What self there is is always present as the subject of the interest that underlies the child's budding intelligence (page 135) and personality. But to confuse the child "self" as the constant subject of his interest with his "self" as the constant object of his interest is an elementary blunder. Anyone relatively innocent of commitment to some school of thought who has watched children has seen that some of their actions are exclusive—the interest is turned back upon its "self," the subject. Other actions are inclusive—the interest is directed outward to other persons and things, both in impulsive curiosity and in impulsive affection. The gradual growth in a normal child is outward, an ever-enlarging identification of his incipient and half-formed "self" with other persons and things. Intellectually the child's own conception of "self," "others," and "world" comes only gradually into existence a bit at a time. We see it in the transition from solitary play through parallel play to reciprocal play, for example. It would be very surprising if the child's world of interest and regard were not closely tied to this gradual intellectual clarification. Indeed, as we shall see in our study of Piaget, there is every good reason, backed up by years of careful observation under relatively normal circumstances, to regard the major phases of intellectual development as strongly reflective of "affective" development.

Let us return, then, to the bizarre hybridization of infant behavior with a vocabulary borrowed from and associated with later stages of development. The connecting point here has already been noticed—in effect: How can there be egoism where there is no ego? Even by Freud's standards the child ought not to be said to have an ego. For one thing, at the outset the infant has no ego ideal, or superego as Freud called it later. If the personality is dynamic, its parts *exist* by reason of their relation with one another. One could make a firm stand *within* the Freudian camp against a child's having any more ego than superego. And as we have seen, Freud himself was somewhat hesitant, in the clutch, about attributing the element of sexuality to the less-than-three-year old. There is a real semantic confusion here; if we then elect to use the term "ego" for the infant impulse, and ignore the fact that these impulses are sometimes directedly inwardly, "exclusively," and other times are directed outwardly, "inclusively," what shall we say of the youth and the adolescent and the adult descendants of this unformed original nucleus of personality, the ego? If we persist in using the same terms, then we must acknowledge that something more has been added, and a "more" so significant that, say, infant and adolescent *differences* as well as similarities are accounted for. For example, an adolescent can hate with a pretty persistent and unbending hatred. This hatred is qualitatively different from the "rage" or "terror" of an infant. Beyond some point this capacity has emerged, a *new* thing. Why shouldn't the same be true of adolescent "love"?

Freud actually is engaged in a circular procedure. He used a terminology—and it makes no difference whether the term is a neologism, like "libido," or is in the public domain, like "love"—whose principal use is in the classification of post-infant behavior, largely that of adults. He then transferred this vocabulary back to the infant and the child, whose own self-consciousness and emotions are at best on the threshold of those stages from which the language is derived. Needless to say, if all the child's actions are interpreted through these categories, rather than being observed as the undefined and ambiguous things they are, the easiest way to get at the adult is through reaching back to his childhood, as understood by those categories. In short, the defense of the understanding of the adult in terms of his childhood is accomplished by interpreting the childhood in adult categories.

Two things save this tautological procedure from total inanity: (1) the need of scientific analysis for simplification of a complex scene (this need contains the danger of reductionism; see page 150); (2) the positive emphasis on the power of childhood influences on adult personality. But this should not be understood as demonstrating continuity of some unobservable "part" of the psyche which deserves the same name throughout its career. The emphasis should be on the *processiveness* of personality, rather than its unchangingness.

In the Middle Ages there developed the "homunculus theory" of human birth. Insemination was the implanting of a tiny human being into the womb. Gestation was the increase in size, without major addition, of this "little man." It is not too much to say that Freud had come close to a homunculus theory of the psyche. His illustration of the apple seed and the bean is a revealing one, in this respect, even after it has been rendered accurate scientifically. He regards human development in the same light as he does the more primitive life of the beans and the apples, an unfolding of the already there from within, under the catalyst of the already there from *without*.

Reductionism and determinism   This final point provides us with a transition to the third area of criticism—determinism and reductionism. The implicit determinism in Freud's theory is no secret. He made much of it. In its particular context with regard to sex and love, it has peculiar significance. It is true that we are offended by Freud's analysis of love which makes the impulse to love an offspring of selfishness and the physical joy of sexual love a thing that has gradually emerged from the sucking instinct and has survived a number of possible perversions en route. But such offense is merely comic prissiness if no other reason accompanies it. Clearly, however, one does: the "nothingbut" quality of the implicit determinism which ignores intuitions that have little to do with tender feelings. The adult is himself a history of decisions. His personality is comprised of the form of those decisions imposed on the raw material of his own previous life, his hereditary endowment, and what fortune offers in the way of coercion and opportunity. It is through his acquaintance with himself as incarnated in these decisions that his intelligence has a right to be said to be self-aware. His consciousness, aware of both his inner self and the outer world, is the outcome of neither an inward heredity nor an outward environment. It is, in some sense, master of them both insofar as it joins them. Nowhere is this decision more intimately known and more central to personality than in the intense personal commitment of adult love. Who offers a deterministic account of this factor offers to dissolve selfhood into its antecedent raw materials and treats the center of a man's life as the outcome of these materials and their chance convergence. His selfhood and his agency are thereby abolished at one blow. But we should perhaps not be offended, for this myth is incompatible with our direct experience of self-awareness, of planning, of choice.

Freud's determinism had two principal roots, one of which is practical, the other theoretical. The roots lie side by side and nourish one another as much as they do the visible plant. The practical root was not only found in practice, especially his practice, but it had *practical* —i.e. utilitarian—features, as well. Freud's patients were people who, in varying degrees and in various ways, were "out of control." The expression is a good one. They were no longer masters of their fate or finders of their own self-fulfillment. Any man can easily be reduced to such a state by factors not immediately psychic. Drugs, physical blows, and systemic as well as pathological diseases can alter personality and/or render a man totally helpless. To the extent that one's life is considered as wholly wrapped up in this one little skintight self, the battle is ultimately lost in any case—to death. But even within life we see men hopelessly trapped and helpless. From this class Freud's patients came. He was not universally successful, and sometimes success was followed by relapse, the most discouraging thing that any therapist or teacher can face, since it is likely to spread the sense of helplessness to the educator or the reeducator. Freud's great courage and honesty faced this problem repeatedly, and we see the signs of it always in his description of his cases.

It is not surprising that Freud gave the most extreme statement to his awareness of the deterministic element in human action. He did not spare any tender sentiments that his young listeners may have. We have already noticed that near the outset of the Vienna lectures Freud spoke of "the determination of natural phenomena," which cannot "at any single point" be abandoned without throwing over "the whole scientific outlook." [88] Furthermore, he said,

> I have already taken the liberty of pointing out to you that there is within you a deeply rooted belief in psychic freedom and choice, that this belief is quite unscientific, and that it must give ground before the claims of a determinism which governs even mental life. I ask you to have some respect for the fact that one association, and nothing else, occurs to the dreamer when he is questioned. Nor am I setting up one belief against another. It can be proved that the *association thus given is not a matter of choice, not indeterminate,* and that it is thus not unconnected with what we are looking for.[89]

Here is the juncture point between theory and practice in Freud's belief in determinism. It is not only that Freud's patients in fact exhibited the minimal degree of human freedom discernible, but that the *theory* of diagnosis required the same determinism. The patient is asked to free-associate (an ironic designation for the action) in order to show other connections in his submerged mental life which will make diagnosis possible. We have italicized a crucial phrase in Freud's statement of this point, to which we will return in a moment. Suppose I have chest pains, persistent, recurring, distracting. I want relief, but I fear a deep and sinister difficulty. I go to the doctor and he announces that nothing is really wrong with me; these things just pop up out of nowhere without reason. I assume then that either the doctor or his science is inadequate—or both. I can't tell myself *there are no reasons*. In short, diagnosis presumes causes and looks for them. When it stops that, it stops being diagnosis. Insofar as psychoanalysis is diagnostic, it must be deterministic, like any science.

There is, however, another side to psychoanalysis. No matter what the method or even the school of thought involved, all psychoanalysis aims at cure. As a rule, medicine in general is primarily aimed at the removal of not just symptoms but their causes. In psychoanalysis the symptoms may be of a vast variety, but the cause is supposed to be personal inability to conduct the course of one's life for oneself. Self-knowledge is at least part of the cure. Much of Freud resembles the familiar "You shall know the truth and the truth will make you free!" There is something paradoxical in being liberated by the news that one is not free. It is equally paradoxical to insist on self-knowledge, if the self as thus known turns out to be nothing on its own but the mere coming together of forces and conditions prior to and external to itself. Either the self is something over and above these materials, or it is no self. It seems unlikely that even Freud intended that psychic cure should be the exchange of one set of masters for another, in which the entire psychic gain was pleasure or release from pain. For example, pleasure about what? Sooner or later all these pleasures have to be interpreted in terms of their parent wishes, sexual gratification, aggression, death wishes, and any other primitive forbears one may *reduce* his complicated and intricate psyche to.

The hard core of Freud's determinism is *reductionism*. A reductionist is a "nothing-but" thinker. Such a person unwittingly denies the reality of the passage of time. He argues that my complex present psyche is really *nothing* but those primordial drives plus subsequent adaptations. There are "sublimations" and "transformations" of these unchanging basic drives. My love of money is the deterministic descendant of my early fascination with faeces and the pleasure both of withholding bowel movements and releasing them.[90] The artist's life is similarly derivative.

> The artist has also an introverted disposition and has not far to
> go to become neurotic. He is one who is urged on by instinctual
> needs which are too clamorous; he longs to attain to honour, power,

riches, fame, and the love of women; but he lacks the means of achieving these gratifications. So like any other with an unsatisfied longing, he turns away from reality and transfers all his interest and all his libido too, on to the creation of his wishes in the life of phantasy, from which the way might readily lead to neurosis. . . . Probably their [artists'] constitution is endowed with a powerful capacity for sublimation.[91]

In this passage we see an implicit answer from the reductionist to his questioner. One may rightly demand, "Aren't these sublimations and transformations—granting your theory of origins—just what make the difference? They don't just happen of themselves. It takes effort and self-remolding to face the social task and transform and rechannel one's internal energies. This is where we find the self different from the materials; in altering them, we thereby bring the self into being." But Freud's answer was evident: "Their constitution is endowed with a powerful capacity for sublimation." And here the bankruptcy of this branch of the analysis comes out in the open. We are faced with changes, even assuming Freud's theory of primordiality. These changes are said to be the "same" thing in a "sublimated" form. If we then say, "How come the sublimation? Is not sublimation just the new thing that your genetic account regards as impossible?" "Oh, no, that's the result of an original endowment too, a powerful capacity for sublimation." Aside from the fact that a capacity still has to be somehow put into action, in order to be a cause, there is a deeper problem: *How should we know of such "capacities" except by their "results in sublimation"?*

Again we have run into a circle. Determinism is defended by saying that present complex features of personality are direct deterministic descendants of earlier basic drives plus adventitious events in the person's history. If we find them not to *appear* to be so, we are told that they are just sublimations. If we then ask how the sublimations occurred, the answer is from a capacity to sublimate. But the evidence for such *capacity* to sublimate lies in the alleged occurrence of the sublimation. The sublimation is defended in terms of the capacity, but the capacity to sublimate is known only through the alleged actual sublimation.

This short and vicious circle is a vital part of Freud's determinism. It features a form of the "Men are really" or "Human life is nothing but" sort. The analytical procedure encourages us to think of what we analyze as nothing but the least units of which it is composed, or nothing but the roots from which it came. The two fallacies—reductionist and genetic respectively—are closely related. The former fallacy renounces the reality of wholes—*Gestalts,* as they are called—in favor of parts. The latter ignores the reality of the present—we may call it freedom—in favor of that of the past which is supposed to have contained everything, in embryo, waiting to unfold automatically, like a Japanese water flower. In one case our *Gestalts* fade into ultimate physical particles, electrons, protons, and the like, and in the other the causal past rushes away from us, over the hill, out of sight. Neither of these myths or mysteries has much to offer in competition with those other superstitions that Freud wished to dispel. And they have the extra disadvantage of offering intellectual respectability to the defeatist.

Freud himself was fortunately not among those whose practice was a vindication of what he claimed. The Vienna lectures begin with a stirring appeal to the young doctors to throw off the inhibitions and complacencies of conventional medicine, to run the risk and reach for the rewards in the high adventure of seeking out new paths of understanding and new insight into mental disease. The language is almost dramatic in its invocation to the students to throw off the shackles. They had nothing to lose, it was once said, but their shames. Freud was manifestly dedicated to the freedom of his patients. This prizing of self-dependence on his part brings us back to the coupling of indeterminism with freedom of choice in the passage on page 149.[92] Freud seems incapable there of distinguishing between freedom of choice and indeterminism. A genuine choice, however, is an act of self-determination. The determination comes with the self which continues to create itself in and through the act of choice. Thus the state of being indeterminate and the state of having freedom to choose are identical only if all determinateness refers only to the past, and the past of the past, indefinitely. There is no place here to follow the twists and turns of this problem in technical terms, but we see again that curious doctrine which regards the passage of time as the mere unfolding of what was already "there."

Yet this is only Freud the theoretician of analytic diagnosis. Freud the therapist, who would give men back their freedom, and whose own life was an almost continuous struggle even when he became famous, reveals again the opposite strain of thought. Of the patient suffering from resistance (lack of candor in facing his symptoms) he says, "If he can be successfully *helped* to overcome this new resistance he regains his *insight* and *comprehension*. His critical faculty is not functioning *independently,* and therefore is not to be *respected,* as it were; it is merely a maid-of-all-work for his affective attitude and is directed by his resistance." [93] The italics are ours; they indicate words that must be talked out of existence—transformed, or reduced, if you will—in order to be introduced into the vocabulary of determinism.

Intellectually, determinism is without support. It claims that all that comes to be does so exclusively because of prior occurrences and they likewise ad infinitum. The claim is a shade pretentious. Judgments using the word "all" should be prepared either (1) to show all the actual cases, or (2) to show, on logical grounds alone, how no exception can be conceived. Determinism is hardly prepared to exhibit occurrences that haven't taken place, and there certainly is nothing logically contained in the idea of an occurrence to demand that all of its ingredients point to the past. Many philosophers and some scientists, recognizing this fact, have decided to abandon the idea of "cause" entirely. When the idea of cause vanishes, however, it takes the idea of "determinism" with it.

There is one important way in which the "all" judgment gains credibility. It is methodologically required for any scientific enquiry. If, scientifically, I demand "Why did that happen?" I must be prepared to submit any answers given to the same question all over again. I must explore the web of causal connection that joins the present with the past. But sooner or later this systematic ordering of the world that we observe will run off the map. We will encounter explanations, including things and occurrences whose deterministic analysis is dubious, at best. These occurrences are decisions and the things are persons. When we encounter them, our scientific method is usually modified and curbed from any pretense to being the sole sure method of human knowledge, by empathy, by reflection, by projection of our admittedly limited understanding of ourselves into other persons. Just as in the scientific mode we may err, so may we also in the humanistic mode. What is important is that the modes are—and should be—distinguishable. Moreover, the humanistic is not always the most humane. It is, after all, the deterministic mode of thought, in some degree, that has modified the brutalities of criminal procedure and of social ills and that has given us the modern awareness of the causes of, say, juvenile delinquency. The old voluntarism held a man responsible whether he was or not.

The distinguishing feature of the humanistic mode of understanding, as opposed to the scientific, deterministic one, is that self-awareness is the indispensable basis of it. In scientific observation, self-awareness has no place. Only two modifications of this view have appeared. In relativity, the relative motion of the observer's body must be taken into account, but this is itself the body mostly as observed, not as lived. The other is the problematic—and debated—role that the observer plays in interfering with the data he observes, especially in the case of the observation of very small particles. But these also are at the bodily end of the spectrum of self-awareness. In humanistic understanding, however, the exact opposite is the case. The fullest resources of self-awareness are required, and these resources must be the constant companion of men understanding one another. For them to ignore or deny this mode of knowledge, tricky and unreliable though it be, is quite impossible.

We came to the subject of determinism by way of the subject of adult sexual love. This love is one of a vast family of humane relations without which human beings are not human. So is the merest moment of wondering how one appears in another person's eyes. Reflective self-awareness of this sort is the starting point of the interrelations among men. It thus starts with what is farthest removed from the scientific aim of a system of impartial observables in the physical world. Such self-awareness is, at the end, the only possible excuse we can have for incorporating the humanities and the social sciences in our curricula. Their objective is just the self-awareness which musters more than the sheer power of objective observation and causal analysis as essential features of human development. Because of this distinctive set of aims and methods, no humane discipline can accept any procedure having other aims as universally binding upon itself. It can, of course, equally not afford to ignore all that can be discovered about men as objects. What cannot be done is treating them as merely objects.

Freud's virtues and weaknesses are largely to be found in one cluster. We may call this collection of characteristics his objectivism. Before Freud, the dominant mode of thought about the inner and not directly observable lives of men was that they are of a radically different order from the commonly observable world. This basic conviction is still true, in our view. But the form of it that Freud confronted badly needed ventilating. Much of the religious superstition which has most damaged religion found shelter from criticism in the idea that scientific objectivity has no role to play in understanding the human psyche. Part of Freud's critique of religion arose from outrage at the human damage done in the name of religion. Further, where religion might shrug its shoulders or allow some form of demonology as accounting for insanity, Freud's analysis exposed the rationale and often the cure for tormented people whose fate was either to be locked up, if they were poor, or expensively cared for, if they were well off, but in any case never to be treated for their illness.

Freud was thus a new kind of rationalist. He was no prizer of reason as lying at the heart of human nature. Far from it. For him reason was a poor thing as a guide to existence, easily overwhelmed by emotional storms and pressures. But he knew that in the eye of the observer, the analyst—the scientist—reasons can be found for whatever occurs, at least on principle. No doubt this accounts for part of his austerity, by modern standards, with his patients: reason is strong enough to discover the logic of action, if it does not cloud its vision with emotion. In the domain of action he found rationality not powerful; in the domain of observation it is the final test of all explanation. His determinism is a necessary corollary to this explanatory rationalism. The same is true of his objectivism—the treating of data as reliable only if they can be put in some form which can be seen by any calm and trained observer. This is the true scientific posture: the demand for objective data—the same for any observer—plus a coherent and logical pattern of cause and effect to bind them together. We have tried to show how this is not only a view which serves in bringing cures to wretched souls, but—when taken in its sociological form—further inspires the humane effort to better the spiritual, physical, and social environments of men in which crime, misery, and poverty are generated. Social reform—in which Freud was not primarily interested—also makes humane use of an at least partial determinism.

Yet there arises from this objectifying and deterministic understanding an attitude in education, rather than an outright doctrine, which ultimately contributes to the current student discontent with education. What happens if we take the doctrines of objectivism and determinism as exhaustively true for human nature; if we decide that the subjective can be dealt with only when it is objectified; if we try to understand everything that occurs as merely the outcome of circumstances which preceded it and from which it arose? Such themes and presuppositions, like any others about human nature, must be reflected in education. In our liberal atmosphere, students more often feel such doctrines than have them preached to them, but too often they find the human being treated explicitly as a machine, usually in the introduction to biology texts. They see the methodological successes of the sciences carelessly made into ontological systems, and they are tempted by the success of causal analysis to assume that determinism as a world view is very plausible. If they soak up the idea that the problem in education is to enlarge intellect, learn laws, memorize the crucial data, become skilled in method, and so on, a few will rebel, then more and more, as from within their own inner lives they discover the primacy of emotions, the dependence of real meaning upon values, however one may objectify both meaning and value. They will turn away from a disordered society where—for reasons too complex to analyze easily—persons have been far too objectified for one another, manipulated, and ignored. To shorten a story that is familiar to any college professor who has taught during the last ten years, they will find their education *irrelevant*.

There is a long tale to be told about this irrelevance and no room to tell it here, but one final point should be made. The form in which the debate about relevance is usually conducted is somewhat off target. Colleges could hardly convert themselves to education for the current crises. The very currency of these crises means that they mutate to other crises later. Education directed toward crises is automatically dated, yet clearly something is needed. Perhaps educators should look at how the drop-out or the student in summer chooses to live. Many distinctive activities and current practices tell a simple and direct story. Every summer, for example, thousands of youngsters from Europe and America, living together and working for bare living accommodations, engage in archeological digs. The routine and the drudgery are as stiff as any school demands on them could be. What draws them is existence in a face-to-face society, a combination of intellectual and physical—dominantly physical—life and the sense of participation in discovery. Again, consider the student "communes," the sad struggling hippy colonies, the "families," the recent involvement in Vista and the Peace Corps. What of the youth-helping-youth drug centers, help lines, job agencies? None of these occupations requires any kind of education at all. The one element they all have in common is what we might call the primacy of the personal and its *subjective* validity. Clearly what has been wanting in education at all levels is the education of the emotions. Think of the T-groups, the sensitivity groups, the encounter groups, the Zen groups, the yoga groups, the Esalen movement; these have been seized upon by people of every age from midteen on. In every one of these activities there is the promise of the enlightenment of mental, spiritual, or physical *feelings*.

The vast spread of groups of adults devoted to heightened sensitivity and heightened awareness indicates a deprivation or deformation in some earlier aspect of development. In our opinion, the analogous phenomena among young adults and teen-agers—the appearance of communal living groups *of all sorts,* the drop-outs, the great rise in undergraduate marriages, the spread of student interest in teaching and in education, the critical attitude toward the "whole educational system" are all basically part of the same movement, a protest on behalf of the personal. It is hard not to find evidence of this protest. Rock music has replaced jazz almost entirely in the musical imagination of young people. In it are embodied sentimental lyrics, autobiographical revelation, emotional portraits of current life, political protest, a great outpouring of persons singing to persons—and being listened to. The jazz that rock replaced had no lyrics and was enormously subtle, almost cerebral. It had lost its voice, lost its feeling, lost its personality. It had become rarefied, exquisite, experimental, and a bit self-destructive. All that it had lost in its sophistication, rock restored. Elegance, poise, form, subtlety are no good when you're hungry. Rock satisfies the hunger. It is not too much, perhaps, to say that what rock was to jazz, the free university, including some comical proposals and activities, is to standard college education. Somebody is trying to tell us something. We may not be listening loud enough.

NOTES

1. It is necessary to use here Nora Barlow's edition, the first one that is complete and unabridged: *The Autobiography of Charles Darwin 1809–1882, Edited with Appendix and Notes by His Grand-Daughter Nora Barlow,* New York, 1958.

2. *A General Introduction to Psycho-Analysis: A Course of Twenty-Eight Lectures Delivered at the University of Vienna,* trans. Joan Riviere, New York, 1935 (hereafter cited as *GI*); *New Introductory Lectures on Psycho-Analysis,* trans. James Strachey, New York, 1965 (hereafter cited as *NL*).

3. *The Interpretation of Dreams,* ed. trans. James Strachey, New York, 1955.

4. *NL*, p. 5.

5. See R. S. Brumbaugh and N. M. Lawrence, *Philosophers on Education,* Boston, 1963, Chapter 2.

6. See Lancelot Law Whyte, *The Unconscious Before Freud,* New York, 1960.

7. Freud wanted to regard this view not as conventional hedonism. He regarded the pain as the experience of an "excitation" or "stimulation" which the organism seeks to avoid and to restore to "equilibrium." Pleasure would then be the "experience of satisfaction." (See David Rapaport, *The Organization and Pathology of Thought,* New York, 1951, pp. 317–318, especially footnotes and comment on Freud's text.) Nevertheless, Freud says in the third part of *GI* (which Ernest Jones refers to as "much more advanced than the earlier two parts"), "It seems that our entire psychical activity is bent upon *procuring pleasure* and *avoiding pain*" (p. 311). It should be noted again that these lectures were given in the winter of 1916–1917, more than a year after all but one of Rapaport's references.

8. *GI*, p. 311.

9. *GI*, p. 310.

10. See *Philosophers on Education,* Chapters 2 and 3.

11. *GI*, pp. 286 ff.

12. *GI*, p. 137.

13. E.g. *GI*, p. 359.

14. *GI*, p. 169. But the old Freud is said to have remarked, "There are times when a cigar is only a cigar."

15. *GI*, p. 136.

16. *GI*, p. 177.

17. *GI*, p. 316.

18. *GI*, p. 149.

19. *NL*, p. 88.

20. *NL*, p. 107.

21. *GI*, pp. 131–132.

22. *The Psychopathology of Everyday Life,* trans. A. A. Brill, New York, 1951.

23. *GI*, p. 27.

24. See *Philosophers on Education,* Chapter 5.

25. *GI*, p. 118.

26. This is a major theme in *Civilization and Its Discontents,* trans. James Strachey, New York, 1962.

27. *GI*, p. 151.

28. *GI*, p. 116.
29. *GI*, pp. 113–115.
30. *GI*, p. 116.
31. *GI*, pp. 137, 171.
32. *GI*, p. 202.
33. *GI*, pp. 160, 119–120.
34. *GI*, p. 212.
35. *NL*, p. 17.
36. *NL*, p. 22.
37. *GI*, p. 311.
38. *GI*, p. 193.
39. *GI*, p. 195.
40. *NL*, p. 109.
41. *The Ego and the Id*, trans. Joan Riviere, London, 1927; *The Future of an Illusion*, trans. W. D. Robson-Scott, London, 1928.
42. *NL*, p. 105. See Georg Groddeck, *The Book of the It*, trans. V. M. E. Collins, New York, 1961.
43. *NL*, p. 72.
44. *NL*, p. 73.
45. *NL*, p. 74.
46. *NL*, p. 75.
47. The pungently sexual character of this simile may have escaped Freud. Had it been called to his attention, he surely would have acknowledged the fact.
48. *NL*, pp. 70–78.
49. *NL*, p. 78.
50. *GI*, p. 37.
51. *GI*, p. 37.
52. See critique at end of chapter, pages 140–157.
53. *NL*, p. 60.
54. *NL*, p. 64.
55. *NL*, pp. 60–61.
56. *NL*, pp. 103, 109–111.
57. *NL*, p. 111.
58. *NL*, p. 109.
59. *GI*, pp. 310, 311.
60. *GI*, p. 392.
61. *Philosophers on Education*, Chapters 4 and 5.
62. This theme, void of much of the Freudian trapping, reappears a bit more modestly in R. M. Jones, *Fantasy and Feeling in Education*, New York, 1968. See Chapter 10.
63. *GI*, p. 273.
64. *GI*, p. 274.
65. *GI*, p. 285.
66. *GI*, p. 311.
67. *NL*, p. 147; emphasis ours. It is here that Neill parts company with Freud.
68. *NL*, p. 149.
69. *NL*, p. 150.
70. *NL*, pp. 149–150.
71. One of the authors lives in a town where the children of one kindly pillar of the community are reared to think that a "devil inside" is responsible for childish wrongdoing.
72. *NL*, p. 150.
73. *NL*, p. 152.
74. *GI*, p. 21.
75. *GI*, p. 220.
76. *NL*, pp. 161–162.
77. *NL*, p. 163.

78. *NL*, p. 168.

79. William James, *The Varieties of Religious Experience: A Study in Human Nature,* New York, 1902; see especially the first two chapters and the concluding chapter.

80. He "quotes" on p. 27 of *GI,* " 'Not one sparrow shall fall to the ground' except God wills it." There is a possible translation problem here, but no such difficulty can account for the fact that the text reads, "except your heavenly Father knoweth of it." It is ironic that Freud's memory failed him in this section, which is on slips and errors.

81. Dr. Boss is also Professor of Psychology and Head of Training at the Psychiatric Clinic of the University of Zurich. Those interested should read the very balanced and significant case study which comprises Chapter 19 of his book *Psychoanalysis and Daseinanalysis,* trans. Ludwig LeFebre, New York, 1963.

82. *GI*, p. 285.

83. *GI*, pp. 285–290.

84. *GI*, pp. 23–24, 302.

85. *GI*, p. 274.

86. *GI*, p. 181. See Neill's adaptation of this theme in Chapter 7.

87. *NL*, p. 100.

88. *GI*, p. 27.

89. *GI*, pp. 94–95; emphasis ours.

90. *GI*, p. 276.

91. *GI*, p. 327.

92. *GI*, pp. 94–95.

93. *GI*, p. 258; emphasis ours.

7

Total Self-Realization: Neill

In a century which has seen the rise and decline of what is loosely called "progressive education," one figure stands out strikingly. A. S. Neill's success at Summerhill in a small town in Suffolk, England, is legendary. His studies have been translated into languages as improbable as Hebrew, Japanese, and Hindustani. His students have come from Scandinavia, South Africa, the United States, and Canada.

Few men of any sort have exhibited Neill's courage—for it takes courage to employ radical and penetrating methods in education. Not only must one go against the public grain, suffer slander and false representation and genuine ostracizing. These are familiar risks. One also has to face a real terror: he may be dead wrong. He may be ruining the very children to whom he wants to bring self-realization. Neill's courage was the courage of extremity, a willingness to stick to principle even where the losses are severe. In his single-minded task of letting children find their own road to self-fulfillment, his watchword was "freedom." The freedom sought was both the method and the end. Most educators will quickly claim that freedom is every educator's aim, the freedom of self-realization, the pleasure of social and professional success, a balanced and useful role in the prevailing society. But how many educators will let the child choose his own means to that end, with virtually no restraint, trusting that primitive and inborn goodness and interest will emerge if the heavy hand and handicap of a frustrated, inhibited, crippled, and crippling society is removed? Think of a school where a student—so-called—exercises his option never to attend a class, and does so for years on end; where the six-year-old student and the headmaster each have one vote in the making—and *rescinding*—of laws; where the student may tell the headmaster to get out of his room, and the headmaster does; where the frankest talk about sex is open to all students of all ages; where freedom of speech includes the right of profanity. This apparently insane set of permissions was summarized by Neill in these words: "I believe that to impose anything by authority is wrong. The child should

not do anything until he comes to the opinion—his own opinion—
that it should be done. . . . external compulsion . . . is fascism." [1]

Neill's work was the outcome of a rare combination of faith, insight,
and confidence. He also had—at least at the outset—one great
advantage: many of his earliest students had nowhere to go but up.
And even later Summerhill had its "problem children." But it was
Neill who, so far as we know, first stated the epigram that there are no
problem children, only problem parents.[2] This overquoted epigram
verges on the banal, if it be taken by itself, since problem parents were
themselves once children and probably at least brought the seeds of
their problems from their own childhood. Neill continued his reflections on problem children and problem parents by suggesting that
perhaps the best statement would be that there is only a *"problem
humanity."* [3] A few children, nonetheless, have not been accommo-
dated at Summerhill. The test is simple: when sustained tolerance,
love, and patience produce no result but a permanent threat to the
happiness of the entire community, then the child is sent home.[4]

The other built-in advantage of Summerhill is the relative simplicity
of the child's environment. In a small school, with a population varying from forty-five to seventy students, with most standard restraints
gone, with authority at the minimum, with all activities optional,
much of what makes a youngster itchy has gone, and he has nothing
to become but better and happier.[5] In a complex world these children
lead simple lives. Moreover, for children who must have some outlet
for resentment, Neill had the great advantage of being able to place
the blame on the outside world from which they came. Thus the
enemy could always be externalized. This was no device. Neill seriously believed in the inherent goodness of children—all children—
and thus placed the entire blame for their misery and misdoing on the
environment and family that spawned them. This honestly held opinion put the children automatically in league with Neill. He was on
their side, and it gave him unusual privileges in straightforward talk
about what ailed them. For a child to live close to an adult who
knows him well, is interested in him, and exonerates him from all
guilt, laying that at the door of a stupid society, is to produce a sense
of trust and confidence—even relief—that only a very few children
have been able to resist.

It is risky to generalize from a particular school having highly individual characteristics, administered by and even permeated by a man
with a unique personality. Nevertheless, Neill's success should be
looked at from a variety of angles. Much of modern educational speculation has asked if the child—and indeed the college student—should

grow up in an educational environment which is separated from the world at large. In the United States, from the time of John Dewey and even a bit before, there have been schools aimed at dissolving the walls of the classroom, at integrating studies with society. Many educators asking themselves "What can be bettered in school practice?" have found the school too isolated. Their cry is now taken up, as we know, by the student demand for "relevance." Neill, certainly a man as independent as any, deliberately engineered an enclave school. The school is not without visitors, nor without its visits to the village, but its day-to-day life is intended to provide just those conditions for education which the student could *not* find in society as a whole.

We have drawn this contrast sharply partly to indicate that there is often little agreement among educational reformers. This situation is partly the outcome of abstract concentration on one ailment or another. It is also partly a question of the nature of the students one is working with and their educational level. Many of Summerhill's pupils had led lives of inhibition and/or neglect. Such children fare best by being taken out of the environment which has permitted such difficulties to arise. Many of the children with whom John Dewey was concerned had been advanced too rapidly along an assembly line of verbal and intellectual training void of operational or functional meaning. Their classroom lives had developed into a kind of alternate existence, often both boring and demanding, disconnected from the rest of existence. The modern college and—increasingly—high school student whose plea is for relevance has been on the educational conveyor belt too long and may need an alternate year, utterly disconnected from school, more than the hybrid activity of classroom-and-current-situation that at first attracts him. If there is a lesson to be learned here it is the warning against massive uniformity in educational procedure or the dream of finding the one thing that stands between us and utopia.

The final test in all such matters is the outcome for the student. Summerhill's problem children have gone back to the world from which they came, full of confidence and the joy of self-discipline, and have become personal successes. In short, the success of the child has lived beyond his relief and his development in the school. And, as for the league of Neill-and-us-kids-against-the-world, who is prepared to say that the child's will is naturally perverse, when it is demonstrable that his home is broken, unhappy, or nonexistent, his school poor, rigid, crowded, and inhumane, his society intolerant, uncaring, bounded and run by adults bent on their own affairs? Not much inspection is needed to make one want to join Neill in his fury as he asked what we think we are doing to our children! As for the problem of the enclave school, Neill said that his job was not reforming a society but rather bringing happiness to some few children.[6]

SCHEDULE AND CLASSES

In this extraordinary and controversial school—in which children understand that they may say "Shit!" only in the school and are accordingly fined if they do so in town—what does a school day look like? Breakfast runs from 8:15 to 9:00. Classes, each less than an hour long, begin at 9:30 after room clean-up. Depending on age, the children stop for lunch at 12:30 or 1:30. Neill said that he did not know what they all do in the afternoon; he spent this time in his garden and seldom saw them about.[7] Games, sports, workshop—these are the things that keep them busy in the afternoons. Town movies, dance, crafts occupy most evenings. The exceptions are talks on psychology for seniors and staff on Tuesday evenings and the all-important General School Meeting on Saturdays. Sunday evening is theater evening.

There is no religious education of any sort. Religious activity—attending church, for instance—is never encouraged or prohibited. It usually quickly dies out among new students in a few weeks. Neill did not mourn. It is clear that his own faith, if any, was Deist and was directed toward the goodliness of God, if not the godliness of good. For Neill, most of what passes for religion is the source of the indignity of man: "original sin," taboo, fear, restriction, and worst of all, hypocrisy. To use his common phrase, it is "anti life." Virtue and love he sang of unashamedly and endlessly, but he did not think they need much, if anything, from religion. He believed that the giving of freedom is the giving of love, and that only love can save the world.[8] Only occasionally did he seem to think that religion may rid itself of its defects. Although he believed that some day we may have a new religion, he also remarked that fundamentally religion (as we now know it) is running away from life, of which it is afraid.[9] There have been many cases of children ruined by religious training.[10] Religion hates freedom, loves authority, and separates body and spirit. These were grave crimes in Neill's book. For him the great hope was that religion would catch up on its delayed evolution, meeting the needs, perspectives, and hearts of the culture which it so long cruelly imprisoned in superstition, fear, and restraint.

The great community gesture is saved for Saturday night: General School Meeting. Like the other extreme liberties of Summerhill, the self-government has an absolute boundary. Student self-government may seem to be unlimited, but its authority is in fact limited to social and group life—including, however, discipline for social offenses.[11] Since students do not have to attend classes, the social aspect of the student's life is the basic one. The more a child at Summerhill is anti-academic, accordingly, the larger part of his public actions fall under the control of his equals. These equals include staff and headmaster, *in their social roles*. Neill told how his proposal to eliminate indoor football (soccer) in the lounge below his office finally carried. His action was based on his dislike of noise when he was working. He got some support mostly from older students, staff, and girls, but it was not enough to carry. However, they kept bringing the subject up and eventually football in the lounge was abolished. Safety regulations are also handled by the General Meeting—against such things as roof climbing, swimming alone, and so on. One should notice in this connection a comment made by the British Government Inspector after a 1949 investigation. He approved the safety regulations and observed that the headmaster approved them only if they were stringent enough.[12]

Throughout Neill's account of Summerhill, one has the feeling that his voice carried the authority of more than one, even when his vote did not. But one also has the sense that this authority derived from his having been right in the past. It derived even more from the children's knowledge that if Neill had a personal interest in presenting a proposal, it would not come in disguised as a principle, moral or otherwise. Neill was not ashamed of having interests and not suspicious of other people who had interests. Nor did he expect the child's interest to have much admixture of altruism until he was well along, as we shall see. Neill told many tales of how his proposals were voted down or materially altered. Such defeats were victories for the children's trust in him and his conviction that the only discipline that counts for anything is self-discipline. This formula which Neill expressed again and again, both directly and indirectly, leads to the question of what the headmaster of Summerhill thought of human nature.

CHILD NATURE AND HUMAN NATURE

Neill repeatedly insisted that he was not a theoretician, and that where he had clear and uncompromising things to say about children, his generalizations were built upon experience. It would be wiser to say that he was prepared to defend his generalizations from the living experience of the school itself. Some of his generalizations—particularly those derived from rather grand Freudian surmises—could not possibly have been based upon experience, but rather upon the appeal of a particularly effective mode of analysis. Thus, for instance, he said, "A burglar who defecates on the carpet after robbing the safe does not intend to add insult to injury. He is symbolically showing his guilty conscience by leaving something of value to replace what he has stolen. . . . Man's moral attitude toward his dung may have much to do with his unnatural diet." [13] Freewheeling speculation of this sort needs to be separated from the context of sensible and grounded remarks on children's toilet training. They show that Neill's resolve to avoid theorizing required self-discipline in the face of strong impulses in favor of theory.

However, anyone who enters a profession with firm prior convictions that largely reject the assumptions of conventional practitioners is a theoretician of the first order. He may succeed in gaining the experience that vindicates his faith. But every revolutionary is a visionary who starts with a barely funded set of ideas to which he is devoted and then sets about creating the situations that will result in experience of a confirming sort. The extreme empiricist never runs a risk. He summarizes only what has happened, and this with little talk of what must happen in the future. What Neill meant by his opposition to theory is best exhibited in two ways: (1) his willingness to submit most of his theoretical convictions to test, without warping the facts he encountered; (2) his candor in admitting defeats, failure of a conviction to work out, and puzzlement—even after years of experience—as to how to solve most kinds of problem. This is not so much antitheoretical as it is antidogmatic. We shall want to consider later the question: How deep into his fundamental convictions did Neill allow disconfirming evidence to go? For the present, let us see if we can clarify certain basic views that Neill held about child nature and human nature, without emphasis on whether the theory generates the experience or vice versa.

Most of what Neill believed about human nature derived from three sources, Jean-Jacques Rousseau, John Stuart Mill, and Sigmund Freud. This is not to say that his acute intelligence and understanding of children was only the offspring of prior theories. But we cannot discover any first premise in his convictions that is not held intellectually by some predecessor. What was unique in Neill was the blend of these ideas and the personal force of putting them into practice—backing them up with his active life. Rousseau's personal life was at a sad distance from his theories. John Stuart Mill, in the essay *Utilitarianism,* seemed to rest his entire hope for a good society on education; but he lived a life primarily of scholarship and political activity. Freud alone lived a portion of his life for the betterment of children. It was a small portion and largely enclosed in the brief therapeutic encounters of early psychoanalytic practice. And the ultimate results of all of Freud's practice, as seen in *Civilization and its Discontents,* for example, was a gloomy counsel of courage against the inevitable sorrows of the human predicament.

The Christian separation between man and nature had been made explicit by Descartes, as we have seen. The Judaic account of creation made men and the rest of the world separate acts of divine creation, thus deriving their joint existence through God. In Descartes, the knowledge of the world is guaranteed by the goodness of God, who would not deceive us. And the knowledge of God, according to Descartes, is the one indispensable idea, outside that of our own existence, which we have.[14] Descartes' argument is logically dubious. But in making our knowledge of the "external" world dependent upon our knowledge of God, he translated the Judaic story of creation into an epistemology: Man and nature are in community only through God.

Rousseau's conviction, a century later, was that a *natural* kinship existed between man and nature, and that civilization—that is, the life of the *civitas,* the city—unnaturally divided man from nature.[15] To restore this natural relationship he reared Emile in simple pastoral surroundings in which he could, like other untrammeled creatures of nature, develop in an unforced and natural manner. These two basic propositions—that children should be reared in "natural" surroundings and that they should be allowed to develop their own natures from within—were main stones in Neill's foundation. The focus of civilization's ills was in the family:

> Civilization is sick and unhappy, and I claim that the root of it all is the unfree family. Children are deadened by all the forces of reaction and hate, deadened from their cradle days. They are trained to say *nay* to life because their young lives are one long nay. Don't make a noise; don't masturbate; don't lie; don't steal.[16]

These don'ts, which Freud felt were necessary to civilization, Neill felt would be wholly unnecessary if children were permitted to live through the stages and impulses which the don'ts are intended to inhibit. His school has been made what it is by adhering to the ideas of not interfering with the child and not putting pressure on him.[17] There is what he called a "gangster period" that must be gone through, and at that stage we can expect furniture to be destroyed.[18] Children enjoy playing to a considerably older age than civilizations have ever admitted.[19] Probably no child has ever had enough play, and it might be more realistic if children were not asked to work until the age of eighteen.[20] Neill offered Peter the bedwetter three cents for each time he wet the bed, encouraging Peter to remain a baby until he had outgrown that phase.[21] He spoke of the child's "living out" his "dirt complex" and of tidiness as one of the "seven deadly virtues."

Closely related to the natural, active upbringing in which certain pre-established stages are lived through was another Rousseauian idea: that the early stages of a child's life are and ought to be self-centered. Neill agreed with Rousseau that the child is naturally an egoist lacking the ability to identify himself with others, usually until the commencement of puberty.[22] (Rousseau, however, thought there was a difference between boys and girls in this developmental pattern.) A child under eight cannot be regarded as "selfish," for he is simply an egoist; [23] and at Summerhill the egoism is lived out and expressed.[24] Moreover, the child should be left to grow at his own rate. For this peculiar task parents are somewhat unfitted, by reason of their emotional involvement with their children.[25] To the parental cry that parents, too, have rights, Neill replied that they do not have any during the first two—or possibly the first four—years of a child's life.[26]

The core of this development is the gradual transition from egoism to altruism, the latter being a relatively late arrival which can never completely eliminate egoism.[27] Self-centeredness as the primary motive that later generates altruism, phases of development that must be lived through, youthful education in terms of action, self-guidance, self-discipline: these were the things that Neill took from the Rousseauian tradition. We find him both more and less extreme than Rousseau. He never said the city is by nature evil, although he was well aware of the risks in slums and the impersonality that goes with them. Emile's tutor showed guidance, wisdom, concern, but also some noticeable preplanning; Neill was a firm believer in keeping hands off. A crucial ideal of Summerhill is a release that allows the child to live with and to follow out his natural interests.[28] Emile may have begun to read late by modern standards, but at Summerhill an extreme case went to school for thirteen years with no classes and was hardly able to read at the end. Neill stressed again and again that the child must grow at his own rate.[29]

Neill's patience with academic progress was repeatedly rewarded. When the disinterested child began to take an interest in academic matters, he galloped. Rousseau treated Emile as if he represented a standard or norm of development; Neill emphasized the importance of different rates and types of interests. He often talked as if the mosaic of interests were genetic in its formation; at the same time he stressed the likelihood that prenatal influences were not sufficiently weighed.[30] Emile's tutor was a constant companion and the only intimate friend. Neill spoke again and again of the love that must be given children, in addition to the company of other children around him with whom he would learn the elements of social conduct by participation. But he made it clear that the love is not the sentimental dependency which a saccharine parent uses to trap a child.

The love that Neill spoke of is the love which he found in the work of Homer Lane. Little Commonwealth, Lane's "reform camp" for delinquent children, was the inspiration for much of Neill's conviction about the deforming of children's characters. Little Commonwealth apparently died with its founder in 1925, four years after the founding of Summerhill, but from Lane Neill had learned his conviction that a child's bad motives were good—or at least allowable—motives corrupted by influences he could not control, and that delinquency is a sickness that can be cured.[31] The love is the love that understands and presumes basic goodness. This love, of which Neill made so much, in recognizing the natural self-centeredness of children—the egoism mentioned earlier—must accept the self-centeredness as good. This conviction was one of the main clashing points between Neill and conventional Christian convictions. The part of religion which Neill deplored may agree that it is natural for children to be self-seeking, but it does not agree that what is natural is therefore good. Natural self-centeredness is the prime evidence of original sin, the doctrine that justifies the cruelty, the punishment, the lack of understanding, and the suppression meted out to children as "discipline."

Rousseau's naturalism leads us by way of Lane to John Stuart Mill. If self-centeredness is natural and good, then discipline must arise because the self wants it, ultimately in the form of self-discipline. The primary principle is happiness. None other can surpass it, nor should it. Neill equated happiness with goodness, the evil in life with everything that limits or destroys happiness. His statements on this theme could almost have come from Mill's *Utilitarianism*. Corresponding to this doctrine and really just another way of stating it is the radical doctrine of freedom in Mill's *On Liberty*. According to this view, a man may do anything he likes for his own interest or on his own impulse, provided that it does not impair the rights or liberties of others. The root of civilization's ills is the "unfree," the "anti-life" family.[32] Families are unwilling for the child to be "selfish—ungiving—free to follow his own childish interests through his childhood." [33] Happiness is the "state of having minimal repression." [34] Neill believed that no one is completely free emotionally, having been preconditioned to be unfree by *his* parents before him.[35] Nonetheless, teaching a child how to behave is needless. A child will learn what is right and wrong in due time.[36]

In addition to his conviction that there is a loss of right and privilege where purely personal liberty is curtailed, Neill took from Freud the doctrine that it is positively harmful—not merely a denial of right—to do so. According to Freud, an unfulfilled wish survives unsated, yearning still in the unconscious lives of persons. The severity of this repression may become bad enough to give rise to serious disorders. For Neill it was the cornerstone of the "anti-life" attitude.

Is there no limiting the freedom of children? There certainly is, according to Neill. It is very easy to draw the line, it would seem. The limit is that each individual can do what he likes so long as this does not infringe on the freedom of other individuals. Neill thought this aim could be realized in any community.[37]

This again is an idea in close agreement with Mill; it is exactly in the spirit of *On Liberty*. Mill and Freud agreed that the primary aim of life is happiness. For Mill the impediments were unnecessary and improvable. Social reform and the cultivation of sensitivity would provide the machinery and the desire to improve the lot of man. Mill's views were in the mainstream of liberal thought: the realization of human happiness through social reform. For Freud, the problem was the same, but it was essentially unresolvable. In *Civilization and its Discontents* Freud made it plain that the surcharge of emotions in the id must always be rebuffed by the superego, which aims at group survival rather than at free individual expression.[38] Full, free expression of the impulses in the id would create a social chaos that the great collective beast we call society cannot and will not tolerate. The conflict, as Freud saw it, is thus inevitable and can at best only be mitigated by understanding the problem and its dynamics.

In 1931, as Hitler rose to power, Freud wrote an additional last line to a later edition of *Civilization and its Discontents:* "And now it is to be expected that the other of the two 'Heavenly Powers' [the first is death], eternal Eros, will make an effort to assert himself in the struggle with his equally immortal adversary. *But who can foresee with what success and with what result?"* [39] Freud indicated earlier that we ought to be grateful that a few people can "salvage" some of the "deepest truths, toward which others grope." [40]

Neill was a curious blend of Millian optimism, represented in the conviction that restructuring society (in this case through education) will release the natural goodness of men toward happiness, and Freudian depth psychology with its heavy emphasis on natural aggression and sexuality. Where Freud spoke of his "intention to represent the sense of guilt as the most important problem in the development of civilization and to show that the price we pay for our advances in civilization is a loss of happiness through the heightening of the sense of guilt," [41] Neill was in hearty agreement. Freud added in a footnote to the above passage, "That the education of young people at the present day conceals from them the part which sexuality will play in their lives is not the only reproach we are obliged to make against it. The other sin is that it does not prepare them for the aggressiveness of which they are destined to become the objects." Neill agreed again, but he saw no justification for assuming that the failure to educate children about sex or accepting aggressiveness is inevitable. Education can be reformed and can in turn improve society. This Millian view was a direct rebuff to Freud's pessimism, though Neill had accepted far more from Freud than he had rejected.

Neill said,

> I think the Freudian emphasis on aggression is due to the study of homes and schools *as they are.* You cannot study canine psychology by observing the retriever on a chain. Nor can you dogmatically theoretize about human psychology when humanity is on a very strong chain—one fastened by generations of life-haters. I find that in the freedom of Summerhill aggression does not appear in anything like the same strength in which it appears in strict schools.[42]

Neill had his own experience to guide him here. He said that the child's reaction to freedom shows up as a decrease in aggression and greater "serenity and charity." [43] But this freedom does not get its results rapidly; years and great patience are sometimes required while the evils of repressive and anti-life education are allowed to peel off like so many coats of paint.[44] A bit sadly Neill went on to say that the clever child can use freedom better and that he will, when the time comes and he has worked his way through the vital play so necessary to his development, do eight years' work in just over two.

These were stunning claims, and there was every reason to believe them. The Royal Commission was not particularly impressed by the educational gains at Summerhill, for all they were clearly disposed to admire the school, controversy and all.[45] But Neill pointed out that it is in the terminal precollege years that the child who *wants* to pass entrance exams and has the ability to do so tears into his work with great fervor. He has learned to hitch his actions to his aims and is now old enough to have aims that loom in the remoter future.

Neill was thoroughly consistent in his beliefs about sex and freedom. He felt that promiscuity is unnatural—free love would not exist among truly free people. He agreed with Freud that "sex is the greatest force in human behavior," but found that it had been exaggerated by a moral code that regarded sex as a sin. Indeed he said that sex "is the basis of all negative attitudes toward life" [46] and he went on to remark that children who have no sex guilt never seem to need religion or mysticism. He plainly was interested in *no* restraint in sexual matters whatsoever. "Every older pupil at Summerhill knows from my conversation and my books that I approve of a full sex life for all who wish one, whatever their age." [47] At the same time, he recognized that steadfast adhering to his principles would have resulted in closing his beloved school:

> If, for example, I tried to form a society in which adolescents would be free to have their own natural love lives, I should be ruined if not imprisoned as an immoral seducer of youth. Hating compromise as I do, I have to compromise here, realizing that my primary job is not the reformation of society, but the bringing of happiness to some few children. [48]

The fault lies in our society, where proper sex is denied to youth, and as a result films and novels rouse the young sexually and lead them to masturbation. [49] Neill repeatedly refused to condemn masturbation, save possibly by implication in this one passage. Plainly what he had—if anything—against masturbation was that it is the source of abusive discipline, guilt, misunderstanding, and deformation of a healthy attitude toward sex.

It is here that Neill differed most strongly from the admired Freud. Freud seemed to think that the conflicts arising from sexual and aggressive impulses were inescapable. Neill apparently thought that a consistent freedom in sexual matters—including total lack of censorship of any sort—would allow sexual development of go through the proper phases. And he further thought that the aggressive impulses— as we have seen—could be sharply reduced by giving full play to the desire for freedom, with only very minimal restraints.

Finally, Neill did not pin much hope on psychoanalysis: we cannot analyze the world. For him, the solution did not lie in curative work with individuals but with proper child rearing in the entire culture. [50] A paradigm of this conviction that the betterment of men begins with the reform of reformable people and works out, by way of institutes, to other people was given—probably without intent—by Neill himself and on the very subject of adolescent sex. He told of finding two new students, a boy of seventeen and a girl of sixteen, alone together late at night. He told them he didn't know what they were doing and didn't morally care. But, he said, if Kate has a child my school will be ruined. If you'd been here awhile you would have some love for the school that gives you freedom; it would be unnecessary to speak of the matter. But since you are new, naturally you don't have this feeling. His point apparently was understood; there was no further trouble. [51]

The story is also a paradigm of one of the two types of limits on freedom that Neill saw. The one was the common-sense elements of safety—locked chemicals, supervised swimming, and so on, mentioned above. The other was the noninterference with the liberties of others.

Everything should be permitted that was safe and infringed upon the rights of no one else. The rule was the same for adults, but they were no longer able to follow it.[52] It was this theme, that men may act as they please provided no one else is harmed, that served to raise questions worth looking at.

Neill's success with his school was partly composed of success with individual students. There were failures that he took pains to tell us about. And there were problems that he regarded as insoluble. Crisis situations, however, like the one in which the students decided to abolish all law and have chaos, were handled with relaxed confidence. Individual tough nuts were left alone to crack themselves, and usually they did. Some of his success, at least as abbreviated into anecdote form, almost seemed magical. Neill's work should be read about, if only to see the firm but patient teacher in action and to pick up cues on the mechanics of recalcitrance and backwardness.

Such success cannot be argued away. It can possibly be argued with, but not readily. Neill met objections to his school usually with a presupposition that the objector was deformed by his society and consequently in no position to judge; if one's own values have been shaped by inhibition, punishment, phony morality, the lesser side of religion, and in general an anti-life attitude, one naturally judges from the background of these values and must judge ill. However much it is backed by success and admirable devotion to life and its betterment, this form of argument is irritating because it is unfair. The young man who says, "I can't speak to anybody over thirty because if he's over thirty he won't understand me" might be cheered by Neill but would be in the same fallacious position, at least in the form of his argument. But as to substance we might also rejoin, "Don't wail over lack of communication and then rebuff efforts at communication. Maybe you didn't start the generation gap, but why are you working so hard to preserve it?" The psychoanalyst who undertakes to discover the deep reasons for someone's being opposed to depth analysis is involved in a very similar fallacy. The former examples are variations on what the logicians call "poisoning the well," a methodological form of begging the question. They are at bottom the same, techniques of employing or rejecting the point at issue instead of making it the object of inquiry. One of the authors of this book once maintained pleasantly and informally to a group of students that *meaning,* however we strive to pin it down, is fuzzy around the edges, always has a growing tip, and deserves to be regarded as at least ambiguous. One of the students peered earnestly up from a book he had been reading and said, "Yes, but just *exactly* what does that mean?" The class howled.

The most serious aspect of this problem is that in substance the claimant may be right. The critic may indeed be hopelessly disqualified for recognizing the good and the pure when he sees it. The man over thirty may indeed not be worth talking to (it is true of men under thirty also, although there may be more hope for them). The objector to psychoanalysis may indeed have erratic and deep-seated antagonisms badly in need of analytic relief. But the form of the argument would never reveal this. The form of the argument presents only two alternatives: accept the basic suppositions and reform your ways, or stand forever beyond the gate of truth.

The critic trying to communicate with an admirable but adamant position thus has the burden of ingenuity placed upon him for finding a way to set up a dialogue where none seems to be too earnestly solicited. It will not do to condemn dogma and yet hold that those who challenge your convictions are of too limited perspective to take the larger view. There are three areas in which we feel the dialogue with Neill is not quite closed.

The notion that altruism grows out of egoism is an old one and is probably right if we say steady altruism grows from a background of erratic or even dominant egoism. But in point of fact it is difficult to watch children without coming to the conclusion that they exhibit a strange mixture of impulsive egoism and impulsive altruism. To say that the child's impulsive altruism is really disguised egoism—a desire for love, approval, or what have you—is to be on the edge of making the very mistake that both Neill and Rousseau—and Kant, Dewey, and Whitehead, as well—protested: reading adult categories into childhood actions. It would be wiser to speak of protoaltruism and protoegoism mixed. Real "isms" are liable to conflict; impulses replace one another experimentally, especially in the child and the adolescent. The very plasticity of the child, which makes education possible, warns us not to define his impulses too finally or sharply. It may even be that altruism grows out of egoism, "enlightened self-interest," as a whole host of English philosophers—Butler, Hume, and Mill among them—have maintained, but this might be said to argue for the radical *difference* between the two feelings. In breathing, expiration grows out of inspiration, death comes only to what was alive, independence —as Neill would admit—from dependence. Perhaps altruism does appear gradually from a background of egoism, but to hold that adult altruism is based on adult egoism is merely careless. If the altruism is defined as a way of obtaining approval (whether the approval be mine or someone else's) for myself—as I might get a piece of candy, an automobile, or a job—the definition is fallacious, at least for the purpose of the arguer. For altruism is autonomous, an end in itself, or else it is not true altruism. If I am altruistic for the sake of approval *and know it,* then the altruism is not for its own sake but appears merely as a means, a device. The desire for approval then becomes the real end and replaces the altruism which it approved. Certainly I can hardly expect approval for desiring to be approved. I can have such approval only if I do not seek it.

The doctrine of the rights of the state over those of the individual is indeed fascism, a group madness in men more terrifying than any individual madness. History is full of concrete examples of this doctrine, of such plunges into deliberate self-erasure, a great glory in being swallowed up by the massive whole. It is madness whether it issues in military action or not. And nobody is safe from it. In search of enlarged and more powerful selves, we lose ourselves in the more powerful group. Aggression is only one form the madness takes. But to recoil from this conception and to argue that the social and political aspects of life are devices made by men whose natural dispositions are primarily self-seeking and whose individual privilege is infinite if it can avoid bumping into another is not necessarily the only alternative.

In the first place the metaphors of contest between claims or forces or of the weighing of rights on a scale are themselves misleading. The first appeals to the very conflict which Neill felt was dispensable in adult civilization; the second talks of rights as if they were possessions to be measured by weight, cost, or market price.

Likely, rights should be discussed in the language of many metaphors—literalness of language being surely impossible here. Suppose we drop the metaphors of battle, the physical, the mechanical, and employ the metaphors of living things instead. Perhaps there are "roots" of rights that spring from each healthy child seed. These, well cared for, mature into actual rights, rights that carry forward into the next generation. Perhaps there is an ecology of rights or a symbiosis. Plants take from the soil and they give back to the soil. They take oxygen from the air but give it back—more of it, as a rule, than they take. In this way the spread of life on this planet has occurred. If one is pro life, he should ask what all the main components of life are, not just some. Religion, for example, may be a contemptible shambles of ideals lying in the fief of a tyrannical authoritarianism, but the ideal of losing one's life to save it can be separately evaluated.

Does being pro life mean just being pro my life? Neill would have been the first to deny it, of course. Yet the doctrine that altruism comes from a background of egoism that it never loses might be easily understood as saying that being pro life means being pro my life and being anti anti your life. My obligation is to see that my exercise of my rights doesn't get in your way and that others give you the same freedom. But isn't it possible that I really owe society something—

even if society is a big subhuman brute? Society is never just a collection of agreeing persons. There are common ends and common purposes, the presence of which is not mere consensus or contract. The life that I should be pro: does not society mediate between me and it?

We are led to the closely related point about atomic individuals. What are these rights that when exercised intrude on no one else? I like honey on my toast. Fine. Usually I'm left alone. Or I'm nineteen and my hair is almost long enough to braid. I come home and my parents set up a terrible yowl. It's not hurting them; what's the gripe? Maybe it does look crazy to them, but I like it. It's my hair and my life. Or I'm twenty-three and my mother depends on me for her financial support: she is crippled. I take to drugs, lose my job, and she takes in washing and does fine stitching, ruining her eyes. Likely Neill would argue that my privilege impinged on hers. But suppose she was well off and I ruined my health with drugs, turning into a blob, a moving vegetable, a vast wreckage of lost opportunity. Mill argued that any man has the right to ruin his life, provided it hurts no one else. But this does hurt someone else. Is my father's interest in my well-being and love and hope he invested in me sheer unwarranted possessiveness? Neill would likely blame my home and my society for my errant ways. But blame is not the issue here. The issue here is my *right* to do as I please, provided it harms no one else. What of the admiration that young adolescents have for me? They wish to emulate me and take to drugs also. Do I owe them nothing? No doubt their society and their parents rendered them susceptible to looking for kicks or relief, or a distorted kind of adventure. That's not at issue. What is at issue, in Neill's view, is: Am I harming another? This distinction between what concerns me and what concerns another is verbally easy but practically very difficult. The great question is: In what things am I really isolated, really alone? Where do vibrations from myself pass no farther than my strictly private affairs? In a world overpopulated, interdependent, specialized, and with far too much togetherness, how much of this negative freedom do I have?

This problem runs in many directions. If I am to have exclusively personal rights, I need to ask myself how far I can extend my personal sensibility. Summerhill is ideal in its direct personal contact. The staff is steering the boat. The children can and do navigate and even steer where they make up their collective mind. Everyone knows everyone else. Loyalty and personal confrontation are high. Anonymity is all but impossible. Responsibility in these circumstances sprouts and flourishes. A decent respect for the dangers of power is easily discovered. Social needs are recognized and in large measure satisfied. The school is—and should be—a haven for the person and personal rights at their best.

Between what is personal and what is wholly public lies the civic, the social, the political. It is in this area that men struggle to make and even live by moral codes. Not all decency can arise from sheer interpersonal relations in small communities. Larger groups with whom we are related loom vaguely in the moral distance. If we live in a massive society there must be massive laws. These are made in an atmosphere of impersonality and anonymity and are similarly obeyed. In such an atmosphere some of the worst features of humanity can emerge: cruelty, envy, hatred, disguised as moral rectitude. But this does not mean that external discipline and restraint are nothing but disguised viciousness, socially inherited.

Any small community can live with just a few laws which are made by all, understood by all, and immediately accessible to all. There is a great lag in the understanding, the making, and the access in a great society. There is much mediation between person and government. If a law seems to me unworthy or mistaken, change is difficult, slow.[53]

It looks as though Summerhill's graduates have capabilities for becoming surviving islands in a massive society. The self-government at Summerhill is astonishing. It not only works, it generates loyalty and docility and neither fear nor resentment.[54] One could hardly ask for more. The question one asks is: Is this personal self-government in a child's Utopia adequate preparation for the adult life in a complex society? The answer seems to be "Yes," if we think only of the person. If we ask how such a person can contribute to the betterment of society, we should not be surprised if he does not do so. Why should he, when he has been happily raised in an atmosphere of dispassionate condemnation of that same society, when it has been a case of we-who-understand against all-those-others, from swearing to sex?

The separation of the school from the rest of the life of the country borders on the absolute and reflects Neill's own needs. If he had tried to reform society by action, he said he would have been killed as a public danger.[55] As an example of the difference between Neill's attitudes and "society's," he commented that most political newspapers are full of hatred.[56] Even movements seemingly concerned with the poor seemed to him often to arise out of no love of the poor but rather a hatred of the rich. Freedom for children means avoiding "religion, politics, or class-consciousness."[57] The students at Summerhill are middle-class children who have never had firsthand encounters with poverty.[58] Although Neill spoke of "abolishing the slum" in a context of praise for the social worker, it seems as though none of the students of Summerhill has ever become one, and very few have themselves become teachers. Summerhill, which viewed from some angles is almost ideal in its operation, seems deficient in self-replication. Neill himself doubted that the Summerhill method would ever come into widespread existence. But he believed that the world must find a better way of ordering its affairs, particularly its attitude toward children and its scheme of education, if it is to improve. "Politics will not save humanity. It never has done so." [59] In this matter Neill differed radically from the reformer Mill, whose liberal notions Neill inherited and whose political effectiveness helped to create the liberal England that brought forth both Neill and the few sterling souls who trusted him.

England and the world could use many Summerhills. Is it possible that the real Summerhill weakness is that, in emphasizing the emergence of altruism from egoism, it has succeeded in bringing happiness to the lives of a fortunate few, but has failed to create the contagion of personal enthusiasm for public service which lies in the base of Neill's method? Will Summerhill insight and experience go the way of its inspiration, Homer Lane's Little Commonwealth?

NOTES

1. A. S. Neill, *Summerhill: A Radical Approach to Child Rearing*, New York, 1960, p. 91.
2. *Summerhill*, p. 104.
3. *Summerhill*, p. 103.
4. *Summerhill*, p. 54.
5. *Summerhill*, pp. 21–22.
6. *Summerhill*, p. 23. A more serious objection may be made, however. Neill plainly saw his work as curative. How far can what is at least semitherapy be used as a basis for educational reform in general? This question has properly been asked of at least two modern psychiatrists concerned with education, Erikson and Jones, and they have given significant answers. See Chapter 10.
7. *Summerhill*, p. 13.
8. *Summerhill*, p. 92.
9. *Summerhill*, p. 241.
10. *Summerhill*, p. 243.
11. *Summerhill*, p. 43.
12. *Summerhill*, p. 77.
13. *Summerhill*, p. 175.
14. See Chapter 3.
15. See R. S. Brumbaugh and N. M. Lawrence, *Philosophers on Education*, Boston, 1963, Chapter 4.
16. *Summerhill*, p. 102.
17. *Summerhill*, p. 91.
18. *Summerhill*, p. 86.
19. *Summerhill*, pp. 74, 64.
20. *Summerhill*, p. 61.
21. *Summerhill*, p. 333.

22. *Summerhill,* p. 277.
23. *Summerhill,* p. 315.
24. *Summerhill,* p. 330.
25. *Summerhill,* p. 331.
26. *Summerhill,* p. 336.
27. *Summerhill,* pp. 181, 163.
28. *Summerhill,* p. 115.
29. *Summerhill,* p. 362.
30. *Summerhill,* p. 95.
31. *Summerhill,* pp. 282–284.
32. *Summerhill,* pp. 102–103.
33. *Summerhill,* p. 114.
34. *Summerhill,* p. 356.
35. *Summerhill,* p. 258.
36. *Summerhill,* pp. 254–255.
37. *Summerhill,* p. 155.
38. Sigmund Freud, *Civilization and Its Discontents,* trans. James Strachey, New York, 1961.
39. *Ibid.,* p. 92; emphasis ours.
40. *Ibid.,* p. 80.
41. *Ibid.,* p. 81.
42. *Summerhill,* p. 20.
43. *Summerhill,* p. 113.
44. *Summerhill,* pp. 115–116.
45. *Summerhill,* pp. 75–85. Here Neill reproduces the report.
46. *Summerhill,* p. 206.
47. *Summerhill,* p. 215.
48. *Summerhill,* p. 23.
49. *Summerhill,* p. 374.
50. *Summerhill,* pp. 345–346.
51. *Summerhill,* p. 58.
52. *Summerhill,* p. 344.
53. In 1968 there was an unprecedented national frustration as voters realized that the second most popular candidate in each political party would be chosen as the presidential nominee. For some this meant that only revolution can revise a rotten system; for others it meant that more public participation is needed in politics.
54. *Summerhill,* pp. 50, 51.
55. *Summerhill,* p. 23.
56. *Summerhill,* p. 93.
57. *Summerhill,* p. 111.
58. *Summerhill,* p. 354.
59. *Summerhill,* pp. 91–92.

8

Learning as Conditioning
of the Organism: Skinner

The doctrine of evolution stretches into almost every aspect of men's thoughts about themselves. It is not so much a wave as it is a ground swell. It permits them to believe themselves entirely parts of the natural world. It also opens new paths of inquiry. One such path leads angularly, but without break, to B. F. Skinner, one of the most comprehensive of modern American experimental psychologists.

Skinner consciously inherits from E. L. Thorndike a question rising from the acceptance of evolutionary theory: "How is human mentality different from animal mentality?" Skinner's response to this question reveals both his theory of human nature and his conception of education. His theory of human nature is important in two ways: (1) It represents a consummation of past tendencies in American clinical psychology which have attempted to develop a scientific study of man. (2) It contains a small set of far-reaching, somewhat original notions embodied in experimental psychology and in applied psychology, including advertising and politics. Skinner's theory of human nature naturally bears on his conception of education. His educational theory appears in two forms: (1) He is the author of a novel about education, in the broad sense of education as directed development. The novel, a Utopia called *Walden Two,* puts flesh and clothes on some of the theories which appear in his professional studies. (2) Also, it was Skinner who rescued the teaching machine of Pressey from obscurity, revised it as he had done previous psychological theories, and placed it squarely in the public domain and interest. It is now permanently lodged there and must be continuously assessed for what it can and cannot do. Skinner's study, *The Technology of Teaching,* will likely be a landmark in the most important *technological* development of twentieth-century education: programed learning.

SKINNER'S IMMEDIATE INHERITANCE

Darwin's *Origin of Species* introduced the question mentioned above. Let us state it another way: in the continuum of development from simpler forms of animal life, how different is man from his predecessors and from his contemporary cousins? [1] In particular, what of man as a *rational* animal, as Aristotle had classified him? Or, a little less grandly, what is thinking? Do animals think?

Before Darwin's century was ended, Thorndike fell to judging whether or not a cat could think. He tested cats to see whether they could "learn" to get out of a box with an internal release mechanism. And they did. The more often you put the same cat in the same release situation, the faster he gets out, up to a point. Speaking popularly, something is retained from the earlier escapes. This something is employed to eliminate random trials. It matures gradually into a schema of action—one of a large number of behavior patterns which Skinner will call the cat's individual "repertoire." But how can we say that we see the cat thinking or that someone has *observed* the cat *learning*? Just exactly what do we see? Some standard of observable behavior is required. The standard devised in this experiment was the shortening of the time interval between the cat's entry into the escape box and his successful use of the escape mechanism.

But now an interesting question arises. Skinner puts it this way: "Did the observed facts point to mental processes, or could these apparent evidences of thinking be explained in other ways?" The answer here is crucial for the elaborated animal experiment whose results Skinner uses as models for human behavior. "Eventually it became clear that the assumption of inner thought-processes was not required." [2] The steps in this revision of the object of study are worth noting. (1) Since animals are our near relatives, do they think as we do? (Answer: Let's give them a problem.) (2) What kind of problem will test animal thinking? (Answer: Simple avoidance, for example avoiding restraint or captivity.) (3) How shall we test "learning"? (Answer: By seeing if the animal can shorten its escape time in successive identical situations.) (4) Does the improvement require the assumption of "inner thought processes"? (Answer: Not at all; all that is needed is the quite objectively recognizable shrinking of the time lapse.) Skinner is quite explicit on this last point. He says,

> The cat had solved its problem as well as if it were a "reasoning" human being, though perhaps not so speedily. Yet Thorndike observed no "thought process" and argued that none was needed by way of explanation. He could describe his results simply by saying

that a part of the cat's behavior was "stamped in" because it was followed by the opening of the door.[3]

In short, the evidence of thinking has been substituted for the thinking, much as the evidence of a crime is used as a substitute for the actual crime; the crime, like the thinking, cannot be directly observed. This transformation is an example of what later came to be called "operationalism"—the identification of a concept with the operations necessary to get a measurable result. Thorndike calls the rate of shortening the escape time to optimum a "learning curve." The curve is graphable.

Modern educational measurement derives partly from Thorndike's work. Skinner, however, carries Thorndike's emphasis on observation one step further. Having made it already clear that "inner" thought processes, which seem too occult to submit to scientific testing, can be translated into behavioral terms, Skinner asks himself, "Why not bring the method full circle and devise methods for observation of human behavior of all sorts, not just thinking?" In this way obscurantism of every kind about human nature can be swept away by the cool and testable methods of science. The problems will certainly be more complex, because men are more complex, but they should not therefore be, on principle, any more resistant to technological investigation. The task is to improve the technology and the techniques of the observation of human behavior in order to bring man himself, the author of the sciences, under the disciplined understanding of the sciences. In short, what is wanted is a science of man.

The other great influence on Skinner's behaviorism was Pavlov. Pavlov showed that a crude form of response to symbols exists in less complicated animals than men. The idea of a *symbol* is vague and general. Here we use it to refer to that which "stands for" or "takes the place of" something. Pavlov showed that by giving a dog food directly after ringing a bell the dog could be conditioned to salivate upon the mere sounding of a bell, which became a symbol for the absent food.

This "association" is the descendant of Locke's—and later Hume's —conception of how our complex ideas are made up of simple ones. For the most part, Locke went no further than showing that our ideas of things ("substances") are complexes made up of our ideas of simple qualities. He did so for good observational reasons. All that we *know* of things is through their characteristics and their qualities. It may well be asked if there is anything else *to* know. Hume extended the idea of association to sequences of experience. He showed, along analogous lines, that not only do our ideas of complex things arise from associations of simple characteristics, but also our ideas of complex occurrences arise from our association of simple *events* with one another. In particular, as long as we merely analyze what we observe, the idea of cause and effect turns out to be an assumption based on experience alone. All that we *observe* is a familiar set of sequences in which event *A* (say, the striking of a bell) is always followed by event *B* (the sounding of the bell). But from this repeated experience we finally come to say that the striking of the bell *caused* it to ring. When I say that the thrown rock broke the window, I am of course making a reliable practical judgment. But there is a big difference between practical experience and theoretical certainty. I am forced to admit that nothing I *observed* passed over from the "cause" to the "effect" and there is no "logical" or "theoretical" necessity that it do so. To think of a rock striking the window without harming the window, or turning into a three-foot midget, is a strain on my experiential credulity but not a logical contradiction. Since it is thinkable, its opposite is not *necessarily* true. It could have been otherwise. Thus the rule of cause and effect is only a good guide to action, problem solving, and so on. It does not have the logical strength of an inescapable philosophical principle. What Hume wished to show is that philosophical judgments based on the idea that things happen in nature according to a *law* of cause and effect are no more certain than any practical rule of thumb.

Hume's development of his theory is simple and powerful. Only a very few philosophers have at once been aware of the power of Hume's skepticism and yet been able to expose its failures. In the late nineteenth and early twentieth centuries many scientists and philosophers of science accepted Hume's argument and insisted that science not only could but *must* dispense with the idea of causation and should think of the laws of physics as descriptions of regular sequences of events. Nothing more was needed. Such summations of experienced events can be made as precise as you like. They are revisable when counterinstances occur. They can be knit together in larger sets of laws with a greater level of generality. As for causation, who needs it? It is not strictly observed; it is therefore not required in order to develop physical laws. It is a practical shorthand with no place in science; it is excess baggage. At times, as we shall see, Skinner is attracted by this resolve to do away with the idea of cause, but at others he is forced to adopt it.

There are, then, two principal ways in which the English tradition from Locke to Hume (the other principal figure who contributed to this notion of cause was George Berkeley) influences Skinner. The first is the notion of association as the basis of knowledge. Our learning proceeds through an accumulation of encounters with relatively simple stimuli. (Locke called this encounter "sensation.") Through repeated experience we weave simple elements into larger and more complex units of knowledge. We begin with simple sensations; these give rise to simple ideas, which can be rearranged into complex ideas corresponding in various degrees to the reality which we originally sensed. Skinner actually rejects the "association of ideas" because of its vagueness.[4] Nonetheless he uses the principle of association as a *tactic* of teaching, as an *analysis* of learning, and finally, therefore, as a *prescription* for teaching machines. From this tradition Skinner also learned a suspicion of the inner, the hidden, the unobservable. Locke had been forced to say that the "substance" in which qualities inhere is a pure *x*, an unknown, revealed only in its observable characteristics. Hume dispensed with the theoretical necessity for cause because it could not be shown to be either logically necessary or observable. For him it was a practical way of thinking gained through the repeated association of discrete events. Thorndike analogously dispensed with the unobservable inner processes of thought in animal experiments. Finally, Skinner goes one step further and undertakes to make observation the sole discriminator of human thought. We shall see that he nevertheless has recourse to what is unobservable and what is causal.

OPERANTS AND BEHAVIOR

Pavlov speaks of training a dog to salivate at the sound of a bell instead of the appearance of food as "conditioning." More specifically, the stimulus was "conditioned" by being followed by food. The response, strictly, was conditioned only in that it followed upon a conditioned stimulus. In the wake of the response, nothing happened to or for the dog, unless it was the failure of the saliva to be met with food. Skinner, on the other hand, is interested in the conditioned *response,* where the appropriate response is greeted with some further consequence which the "organism" finds agreeable or disagreeable. Many behaviorists speak of this further consequence as "reward" when it is favorable, "punishment" when it is uncongenial. Skinner prefers the terms "negative reinforcement" and "positive reinforcement." Using Skinner's own type of analysis, we may guess that his preference for these terms is conditioned by the association with Thorndike's "stamped in," according to the law of effect.

The fundamental idea in Skinner's analysis of behavior is that of an "operant." An operant, says Skinner, is the "unit of a predictive science," and, he continues, it is not a response but a class of responses.[5] Strictly speaking, the term "response" is misleading, he says; any kind of measurable and countable movement, regardless of origin or cause, is what is intended—whatever *"operates* upon the environment to gen-

erate consequences." [6] Behavior, Skinner goes on to say, "regardless of
when specific instances occur, is an *operant* . . . a set of acts" defined
in a way that permits measurement and counting. [7] In Descartes, mathematics is the model system; in Skinner it is the model instrument.
Descartes wanted certainty of result; Skinner wants objectivity. Just
as Descartes had coveted the certainty and clarity of mathematics, so
Skinner covets the objectivity, the precision, and the systematic organization of the physical sciences.

What has all this to do with learning? The term "learning," says
Skinner, "may profitably be saved in its traditional sense to describe
the reassortment of responses in a complex situation." [8] The phenomenon that Skinner is describing is familiar enough. Suppose I am learning to hit a flat drive in tennis. In Skinner's vocabulary I want to enlarge my "repertoire" of strokes, that reliable set of actions which can
be skillfully called upon to produce desired results. My early efforts result in smart raps to the base of the net. I watch the stroke as I hit it,
tilting the head of the racket back a bit. The balls fly over the fence. I
correct again, trying to keep the head of the racket practically perpen-
dicular to the court. The ball flies at exactly the right height—in the
next court on my right. I add another dimension to the revisualizing
and decide I'm hitting the ball too late. And so on. This is an example of activity that could be called human learning. It is the kind of
behavior that is easily observed, and—what is important to notice—
the "internal thinking" that accompanies the behavior is sufficiently
familiar so that we may experience it vicariously by simply watching
another person. We can plug in, from our own experience, the mental
and the emotional flow which constitutes the personal aspect of such
behavior and attribute something like it to another person, with little
risk. It is just this plugging in, however, which Skinner seems almost
deliberately to ignore in his effort to reduce learning to wholly observable phenomena.

What, in this example, is the "reassortment of responses"? With a
preformed idea of what we want, our actions, we say, are guided by
success and failure. I look at my last stroke, in retrospect, complete
with the ball flying over the fence, and make the oncoming stroke different. I'm not strictly "reassorting" at all. Such manipulation is impossible. I shift the pattern from one try to the next. I somehow abstract
from the past all the relevant features of it, search out the one or two
that seem to be the sources of failure, and make my next response like
the old one, but different from it in significant ways.

The example of learning to hit the ball properly is in one respect
too complex. It is a case of self-testing, where conditioner and conditioned are the same person. Skinner finds some difficulty in treating

these reflexive cases, to even his own satisfaction.[9] Since he primarily wants observables and is suspicious of what is inner, he finds the idea of self-control hard to analyze. It is easier to stick to cases where the conditioner and conditioned are always distinct.

Skinner says of operant conditioning in general that it "shapes behavior as a sculptor shapes a lump of clay." [10] The shaping agency is the process of "reinforcement." Reinforcers are ways of underscoring certain patterns of behavior by giving the organism something it wants or likes when it operates in some particular way. In Skinner's words, the reinforcers are ways in which behavior "pays off." [11] The primary reinforcers, however, are biological: these include nutrition—food and water—sex, and escape from harmful conditions.[12] In general, Skinner believes that biological advantage is the basic reason why a reinforcer reinforces. In any event, a biological explanation of reinforcement power may be as far as we can go.[13] The pigeon that learns to execute unfamiliar, noninstinctual actions can be taught to do so quickly and effectively by simple manipulation. He is first made hungry— observable in terms of body-weight loss—and then reinforced with grain when he does what the experimenter wants. The highly complex behavior of human beings who, in Skinner's language, are conditionable by a great variety of reinforcers seems to be much less biologically oriented, and Skinner, in spite of speculative leanings, refrains from tracing human preferences back to differentiated animal needs. He occasionally follows Freud in an effort to derive developed behavior from earlier behavior. He speculates, for instance, on the attractions of music in terms of the sexuality of rhythms.[14] By and large, however, he contents himself with accepting reinforcers where he finds them.

In *Walden Two* Skinner gives even more latitude to the diversity of human wants and needs. Its founder, whom Skinner calls Frazier, says at one point, "Not many works of art can be traced to the lack of satisfaction of the basic needs. It's not plain sex that gives rise to art, but personal relations which are social or cultural rather than biological." [15]

EDUCATION

EDUCATION AS CONDITIONED RESPONSE

Skinner regards education as a system of well-calculated reinforcers, some of which may even be spurious. There are generalized reinforcers, like money, which can be exchanged for "primary reinforcers of great variety." [16] Among these broad-spectrum reinforcers, or "tokens" as Skinner calls them, are the "marks, grades, and diplomas which he [the student] has received." [17] The tokens used in an educational system form a series of possible exchanges, a lower for a higher, and the cash value of the final token—a diploma, degree, graduation—is ordinarily pretty clear. [18] It is a shade unclear what is meant here, since one does not "exchange" marks and grades for something in the sense that money is exchanged for food. The money is no longer ours; the grades are. Perhaps Skinner means that the significance of school grades as incentives is "taken over" or "supported" by the longer-term incentive of a diploma. [19] But in any case, Skinner is convinced that one job of the educator is to work out consequences—artificial and arbitrary or not—that will have proper feedback. [20] The spurious consequences are grades and the like, used to condition the response called education—something to keep the pot boiling, so to speak. Long-term objectives are sometimes too remote to be attractive.

Skinner believes that the entire educational relationship, from the side of either the teacher or the student, can be analyzed as operant behavior. He does not spend much time on the teacher. Most members of the educational profession engage in it because they get "economic reinforcement." [21] It is also a "good thing to do"—it is approved by the "ethical group." Since many teachers could make more money or even gain more approval (whatever "more" approval might mean observationally) by other professions, the question remains open why they choose to teach; but Skinner's primary emphasis is on the process and the institution. Education, according to Skinner, aims at establishing behavior that will be advantageous either to the individual involved or to others or to both in some future time. [22] The emphasis is on acquiring behavior rather than maintaining it. When religious or governmental or economic control aims at making certain patterns of behavior more likely, educational reinforcement will simply make special subpatterns more probable in special situations. [23]

Education looks to noneducational consequences for its justification. "Education," according to Skinner, "would be pointless if other consequences were not eventually forthcoming, *since the behavior of the controllee at the moment when he is being educated is of no particular importance to any one.*" [24]

What are the reinforcers peculiar to education? Actually, according to Skinner, the present situation is in flux and we are in process of exchanging old reinforcers for new. Established educational institutions use devices to reinforce behavior which are familiar—grades, promotions, honorary societies, diplomas, and so on—all of which are positive reinforcement of approved behavior. [25] As for negative reinforcement, punishment, corporal and other, was used. But the resulting "neurotic by-products" make it useful to look for "other techniques of control." The teacher now must become "interesting; in other words he becomes an entertainer." [26] In *Walden Two* this same point is made by Frazier, that the lecturer must, in the new order, become an entertainer. The problem of the lecturer is solved by dispensing with it, and him. The lecture is, in any case, obsolete and inefficient compared with printing.[27] He goes on to suggest that printed lectures should be handed to students and that what the lecture method has to contribute beyond the printed lecture is "platform chicanery. The public lecturer can still entertain," [28] but this should be known for what it is. Still later Frazier, in a remark reminiscent of one attributed to Henry Ford, says, "History is honored in Walden Two for entertainment. It isn't taken seriously as food for thought." [29] Our curiosity as to what does constitute serious food for thought is shortly satisfied. The students are given, Frazier explains, a survey of techniques of thinking, taken from logic, statistics, mathematics, and "scientific method." That is all they need in the way of "college education"; for they can get the rest for themselves in the libraries and laboratories of Walden Two.[30]

If we follow the informal ideas of *Walden Two* and the more formal theoretical ones of *Science and Human Behavior*, written five years later, we get a fairly clear idea of what Skinner thinks education should ideally accomplish. The shift that Skinner wants is from negative reinforcement devices—for the most part—to positive devices, and from artificial ones to real ones. One of the characters in *Walden Two* feels driven to admit that the contemporary motives operating in educational institutions are "fear of one's family in the event of low grades or expulsion, the awards of grades and honours, the snob value of a cap and gown, the cash value of a diploma." Frazier says that at Walden Two the substitute for these things is simply the absence of them. "We have had to *uncover* the worthwhile and truly productive motives—the motives which inspire creative work in science and art outside the academies." [31] He goes on to speak of the natural curiosity of babies and how this comes to be wiped out. The only problem in Walden Two education is that there is a surfeit of motivation. The children have to be "fortified" against discouragement by making the sought-after reward, "a bit of tune from a music box or a pattern of flashing lights, more and more difficult to obtain, so that persistence is built up." [32]

> We appeal to the curiosity which is characteristic of the unrestrained child, as well as to the alert and inquiring child. We appeal to that drive to control the environment which makes the baby

continue to crumple a piece of noisy paper and the scientist to
press forward with his predictive analyses of nature. We don't need
to motivate anyone by creating spurious needs.[33]

In such an ideal society, punishment is never used.[34] But this does
not mean no guidance; on the contrary, what is entailed is total guidance. As Frazier says, "The fact is, we not only *can* control human behavior, we *must*." [35] The reason given is that behavioral control is already a well advanced technology but often in the hands of the wrong
people: Nazis, advertisers, salesmen. Skinner the psychologist is concerned with the same problem as it appears in education: lack of control.

The current educational institution is in the process of change, and
"at the moment it lacks adequate control." [36] The birch rod, the family discipline, and the "honorific" values of education have all played
their parts in educational control. Transitional results of this change
include the lecturer as entertainer (mentioned above), demonstration,
visual aids, and field trips. In general, "progressive education" has
moved in to provide genuine substitutes for the receding mistaken and
false controls. This means natural rewards rather than artificial ones,
positive reward rather than negative punishment, and prompt reinforcement rather than postponed reinforcement.[37] All of these aims, as
we shall see, are embodied in Skinner's conception of teaching machines. Clearly, the teaching machine is for him only a natural out-
growth of a technology already in progress.

EDUCATION AND HUMAN NATURE

In *Walden Two* it is clear that Frazier's commitment to the control
of human behavior arises directly from his determinism. He says so.
One feels that Frazier is not always Skinner's puppet or projection. He
is often more extreme than the real-life Skinner, more sure-footed and
arrogant, and certainly more successful. Frazier has his Utopia, Skinner does not. But Frazier's determinism is very like that of his creator,
and we can treat them jointly. This determinism is at the heart of
Skinner's theory of human nature and deserves close attention.

Two principal points lie at the basis of Skinner's conception of
human nature. (1) *Human nature is extremely plastic.* Conditioning,
as we have seen, shapes behavior "as a sculptor shapes a lump of clay."
We shall later see that teaching machines for human beings are modeled on experimental work in which pigeons were taught to do tasks
that had no instinctual counterpart and no natural usefulness. (2)
There is a basic conflict of interests between persons and society.
"Each of us," says Frazier, "is engaged in a pitched battle with the rest
of mankind. . . . That's our original sin and it can't be helped. Now

'everybody' else we call 'society.' It's a powerful opponent, and it always wins."[38] Skinner here is a direct descendant of Thomas Hobbes. Hobbes said, "I put for a general inclination of all mankind, a perpetual and restless desire of power after power that ceaseth only in death." Furthermore, Hobbes argued that men were naturally at war, "of every man against every man," and that government is needed to have peace.[39] Hobbes, incidentally, not only provided his successor John Locke with some of the materials for an early theory of learning by association, he was—unlike Locke but like Skinner—a fully committed determinist.

We notice that the doctrine of innate characteristics and the plastic moldability of human nature are not only compatible with determinism but virtually required by it. However, determinism must have more than these two doctrines, since any account of human nature would acknowledge these two factors. What determinism demands is that there be *no other* factors. Indeed, these two factors have familiar names and doctrines—our fate is determined by two forces: environment and heredity.

The "pitched battle" that Frazier speaks of is a major concern of Skinner's. This natural conflict—labeled "aggression" in so many current treatises—represents the point of moral contact between Skinner the laboratory experimentalist and Skinner the theoretician of man in search of a science of man. The frightening tragedies and near tragedies of our time appall him, as they should. We got past the risk of a chain reaction, as we fiddled with early nuclear fission, but it is not at all the case that two devastating world wars in the past single half century offer much assurance of a lasting peace.[40] Nonetheless, Skinner seems to hold not that there has been too much science but that there has been too little. We can control and predict nature remarkably, yet so far we have made little progress with a science of man.

The theme of a science of man dominates the whole of *Science and Human Behavior*, as the theme of cultural design—Skinner calls it "engineering"—does *Walden Two*. As a result, he begins and ends *Science and Human Behavior* with an attack on what seems to him the illusion of freedom. Why? For reasons that are very familiar in the history of philosophy:

> The hypothesis that man is not free is essential to the application
> of scientific method to the study of human behavior. The free inner
> man who is held responsible for the behavior of the external biolog-
> ical organism is only a prescientific substitute for the kinds of
> causes which are discovered in the course of a scientific analysis.[41]

If we are to have a science of man then such a science must search out causes. No causes, no science. "You don't have a science about a subject that hops capriciously about," says Frazier in *Walden Two.*[42]

Skinner, as we have seen, adheres to a school of thought which finds the terms "cause" and "effect" misleading. Strictly, he prefers to use "change in the independent variable" for "cause" and "change in the dependent variable" for "effect." These terms ignore the "how" of cause and effect; they emphasize only the "that," stressing the fact that "different events tend to occur together in a certain order." [43] However, he is willing to speak of causes and effects with the understanding that they be understood in the above fashion. In passing, we should notice that the need of science to discover regular sequences which can be expressed in the form of scientific laws does not automatically lead to the acceptance of determinism. We need as well to show that the sequences of cause-followed-by-effect not only do occur but must do so. Secondly, we must show not only that such inevitable sequences do occur and must occur (so that, given event of type *A*, event of type *B* must follow) but that all events that could occur or have occurred are of this "scientific" sort. Many scientists, however, have seen no need to argue that because we have reliable scientific laws, scientific explanation is our only mode of explanation.

We might want to say that if we are faced with accepting determinism in order for there to be a science of man, we have an open choice between rejecting alternatives to determinism and rejecting a science of man. What does this determinism lead to in Skinner's view of human nature and education?

Punishment and responsibility   The answer is clear: determinism revises our conception of responsibility. In the remoter past it has been customary for persons to be held responsible for their own behavior. The backward child was sullen, lazy, perverse, and so on. This was the doctrine of freedom in a horrifying form. In the recent past the causal factors that guide and coerce child behavior—economic, racial, neighborhood, family, and so on—have come out into the open. They have begun to be understood in their awful power. To a lesser degree, the physical factors of heredity are now better understood, as well. From these causal analyses there has sprung a new humaneness in education that should make anyone suspicious of a simple doctrine of human freedom. In educational psychology the result has been to stress positive reinforcement.

Positive reinforcement consists in adding an attractive element to or removing a repelling one from the situation in which a desired result occurs. Negative reinforcement consists in the converse: removing something attractive from or presenting something repelling to the undesired situation.[44] In the positive case we may give food to a pigeon or a good mark (one of the spurious reinforcers) to a student, or we may remove a shackle from a trapped animal or give to the obedient prisoner the privilege of being a trusty. In the negative case we punish, hurt, fine, constrain, and so on. There are good experimental grounds for being suspicious of punishment. The suspicion goes back, as we have seen, at least as far as John Locke, who based his conclusions on unmanipulated experience rather than on experiment.

Both in human beings and in animals we can quite dispassionately see reasons for sharply limiting our recourse to punishment.[45] Its immediate appeal is as a deterrent. But experiments tend to show that well-formed dispositions are not erased by punishment. They are only driven underground and may emerge later, after the deterrent is gone, much in the fashion of Freud's repressions. For a child this may mean that "if the behavior is a function of age, the child will, as we say, outgrow it." [46] And it may be worthwhile to live with a rough phase rather than to punish in a way that will have bad results in the future. What bad results? Those negative feelings which we call shame or guilt are only one result. There is a further complication. The behavior that removes the sense of guilt or overcomes it when it appears tends to be self-reinforcing. One may get more and more addicted to behavior which assuages guilt; the result is a condition which Skinner —along with Freud—calls "anxiety." We are all familiar in life and literature with the related "once-fallen" young woman who overreacts to her guilt by turning into a prudish and repressed old maid. She is uncommon nowadays, but the wild and irresponsible youth who hardens into a stern and demanding father once he matures is still familiar. The timid or insecure person, the more obviously "anxious" sort, is likely to come from a background of severe punishment erratically administered.

Punishment exacts too high a price, it is concluded, and gives not much back in reliable return. One further hazard not mentioned by Skinner but pertinent to the problem of punishment, is the following suggestive conclusion drawn from animal experiments:

> . . . we have also seen that there is a danger in animal experiments that the animal will avoid not only a particular wrong response but also the whole situation which involves punishment. It might therefore follow that human beings would avoid not merely the actions which lead to punishment, but also the processes in the brain which attach anxiety to those actions.[47]

We might call this the "blown fuse" phenomenon; it has many forms.

The alternative to punishment is positive reinforcement. There must be a "payoff," to use Skinner's engaging term. He mentions the girl who must see that her friend's behavior in dating her should be "suitably reinforced"—if she wants another date. Further, "To teach a child to read or sing or play a game effectively, we must work out a program of educational reinforcement in which appropriate responses 'pay off' frequently." [48] This "frequently" is a familiar theme of Skinner—especially in the education of children.

Plasticity and control   "For one thing," says Frazier, "we don't punish"; in *Walden Two* the ideal of unassisted positive reinforcement is realized. [49] This rule of practice is paralleled by a conviction about basic human nature. The "pitched battle" which we have previously noted is not to be regarded as morally wrong or right. It merely *is*. Apparently Skinner thinks—not too originally—that this factor is rooted in the biological struggle: "By its very nature the struggle to survive cannot give birth to a noncompetitive intelligence." [50] But earlier, "We have no truck with philosophies of innate goodness—or evil, either, for that matter. But we do have faith in our power to change human behavior. We can *make* men adequate for group living—to the satisfaction of everybody." [51]

The eager critic should not assume that Skinner himself is out of control here, concerning what can be done. He is talking about the improvability of man—which is the assumption that underlies every genuine conception of education. We recall that the real Skinner, not the fictional Frazier, is committed to the old-fashioned notion of phases of development. In this developmentalism he is like both Freud and Piaget. This same developmentalism is present in the works of Gesell and Ilg and in the widely used handbook of Dr. Benjamin Spock. [52] Frazier too is a developmentalist, but with a difference. He is committed to phases, but not to the customary conditioning of the early phases in the home nor the normal procedures in school. Of home training he says, "The significant history of our times is the story of the growing weakness of the family." [53] A few pages later he describes the practice in Walden Two in greater detail.

> Group care is better than parental care. In the old pre-scientific days the early education of the child could be left to the parents and indeed almost certainly had to be left to them. [But the scientific rearing of children is an intricate business and the mother hasn't either skill or time to do the job.] Home is not the place to raise children. . . . Our goal is to have every adult member of Walden Two regard all our children as his own, and to have every child think of every adult as his parent. [54]

The social import of this theme seems evident. If you want a genuinely cooperative society, don't let the outmoded family structure intervene in the crucial years.

Not only does Frazier wish to all but do away with the family as early and continuous educator, he also finds that "at least half of the high school years are a total waste—and half of college, too, as our more emancipated educators are beginning to discover." [55] The curriculum we have already encountered shows what Frazier means. Finally, of the period normally associated with this educational phase, Frazier says, "Adolescence is seldom pleasant to remember, it's full of unnecessary problems, unnecessary delays. It should be brief and painless, and we make it so in Walden Two." [56]

This last remark, where phrasing suggests that Frazier's fictional (Skinner's real?) adolescence was unhappy, shows that while Skinner is a developmentalist, he is a very special kind—one who sees no particular length of time for the given phases of development, one who would like to see the task of maturation speeded up to get through what he regards as a nuisance at best, and finally one who regards the family contribution as an impediment to development. What is invariant in phases appears to be their order, not the period of time required for each or even for all.

If we condense the foregoing themes into a single theme, it comes to this: The plasticity of personality not only permits early and highly skilled manipulation, it demands it. The aggressive intelligence which the struggle for survival has bred can be rechanneled by early and carefully guided "behavioral engineering." [57] This last concept appears under this name and others through both the technical and the popular works of Skinner. But the engineering must be professionally undertaken from the outset. "All our ethical training is completed by the age of six." [58] For Skinner it must be directed at the very core of each person's development, at the deepest level of motivation. "Our members are practically always doing what they want to do—what they choose—*but we see to it that they will want to do precisely the things which are best for themselves and the community*. Their behavior is determined, yet they're free." [59] The watchword for the entire process is *control*. Its meaning is "positive reinforcement." The process is called "operant conditioning." Positive reinforcement seems to range over the full scale of noble human emotions. "We make every man a brave man," says Frazier.[60] Elsewhere he says, "What is love, except another name for the use of positive reinforcement?" [61] Again, Frazier speaking of control praises Jesus: " 'Love your enemies' is an example —a psychological invention for easing the lot of an oppressed people. . . . Jesus must have been quite astonished at the effect of his discovery." [62] This tactic is a special form of what Skinner, as laboratory technologist, calls "extinction," a term taken from Pavlov. Extinction is the tactic of conditioning someone to "do something else" by positive reinforcement.[63] Its extreme form is doing the exact opposite of the behavior to be extinguished.

But control remains the central notion, since it embodies the causality that—as we have repeatedly seen—characterizes all courses of events. The intelligent and experimentally guided use of this fact is "control."

Control and interiority   The theme of control brings us full circle to determinism again. Skinner, we know, believes that science requires determinism since it searches for causes; moreover, he evidently thinks that all events come under scientific comprehension; hence all events fall under the causal analysis; thus there is no such thing as a spontaneous freedom. Everything that comes about does so for reasons that antedate it and generate it. The task is to put oneself in a critical position in these processes: "when we reinforce with food, we gain control over the hungry man." [64] Again, "in order to get the pigeon to stretch its neck, we simply make it hungry." [65] The prime aim of science is prediction and control, and behavioral science follows the physical sciences in these aims.[66] Not only is control the aim of science and the means for bettering human behavior and, to that extent, human nature, the desire to control comes perilously close to being an innate drive. At least it manifests itself as early as the baby's repeated delight in crumpling a piece of paper.[67] It is, moreover, one of the class of entities which Skinner calls "generalized reinforcers." These generalized reinforcers are reinforcers which have an appeal—are effective—because they do not need to be understood in terms of some particular deprivation, like hunger.[68] They include such things as "tokens," e.g. money, the "submissiveness of others," so that we have our way, "approval," and the desire "to control the physical world." Actually, the "submissions of others" would seem to point to a desire to control the personal world as well as the physical world. Since reinforcers have no specific antecedent deprivation, Skinner thinks ill of their being said to be "needs," e.g. the need for approval. He goes so far as to say they *seem* to be autonomous.[69] Since "autonomous" means "law unto itself," "not ruled by anything else," and science is the search for order and law, it would seem that we have here what some might call "primary drives," "basic urges," and so on.[70] But Skinner does not accept this conclusion. The reason he does not do so is critical. It seems to introduce the subject of interiority or privacy, a subject of unusual importance for the behaviorist, since he leans heavily on the publicly observable. The reason is straightforward:

> . . . a capacity to be reinforced in this way [by general reinforcers] could scarcely have evolved in the short time during which the required conditions have prevailed. Attention, affection, approval, and submission have presumably existed in human society for only a very brief period, as the process of evolution goes.[71]

Money is even more recent. What is needed to make this argument sound is the idea that evolution of man is to be understood in terms of physiological characteristics alone—posture, skull shape, brain capacity, dentition, etc. In this view, human evolution has not advanced one whit since the appearance of the biologically recognizable *homo sapiens.*

TEACHING MACHINES

From the time of S. L. Pressey to the present, close onto fifty years, the phrase "teaching machine" has been able to trigger controversy. In 1924 Pressey realized that the routines present in teaching might well be mechanized. He may properly be called the "father of the teaching machine."

In our estimation, knee-jerk emotionalism about teaching machines can be quieted by pointing to those features of the educational process which in point of fact are mechanical. If there are routines, then, *why not save the subtle and highly diversified talent and training of the teacher for human and unduplicatable efforts?* In our opinion this motto of the teaching machine advocate can never be brushed aside.

Pressey's machine actually combined teaching and testing in a single act. The machine mechanizes the multiple-choice test. It has four keys, one for each of four possible answers. A correct answer automatically rolls a new question into view. The machine counts the correct answers, so the student has his test grade immediately at the end of the test. Skinner's machines were conceived between the time of Pressey's machine and the more recent one devised by Crowder.[72] Skinner clearly owes the basic idea to Pressey. Pressey's machine can be run again, so that the student can improve his score—a "reinforcement" factor, in Skinner's language. It can even be made to pay off in candy for a certain percentage or better of right answers.

However, Skinner finds that Pressey's multiple-choice programs stress recognition rather than recall. We should produce answers from our own resources, not merely identify them. Skinner's teaching machines all work on the same principle: there is a routine to be learned, a skill, or whatever.[73] In every case the machine is programed for a series of small steps to lead to another small step. The steps may be small in many ways: rhythm is taught a child through having him match, by pushing a button, a series of clicks played by the machine. The machine can be adjusted to permit the child to be off timing a bit at the outset and demand greater precision later. Tone matching is similarly done. Verbal sequences for teaching the verbal, nonexperimental side of physics ask for a correct word to be entered in a blank.

Occasionally either one of two words is allowed by the program, but usually not. The sentences are ordered in an ascending scale of application and relation or both. The student reads the sentence, fills in the blank, then uncovers the right answer, and goes on.

Aside from incremental stepping, what makes the machines work? "A teaching machine is simply any device which arranges contingencies of reinforcement." [74] Skinner occasionally uses "reward," but for more ultimate goals. Reinforcement, we recall, is what keeps the educational process going. What is rewarded—or "reinforced"—is "operant behavior." We recall that operant behavior can be called a "response" but without the implication of an identifiable "stimulus." [75] It is any kind of "behavior defined by a given consequence." [76] The reinforcements are satisfaction of the desire to know, curiosity, and so on. They may be quite arbitrary—like grades and diplomas. Or they may be quite plainly tangible. For example, Skinner shows a picture of the tone-matching machine with a little box on top of it which dispenses "tokens, candies, or coins" as additional reinforcement.[77]

We recall Skinner's opposition to "negative conditioning." This he calls "aversive"; it constitutes one of the prime weaknesses of traditional education. He strays close, however, to aversive control in getting a twelve-year old, whose congenital cataracts had recently been removed, to wear the glasses which would save him from blindness. The child refused to wear the glasses; "it was necessary to allow the child to go hungry so that food could be used as an effective reinforcer." [78] Gradually the touching of frames without lenses was reinforced with food, then carrying them, and so on. There is a thin line between allowing pain to arise and creating pain. But Skinner's account gives us a peep-hole on the hungry thief in *Les Misérables* or the panorama of rioting blacks in Watts, surrounded by opulence. The blacks, their hunger for possessions exacerbated ("conditioned") by massive advertising, raged and looted through stores and were selectively shot by frantic police; Los Angeles pigeons, we might call them.

Skinner's work indeed has grown out of the conditioning of animals by controlling the food supply. Hungry behavior seems common to all life and certainly to animal life. Pigeons are among Skinner's favorite experimental subjects. In an article in the *Scientific American* he said, "Much of our work has been done with the pigeon, a healthy, docile animal." [79] Its behavior can be "shaped as a sculptor shapes a lump of clay." [80] With care used to develop the "learning" a small step at a time, it can be taught to walk a figure of eight to get at a kernel of corn. "The power of the technique has to be seen to be believed." In the article he reveals a contribution to the World War II effort: Project Pigeon. Three pigeons in strait-jackets before screens which pictured the track of a missile were taught a pecking route that guided the missile on target. When the missile strayed, the image on the screen showed it, a pigeon pecked, and the direction was corrected. In another experiment Skinner once got one extremely active and docile pigeon to make a desired response over 73,000 times in five hours— better than four times a second! "There is," he says, "a historical connection between Project Pigeon and our teaching machines. . . . It is true the scrap of wisdom imparted to each pigeon would have been small, but the required changes in behavior were similar to those which must be brought about in larger quantities in human students. . . . Why not teach students by machine also?" [81] And finally, "Machines such as those we use at Harvard could be programmed to teach, in whole or in part, all the subjects taught in elementary and high school and many taught in college." [82]

CRITICAL EVALUATION

Many of Skinner's virtues and vices appear in practical and simplified form in *The Technology of Teaching*. We begin there as an entry point to more general considerations. Chapter V, "Why Teachers Fail," can be profitably read by any teacher, teaching at any level of comprehension. It includes hard questions for teachers to ask themselves about teaching practice in general, but more particularly their own. No philosopher, however, is likely to think of Skinner's discussion of Plato's theory of learning as exhibiting either reflection or— bluntly—even much effort. Again, the painful and familiar difficulty that Pestalozzi had with Rousseau's method is mysteriously brought forward as an apparent critique of both men.

In general, *The Technology of Teaching* is not overburdened with close reasoning. One paragraph, for example, on how children find ways of escaping from school ends with, "Children who commit suicide are often found to have had trouble in school." [83] This remark, incidentally dropped into the discussion without citation or authority, comes directly after a condemnation of aversive control in terms of its evil consequences. An obvious alternate to the implied conclusion that aversive school control generates or aggravates suicidal tendencies is that the prior conditions which lead to school problems also lead to suicide.

Sometimes Skinner's habit of dissecting large tasks into small learnable bits seems to affect his critical powers. He cites Plato's injunction in the *Republic* about avoiding compulsion and letting children's lessons "take the form of play" as a case of positive reinforcement.[84] The context happens to be one in which Plato is suggesting that the child

acting in an unrigged situation will show natural bents which will indicate what kind of education is best for him. Skinner is blinded to
this by his dislike of the idea of "being born that way," which, he says
elsewhere, has little to do with demonstrated facts.[85] Only extreme
haste or lack of interest in the context, again, could underlie the proposition that Socrates' conducting of the slave boy through a mathematical proof is "one of the great frauds in the history of education." [86]
The lifting out of context of a passage from Newman's *The Idea of a
University* leads Skinner to say of Newman that "he recognized a poor
student, but not a poor method." [87] Yet his observation is contradicted
by a citation from Newman, immediately preceding. And consider,
"What he [John Dewey] threw out should have been thrown out. Unfortunately he had too little to put in its place. Progressive education
has been a temporizing measure which can now be effectively supplemented." [88] The identification of Dewey with progressive education does not assure us that Skinner has read much Dewey, nor any of
Dewey's critiques of progressive education.[89] Lest we be accused of similar atomizing, it should be noticed that these cases of pitchman cocki-
ness are softened elsewhere when Skinner feels in a more statesmanlike
mood.[90] Such moods seem most easily reinforced in Skinner's writings
when he discovers precedents for his own opinions. As he says in a
winning espousal of several myths, "Many things please a teacher,
from a polished apple to fulsome footnotes in a thesis, and the careless
teacher will reinforce fawners and flatterers." [91]

These miniature critiques of the thought of other men are only
symptoms, however, of a rather determined focusing on one's own
theories. Let us look at some aspects of these theories.

TEACHING MACHINES

It now seems likely that we will not have a wave of teaching machines brought into the classroom to be teachers' helpers—or substitutes. For one thing, the program alone will apparently often do as
well as the program and the machines. Furthermore, audio-visual aids
of all sorts are beginning to be despaired of by some of their most vigorous supporters. Apparently the problems of training, bureaucracy,
repair, and maintenance are overwhelming enough to give computer
experts grave doubts about the mechanization of education.[92]

The program is likely to remain with us, however, and even if it
does not, it embodies certain approaches to education that should be
examined. In our opinion, programed learning is exceedingly limited as to both scope and its place in the total learning process. We do
not mean to say that only routines should be mechanized or—with
Crowder—that the pigeon is a poor model of a student. The basic lim-

itation is that insofar as education is education for life, programed learning is the very opposite of education. At best it provides factual instruction useful as an adjunct.

Life is integrative　All life synthesizes. A. N. Whitehead put it well when he stated the contrary position, long before Skinner formulated his: "The pupil's mind is a growing organism. On the one hand, it is not a box to be ruthlessly packed with alien ideas." [93]

Life is lived through language　To be a bit redundant, through language alive: spoken, heard, actual. The words on the page, especially words whose total impact is factual, are a rather abstract and nonsocial segment of language. A telling example by an alert teacher —especially in the middle of a quite rigorous drill—adapted to the total classroom situation *now* is not duplicatable by a program, yet it may save the day or even generate real interest where only an interest in getting finished existed before. The machine cannot provide such an educational stimulus, let alone tell when the time is ripe for it.

Life is primarily concerned with value　Canned value claims could be programed, but few educators would favor "value" instruction with neither discussion nor dialogue.

In summary, the social aspect of education can hardly be ignored and certainly can't be replaced by programs. Even Platonic dialogues fall far short of the living situation. We are not speaking here of "getting along with others" or of social poise and related aims which might be part of education at its best. The basic point is that much of mental growth requires sensitive contact with a *responsive* mind. Plato long ago remarked in his *Seventh Epistle* that a book can only give the same answers, no matter who its questioner is. The same is true of the program. We may, as a people, have an excess of togetherness, but we already have too little sociality. The program provides isolated self-improvement in the domain of performance. The Skinner box shows its inheritance from the Pressey machine, that of being an auto-tester. A discernible part of education is routine and factual; it submits to programing. But that is the antechamber. Basic education is social. Programed education is not.

BEHAVIORISM

Skinner is not wholly clear about what is meant by behaviorism. Sometimes he defends what might be called "hard behaviorism": "I would define behavior as the movement of an organism in space, with respect to itself or any other useful frame of reference." [94] If its statements "are useful for scientific purposes, they must be based upon observable events, and we may confine ourselves to such events exclusively in a functional analysis." [95] What are called "causes of behavior" are dubbed "independent variables," but they are external also and "must also be described in physical terms." [96]

What Skinner evidently wishes to disperse, if not deny, is any mysterious entities, relations, influences out of the public sight. They border on the occult and have no place in science. What is reliable is observable. What is not observable is suspect—at least to the scientific attitude. One of the things that call down anger and horror upon Skinner is the coarse, bland pursuit of this theme, coupled with exemplary calm and relative lack of emotional involvement. Critics sense an alien mind, psychologically from some other universe, manipulative, calculating, unemotionally ruthless. It is not hard to make a caricature of him that resembles Dostoievsky's Grand Inquisitor. Skinner lends himself to these caricatures; he sometimes seems as unfeeling about his public image as he is about his pigeons who are doing figures of eight instead of feeding, flocking, and family raising. What is implied in the exclusion of the interior?

Preoccupation with observable data takes two forms in Skinner. His most unflagging rejections are saved for what is nonphysical. He is more cautious about interiority which is often inaccessible, but presumptively physical, such as neural and visceral alterations in cognition and conation. Psychic "inner causes" give us little but confusion. Much common talk ("he changed his mind," etc.) and some technical talk ("Freud's unconscious," for example) are merely inventions. So also with "borrowing ideas," and the like. "In all this it is obvious that the mind and the ideas, together with their special characteristics, are being invented on the spot [!] to provide spurious explanations." [97] Because mental and psychical events "lack the dimensions of physical science, we have additional reasons for rejecting them." [98]

Neural causes and neural events are less treacherous. They are accounts, at least, of physical occurrences. But for the most part, these physical occurrences play little or no part in the observation of behavior. Skinner thinks the way is open for such study, but if a science of behavior were to depend upon it, it might wait forever. "Eventually a science of the nervous system based upon direct observation rather than inference will describe the neural states and events which immediately precede instances of behavior. . . . However, we may note here that we do not have and may never have this sort of neurological information at the moment it is needed in order to predict a specific instance of behavior." [99]

An interpolation should be made here. Skinner, in the last passage, speaks of "predict" rather than, as he frequently does, "predict and control." The early part of *Science and Human Behavior* is saturated with this manifest ideal of prediction and control.[100] References to control are even more numerous. If we put the words "and control" into the above passage, by-passing the impulse to ask a Freudian question about their absence, we are able to guess why Skinner disturbs people with well-developed imaginations. Indeed, the control of behavior by neural implants is proceeding faster than Skinner might have guessed, for instance in the work of Delgado.[101] In addition, the public press lately carries discussion of the quieting of unruly students and convicts by chemical means.

To return to the problem of inner events and inner causes, the worst kind of innerism, for Skinner, is that which lacks *either* psychic or neurological dimensions, e.g. talk of hunger, pugnacity, intelligence, musical ability *as causal* is "merely redundant. . . . A single set of facts is described by the two statements: 'He eats,' and 'He is hungry.'"[102] To say of a person that he has musical ability is to describe the same set of facts as saying that he plays well.

Restlessness surely overcomes any reader at this point. There is an element of self-consciousness that seems to be being ignored entirely— among many other things. Certainly when I say "I'm hungry," it's not the same as saying "I eat." Skinner is not wholly unaware of the difficulties; although his efforts to deal with the problem are a bit unclear, he does not duck it. He acknowledges the problems of "private events" and the "self." "With respect to each individual," says Skinner, "a small part of the universe is *private*."[103] But he goes on to deal with these events as those which occur "within one's skin." There is clearly some confusion here, in which Skinner's own distinction between the two types of interiority, psychic and neural, is ignored. What is within one's own skin would seem to be physical, but when I speak of my feelings or my ideas, I'm not reporting physical data. I can easily distinguish my hunger from my eating, even if the observational, "He eats" and "He is hungry" designate the same set of observable facts. And when I say, "I'm hungry" or "angry," the words may be accompanied by visceral or adrenal events, but it is precisely these events which I'm *not* reporting. When I say, "I'm thinking," I may be designating something that never exists apart from neuronal activity, but I'm not designating neuronal activity. One might as well say that because there are no children without mothers, the term "child" designates the same as the term "mother." Skinner never considers the two-perspective view of thought processes through which alone we could begin to understand or explain our interest in the physiology of thought. It would be very odd to tell of how one physiological process is interested in another, or itself. The very ideal of "objectification" implies our awareness of a nonobjective realm different from the objective and in the last analysis required by it. In brief, observations require observers as well as what is observed, and even where the two are one—perchance—as in self-observation, their functions are distinct and require one another. Objectivity inherently requires reference to subjectivity.

It does not follow that because an object of our awareness is not "externally observable" in the world conceived as a physical order, we must then hold that such awareness refers to internal (within our skin) physical order. Not everything of which we are aware deserves to be regarded as observable, if "observable" means "reducible to sensory data." Skinner's efforts to do so take him into occult entities of the sort he would like to avoid. To say that I've only now acted on an idea I previously had, says Skinner, is to describe a covert response which preceded the overt.[104] He does not enlighten us about why this is an improvement. The postulation of the pre-existing "covert response" is obviously a gratuitous inference, at best implying that there was a pre-existent electrochemical "set" in the organism, when it had the idea. But this set is clearly not what the owner of the idea is indicating by "idea." If behavior is what is observable, let it rest at that, without speculative extension or confusion between mental and physical awareness. The notion of a "covert response" is hazy in Skinner's mind, however; it is not confined to things like ideas, it also extends to "microscopic behavior," which is so small as to be "wholly private." [105] In addition, it refers to tiny actions like the inadvertent finger motions of deaf-mutes, which—since they could be meaningfully amplified—lead Skinner to suppose that the blurred line between "public" and "private" is not fixed and "the problem of privacy may, therefore, eventually be solved by technical advances." [106]

EDUCATION AND METHODOLOGY

There are other difficulties with Skinner's views that extend into the technical theory of learning. For example, he speaks of a response as a unique occurrence which cannot be predicted or controlled, yet shortly talks of the "reassortment of responses," where he probably means the adjustment of a present response to profit from the retention—somehow—of the significance of past responses. The point is not merely technical, since we apparently choose which would-be stimuli we shall allow to be most significant to ourselves and respond accordingly. Searching out the intractability of a response, once it is made, might give Skinner a view of that freedom toward which we educate children—to discriminate the worthy from the unworthy—and whose mention he finds a threat to a science of behavior. But if we follow this line, we should be soon plunged into complicated metaphysics and epistemology and thus carried beyond the area of Skinner's interest or competence.

How shall we look at Skinner's methodology, staying at the same semipopular level which he prefers? We may want to say that he is dealing with an engineering or technical problem. Frazier speaks unabashedly of "behavioral engineering" in *Walden Two*. Engineering techniques should not be considered the same as science. However faint the boundary, most scientists and engineers would insist on the distinction. Science, as its etymology exhibits, is concerned with knowing. Engineering is concerned with prediction and control, those two ideas which so dominate Skinner's thought. One may predict and control the behavior of a child and not know him at all. Indeed it could be argued that overweening devotion to these ends would render the child a total stranger. Control over poliomyelitis is virtually complete; some researchers are almost distressed since the sources of contagion, the incubation period, and even the physiological course of the disease remain almost as great a mystery as they were before the Salk vaccine.

There is a nickname for what is, in effect, not a theory of the nature of something, but the theory of how to make it work. The phrase is "black box." It stands for any situation in which an input into any kind of "black box" whatsoever has been tried in enough different ways so that through experience we can get a desired output. What is going on inside the black box is opaque, unknown. Genuine knowledge, including that of science, consists in the illumination of what's going on inside the black box. An engineer, for example, designs a building, sets up specifications in terms of the tensile strengths of materials. These he gets from tables that supply him the needed information. He moves in a domain of results. He is not interested or informed as to *why* some material has such and such tensility. A crystallographer may spend years—in close research with others— trying to find out what, in a given fusion of molecules, makes one alloy stronger than another. The engineer knows what he needs to know in order to get results. If, years later, it turns out that the tensile strength of a material diminishes because of "metal fatigue" or changes because of unique tensions in unfamiliar modern architectural design, the collapse of his building may show him how limited his black-box approach is. He was betrayed by the unfamiliar or the uncharted.

The applications of the above example should be clear. A substantial part of education is governed by the accepted norms of certain prescribed ends. This is especially true in the case of what are called skills—elementary language and elementary mathematics, for example. As long as we are convinced that what we are after is useful to know, not likely to become passé in the near future, and capable of analysis into small segments without loss of vision of the whole, programed learning as an example of behavioral control serves a useful end. But we need widespread acceptance and justification for the ends. Skinner's example of the neurotic child who is controlled to accept the glasses that will save his sight by food deprivation is a cause for some concern. Most people would agree that sight is a portal to freedom, for which the child can well pay the price of coercion now. But who makes judgments of this general sort, over how much of a child's activities, and so on? One interviewer pointed out that the methods exposed in *Science and Human Behavior* "could become quite effective if, say, a hostile government were to gain control and proceed to shape the development of children, putting such techniques totally into use. Could this not lead to a rather dangerous situation for the world?" Skinner's reply is illuminating:

> There's no doubt about it, but what are you going to do? To impose a moratorium on science would be worst of all. It does not solve the problem to say we must not increase our knowledge or publish what we already know because it might fall into the hands of despots. The best defense I can see is to make all behavioral processes as familiar as possible. Let everyone know what is possible, what can be used against them. . . . I think a science of behavior is just as dangerous as the atom bomb. It has the potential of being horribly misused. We must devote ourselves to a better governmental design which will have some control over all destructive instruments.[107]

Presumably Skinner would on reflection want to say "potentially destructive knowledge," instead of "destructive instruments." But in any case, it is the question of "better governmental design" that may give us pause. Once again it is the technical aspect on which Skinner (unwittingly) rests his hopes. In a sense he must. He holds that the organism is indefinitely malleable—like clay, we recall, in the hands of the sculptor. This being the case, the technique of the sculptor must be highly developed, if good results are to be obtained. But suppose that the clay has a structure of its own? Suppose its growth patterns, however malleable, are predispositions which call for a phased maturation. Or again, suppose the basic education of children must involve feelings which are exposed to opportunities for self-projection, outgrowing, contactual, and projective, rather than receptivity to preshaped values, determined from the outside and stamped in, in the name of tranquility and experience. Indeed, in general, if the theme—now taken up by quite a few biologists, including the distinguished geneticist Dobzhansky [108]—that mankind is evolving at an ever more rapid rate is true, then should we not be more concerned with social education, education for adaptation, and education for innovation, rather than nonsocial education with fixed steps and firm conclusions about unalterably important and thoroughly understood skills? Educational growth has a grain of its own—at least according to Piaget. The training of value responses lies in the eliciting of emotional development, if Richard Jones is right. Isn't there such a thing as intuitive thinking as well as analytic thinking, as Jerome Bruner urges? Hasn't much of the child's educability been decided by emotional factors oblique to or prior to his cognitive and sensory-motor development, as Erikson implies? It is to these acutely modern concerns that we must turn, however briefly, to assess our current educational scene.

NOTES

1. See B. F. Skinner, *Science and Human Behavior*, New York, 1953 (hereafter cited as *SHB*), p. 38, for example. The recent appearance of Skinner's *Beyond Freedom and Dignity* (New York, 1971) does not change our appraisal.

2. *SHB*, p. 60.

3. *SHB*, p. 60.

4. *SHB*, pp. 276, 279.

5. *SHB*, p. 65.

6. *SHB*, pp. 64, 65.

7. *SHB*, p. 65.

8. *SHB*, p. 65.

9. See *SHB*, pp. 237–258, for example.

10. *SHB*, p. 91.

11. *SHB*, p. 69.

12. *SHB*, p. 83.

13. *SHB*, p. 84.

14. *SHB*, p. 293.

15. *Walden Two*, New York, 1962 (hereafter cited as *WT*), p. 125.

16. *SHB*, p. 79.

17. *SHB*, p. 80.

18. *SHB*, p. 80.

19. Compare "verbal stimuli," pp. 407–408.

20. *SHB*, p. 67.

21. *SHB*, p. 404.

22. *SHB*, p. 402.

23. *SHB*, p. 402.

24. *SHB*, pp. 402–403; emphasis ours.

25. *SHB*, p. 405.

26. *SHB*, p. 406.

27. *WT*, p. 42.

28. *WT*, p. 43.

29. *WT*, p. 115.

30. *WT*, p. 121.

31. *WT*, p. 123.

32. *WT*, p. 125.

33. *WT*, p. 125.

34. *WT*, p. 113.

35. *WT*, p. 257.

36. *SHB*, p. 406.

37. *SHB*, pp. 406–407.

38. *WT*, p. 104.
39. *Leviathan*, Part I, Chapters 11 and 13.
40. *SHB*, p. 4.
41. *SHB*, p. 447.
42. *WT*, p. 257.
43. *SHB*, p. 23.
44. *SHB*, p. 73.
45. *SHB*, pp. 184–193.
46. *SHB*, p. 192.
47. D. E. Broadbent, *Behaviour*, New York, 1961, p. 84.
48. *SHB*, p. 74.
49. *WT*, p. 113.
50. *WT*, p. 297.
51. *WT*, p. 51.
52. Among the best known books by Arnold Gesell and Frances L. Ilg are *Infant and Child in the Culture of Today*, New York, 1943; *The Child from Five to Ten*, New York, 1946; *Child Development*, New York, 1949. Dr. Benjamin Spock is the author of *The Pocket Book of Baby and Child Care*, New York, 1946.
53. *WT*, p. 138.
54. *WT*, p. 142.
55. *WT*, p. 136.
56. *WT*, p. 132.
57. *WT*, p. 102.
58. *WT*, p. 107.
59. *WT*, pp. 296–297.
60. *WT*, p. 114.
61. *WT*, p. 300.
62. *WT*, pp. 105–106.
63. *SHB*, pp. 239–240.
64. *SHB*, p. 77.
65. *SHB*, p. 68.
66. *SHB*, p. 17.
67. *WT*, p. 125.
68. *SHB*, pp. 77–81.
69. *SHB*, p. 80.
70. *SHB*, p. 13.
71. *SHB*, p. 80.
72. Norman Crowder, whose recently developed "intrinsic programming" is a return to the multiple-choice technique of Pressey's machine but with branching routes to allow flexibility in achieving the desired informational state. See his "On the Differences Between Linear and Intrinsic Programming" (reprinted and abridged) in *Educational Technology*, ed. J. De Cecco, New York, 1963.
73. What follows in the next three paragraphs can be found in greater detail in B. F. Skinner, *The Technology of Teaching*, New York, 1968 (hereafter cited as *TOT*), Chapters 3 and 4.
74. *TOT*, p. 65.
75. *TOT*, p. 64.
76. *TOT*, p. 65.
77. *TOT*, p. 70.
78. *TOT*, p. 67.
79. B. F. Skinner, "Teaching Machines," *Scientific American* CCV (November, 1961): 92.
80. *Loc. cit.*
81. *Ibid.*, p. 95.
82. *Ibid.*, p. 97.
83. *TOT*, p. 97.
84. *TOT*, p. 149.

85. *SHB*, p. 26.
86. *TOT*, p. 61.
87. *TOT*, pp. 108–109.
88. *TOT*, p. 58.
89. See R. S. Brumbaugh and N. M. Lawrence, *Philosophers on Education*, Boston, 1963, Chapter 6.
90. E.g. *TOT*, p. 153.
91. *TOT*, p. 152.
92. See particularly A. G. Oettinger, *Run Computer Run*, Cambridge, Mass., 1969.
93. *The Aims of Education*, New York, 1929, p. 47. See *Philosophers on Education*, Chapter 7.
94. R. I. Evans, *B. F. Skinner: The Man and His Ideas*, New York, 1968, p. 8.
95. *SHB*, p. 36.
96. *SHB*, p. 35.
97. *SHB*, p. 30.
98. *SHB*, p. 31.
99. *SHB*, p. 28.
100. E.g. *SHB*, pp. 7, 8, 17, 21, 23, 35.
101. See M. R. Delgado, *Physical Control of the Mind: Toward a Psycho-Civilized Society*, New York, 1969.
102. *SHB*, p. 31.
103. *SHB*, p. 257.
104. *SHB*, p. 279.
105. *SHB*, p. 216.
106. *SHB*, p. 282.
107. Evans, p. 54.
108. See Theodosius Dobzhansky, *Mankind Evolving*, New Haven, Conn., 1962.

9

Education as Growth: Piaget

Piaget is like Freud in three signal respects: (1) he gives us a new and more detailed image of man; (2) he directs very little of his total energies to educational prescription or recommendation; (3) he leaves his indelible stamp on everyone intelligently concerned with educational theory and practice. While providing little, comparatively speaking, for educational practice, he inspires and even guides those who make the frontiers of educational reform their business.

BACKGROUND

Jean Piaget will be seventy-seven this year (1973). He is Swiss. He was appointed Director of Studies at the Institut Jean-Jacques Rousseau and became codirector of the Institut as a whole in 1932. He has had a series of distinguished associations and appointments with the University of Geneva, with Bleuler in Zurich, at the Sorbonne, and with UNESCO. Finally, since 1955, starting with a grant from the Rockefeller Foundation, he founded his own Centre International d'Epistémologie Génétique. We may begin with this Center as a concrete embodiment of Piaget's life work.

The Center's very name indicates this work—the interest in what Piaget called "genetic epistemology." This term, in a broad way, dominates Piaget's work with children throughout. The basic theme behind Piaget's method goes back to Locke's "seasons" of learning and more directly to the work of Piaget's great predecessor, Rousseau.[1] Rousseau had insisted that we are taught best, at the outset, by nature and by things. He had insisted that verbal understanding comes as an abstraction from more basic contactual and manipulative understanding, which does and must precede it. Hence Emile is not even exposed to books until he is about to enter his teens. For Rousseau, motivation must come from within; values must therefore be concrete at the outset before they ever can be codified into maxims or moral truths. They must thus begin with *amour-propre*, egoistic self-love, as a basis for proceeding to the more sophisticated level of *amour-de-soi,* self-respect. *Amour-de-soi* objectifies oneself for himself and is the basis of any sustained, nonimpulsive concern for others. It follows that the imposition of artifice by adults on nonadults results in deformation of the child. In doing this, the adults refuse to recognize the intrinsically different mentality and spirituality of a child, however much the phases of his growth from infancy to young adulthood may be leading toward a generally recognizable maturity. In Rousseau's view the phases are themselves intrinsically worthy. They follow a scale from physical movement and contact to abstract and symbolic thought. The scale is a temporal series. The urge comes from within the child as he reaches first toward a world of things and only later to any genuinely abstract or social self-realization. If the order is upset, compressed, transformed, or otherwise not allowed to develop, we should not be surprised to find a flawed adult emerging. In particular, for Rousseau, real freedom can hardly appear in such an adult. Freedom is self-reliance. How can there be self-reliance when the self has not properly developed?

Every one of the above convictions is to be found, with some modification, in Piaget. In Piaget, however, they emerge not as doctrine but as a method of study, characterized chiefly by a willingness to let the child's behavior in prescribed situations dictate a set of empirical norms, proper to his age, exhibiting an understandable and cogent series but by no means corresponding to adult conceptions. Since a great deal of Piaget's work tends toward the descriptive and explicative rather than, like Rousseau's, to the prescriptive and expletive, one does not find much talk in Piaget of freedom and the like. What was in Rousseau a reformer's insight becomes in Piaget an instrument of investigation resulting in a unique approach to and understanding of children.

As other moderns are, Piaget is influenced by the doctrine of evolution, particularly in its emphasis on the recapitulation in individual development (ontogeny) of the development of its kind (phylogeny).[2] Contemporary notions of space, time, causality, morality, and so on have emerged from past ones. So also does the individual adult's thought arise through a series of conceptions that follow an analogous order. A child's world, for instance, is animistic, populated by spirits remarkably—though obviously more flexibly—resembling those of our few remaining Stone Age cultures, where animism is the dominant attitude. (Piaget began life as a biologist. "Began life" is almost acceptable hyperbole. He published his first paper at the age of ten, about a pied sparrow. Before he was twenty, he had twenty publications on mollusks to his credit. He had, indeed, been offered the job of curator of mollusks in the Geneva natural history museum by a man who, inspired by his publications, did not know that Piaget was a student in secondary school.)

Aside from earning a Ph.D. in biology with a dissertation on mollusks, Piaget read extensively in several fields, among them philosophy. He was particularly impressed with Bergson, whose own work can fairly be regarded as a revision of Kant's theory of knowledge in the light of post-Darwinian biology. Kant's epistemology largely approached the problem of human knowledge nondevelopmentally.[3] Kant derived from and shared with Rousseau the latter's prizing of the distinctive phases of childhood as well as of the rights of children to live and grow as children. But it did not occur to Kant to deal with the problem of the theory of intelligence in any other way than in its adult form. One of the themes of his difficult *Critique of Pure Reason* is that the ways in which people understand their factual world fall into twelve necessary categories, inescapable hallmarks of their thought processes through which the world is not merely passively received in sensation but is actively rendered meaningful by "the understanding." These categories are themselves derivable from an exhaustive list of logical forms that characterize the basic structure of all reason, whether or not it relates directly to experience. The categories of the understanding are nothing but logical forms insofar as they are conditioned to apply to sensory appearances. These appearances in turn are the roots of all our experience. We shall find that under the guidance of Bergson, Piaget came to the conclusion that the true order is the genetic order not the logical order, that indeed both child development and the historical development of humanity, insofar as it can be made out, is just the opposite of the logical order. In its extreme form this doctrine insists that no logical form is self-recommending without further warrant. If there be a logical order to the world, then the child's recognition of this order will come about by encounter, assimilation, and accommodation—gradually. The security we feel, then, in logical analysis rests in its being a high-order generalization reached by cumulative experience. Logical thought is a late phase in the late arriving process we call "abstraction."

What in Bergson's biologically oriented philosophy led Piaget to this inversion of the Kantian analysis? The dominant work was clearly *Matter and Memory,* published in the year of Piaget's birth, 1896. The precedent *Time and Free Will* (1889) and the following *Creative Evolution* (1907) contained foreshadowings and echoes of the doctrine respectively.[4] In *Matter and Memory* Bergson made a very telling point about perception.[5] Perception, he said, has been misunderstood too long in the theory of knowledge. Epistemologists, including Kant, have assumed that our perceptual powers are primarily the undergirding of our knowledge and that therefore all knowledge arises from the simple stirrings of sense. But the Darwinian theory shows us what perception is by establishing our kinship with all life, even the simplest sentient forms. *Perception is geared to action.* It is acutely practical; primarily it is an instrument of adaptation, arising firmly to meet the challenge of survival and adaptation. The habits so formed under these natural pressures "float up" uncritically to levels of speculation. We do not notice the practical origins of these habits. Detached from their function, they generate spurious problems for metaphysics.

What Bergson was rejecting was a tradition extending back through Locke's insistence that all our knowledge arises from experience and that there are no innate ideas, to Aristotle's conviction that whatever is in the mind must first be in the senses. Bergson's analysis was complex and requires much reflection to comprehend. He skillfully showed that many traditional philosophical problems were pseudoproblems arising from questionable presuppositions. The keystone of these confusions was the assumption that action-oriented perception was the immediate inlet of speculative knowledge.

Piaget's work began, then, with a view to taking a genetic approach to epistemology, starting with the infant and his need and urge to act, manipulate, and discriminate. This approach could have been undertaken at any time in the history of pedagogy—theoretically. But what gave it force was the post-Darwinian conviction that child development might well give us an image of the historical emergence of consciousness, in this way rendering clearer an approach to our understanding of knowledge which history hardly affords. Thus Piaget's work with children, beginning with his connection with the Binet laboratory, was initially undertaken as a means toward laying the foundation for a genetic approach to the problems of epistemology. His first five books, from 1926 to 1932, were directed toward that end, even though their content was the study of childhood thought. The books tend to be sketchy—even though they include the works most frequently printed and reprinted in English; and by Piaget's own account they rely too much on unsupported verbal exchanges. Since, like Rousseau before him, Piaget eventually comes to recognize that there is a great difference between verbal manipulation and a firm grasp of verbal meaning, his work, to be substantial, must dig in deeper to action, deeper into the overt "sensory-motor" functions of which Bergson made so much in *Matter and Memory.*[6] Indeed, from the highly verbal exchanges in the first of these books, *The Language and Thought of the Child,* to the much more matter-of-fact emphasis in the fourth, *The Child's Conception of Physical Causality,* there is a shift in both what is studied (language and thought to ideas of force) and the way in which it is studied (the discussion of "why" as opposed to giving the child manipulable objects and data).[7] The "sensory-motor" phase itself, which Bergson represented as genetically the underpinning of human thought as well as historically its origin, is taken by Piaget, complete with the name Bergson used, for the earliest of these main periods in the growth and emergence of intelligence.

To put the matter in dramatic brevity: Piaget's projected sojourn in child psychology became a career. Nevertheless, he neither forgot his original interests nor regretted or neglected them. Piaget's early interests are at least partly developed in the three-volume *Introduction to Genetic Epistemology,* which it must be understood gave rise to studies of childhood, not merely to theoretical generalization.

THE THEORY OF CHILDHOOD DEVELOPMENT

The dominant fact about Piaget's work is that it is empirical, much of it straight reporting. His published output runs to about the equivalent of seventy-five 250-page books. Efforts of this sort are likely to outrun the author's capacity to create and maintain a static system, especially since such a system, once achieved, might tend to inhibit the impartiality of future observations. Nevertheless, Piaget groped his way early to a major hypothesis about development which grew as it was confirmed and served him as a guide. Its outlines can be stated rather simply. Its subdivisions, however, are another matter. Accounts of similar subject matter written at different times do not quite jibe with one another as to the distinctness and fittedness of subordinate phases. In this respect he is like Plato who used divisions as pedagogical devices rather than as final ontological compartments.

The earliest stage of child development is sensory-motor, running roughly through the first two years of life. It is the hardest of all to describe for obvious reasons. If the first stirrings of intelligence lie here in their most primitive form, an adult intelligence trying to enter that world of the very young infant is sure to arrive at the border with a set of adult categories marvelously unsuited for the task in hand. But without some categories, some idea of what to look for and how to look, the adult cannot enter at all. The only hope is to use categories of broad application, carrying as few presuppositions as possible.

The child in the earliest stage is an assimilator. He takes in food at the material level. He is aware of such things as skin stimuli, light, and sound. He assimilates these as well.[8] But assimilation of this sort is once and for all. It is general "assimilation" that Piaget usually refers to. The nipple is recognized as the same nipple and later the mother as the same mother throughout the repeated instances. The child's principal problem at this stage is one of "accommodation." *The Origins of Intelligence in Children,*[9] a work based almost entirely on close and tireless observations of Piaget's own children, follows the history of assimilation and accommodation through six principal phases. These phases are accumulative, for the most part, rather than competitive. In a partly spatial metaphor, we may say that the child is something of a vacuum, albeit an eager vacuum. He seems to need everything he can get from the "outside" world or supply from "within" himself. Later, especially in the verbal phase, he will discriminate one item from another. He will improve and correct his explanations, discarding an old one for a newer and more logical one or one with more generality in it. But at this stage his behavior patterns do not merely succeed one another; they enclose one another as the problems of coordination are progressively solved. For example, he differentiates his sucking in terms of different ends it serves—nourishment, recognition, pacification, etc.

Piaget evidently regards certain behavioral patterns as hereditarily donated. He even speaks of "hereditary schemata." These schemata (the term originated in epistemology with Kant, who used it to describe the rules whereby thought and sense are joined to form experience) are but the primitive materials for more developed schemata. Thus there is a sucking instinct, but no instinct to suck *thumbs.* Thumb sucking is a differentiation which is acquired through exploration and discovery. Searching or exploring manifests itself in what Piaget calls (after Baldwin) "circular" reactions, since they involve a sequence of motions that are repeated again and again.[10] Later in the first four months the child will develop from positional anticipation of feeding to purely visual cues, setting the stage for the one sensory area in which human beings may be said to have some considerable dominance among fellow animals.

At this point we must notice that although there are unique phases within stages through which the developing child goes, there are recurrent types of operation through which intelligence sophisticates itself and cumulatively develops. Assimilation is but one function of intelligence; indeed it is but one function of an aspect of intelligence. Coordinate with and requiring it reciprocally is accommodation. Adaptive processes have both an assimilative and an accommodative side. There is no such thing as the kind of pure assimilation which Hume seemed to regard as occurring when we merely passively "have" or "receive" sensations. The reason that no such "pure" assimilation exists is that "by incorporating new elements into its earlier schemata the intelligence constantly modifies the latter in order to adjust them to new elements." Indeed Kant's injunction that we cannot *know* things in themselves since we always contribute something from ourselves is not only true for adult intelligence but manifestly true in the growth of the child's intelligence as well. Piaget continues the above passage as follows: "Conversely, things are never known by themselves, since this work of accommodation is only possible as a function of the inverse process of assimilation." [11] Furthermore, Piaget says, adaptation is no isolated or even isolable function of intelligence; the inescapable companion, he continues, of adaptation is organization; organization is "the internal aspect of the cycle of which adaptation constitutes the external aspect. . . . These two aspects of thought are indissociable: it is by adapting to things that thought organizes itself, and it is by organizing itself that it structures things." [12]

Developing intelligence functions both as an agency and as a patiency. It is in some degree passive before things; this passivity enables it to organize itself. Such organization is not a passivity but an activity which generates provisional schemata, and these structure things. Obviously, our attention should be drawn to the schemata, bearing a Kantian name but serving at best only in a semi-Kantian way. Also the foregoing analysis is too general. What actual data lead us to Piaget's account of the circuit between self and world? We shall find that the infant's growth in the cycle between perception and action serves as a compact micromodel for the higher stages in the development of intelligence.

Before we turn to these matters let us summarize the philosophical problems of knowledge, which Piaget resolves by applying them to problems of childhood learning. Hume, exaggerating one side of Locke, had insisted that all of our knowledge arises from sensory impressions. This is adaptation in its most simple form, as we have already noticed—sheer assimilation, based upon and drawn in parallel to physiological assimilation: eating, breathing. Ideas of these impressions form our stock in trade for knowledge, and the various associative groupings in which we find them comprise our knowledge of the outer world of things and causes. Kant, on the other hand, was interested not in this passive assimilation; sensations are the meaningless stuff of experience. He was interested in the way our own perceptual structuring of sensation—an activity that can only be assigned to our faculty of knowledge—gave meaning to the sensations which they did not have themselves. We range our sensations in space and time, where they fill up "space and time" and have location boundaries, here's and there's, now's and then's. In short, we organize our sensory data by definite spatiotemporal rules, which mathematics expresses, and according to definite laws, which science expresses. Speaking crudely, Hume's conception of experience was of our passivity before it. Kant's emphasis was on our activity in giving meaningful form to what is otherwise the kaleidoscope of mere sensory data.

Both the Humean and the Kantian view have much to be said for them. The issue between them is long and difficult. Piaget's position —speaking equally crudely—is that both are right but that they fail to see they are on opposite sides of a cycle. The needed conception here is adaptation, a notion taken, of course, from the Darwinian theory. In its modern biological form, it refers to the capacity of a species, by eliminating those forms which don't adapt, to take some special place in the complex interrelations of their environment. Animals that compete for the same food supply in the same way don't, as a rule, all survive. The same plain with trees can support only *one* long-necked animal, like the giraffe, which eats leaves off the tops of the tree. The long-nosed anteater has developed special claws for ripping off the shell of the palaces of ants and a long tongue for digging deep into passages to ferret them out. The "balance of nature" is embodied in these adaptations. The choice of the biological term here is not accidental for a man who began life as a naturalist. Moreover, it is an exceptionally happy choice: a second glance at adaptation of a species shows that the species did indeed conform to a need for survival and a way of doing it special to itself; a second glance also shows the environment responding to the adaptation. Trees that cannot stand top cropping will vanish before the giraffe. Ants that cannot multiply in goodly numbers may be eliminated as a species by the animal that feeds on them. The disappearance of these species represents alteration, to which the predator species and the rest of the environment must conform or die. The cycle of adaptation in terms of assimilation and accommodation in nature is endless. So also for the long process of maturation that perception and intelligence travel: they develop in a spiral of assimilation-accommodation.

It follows that when we speak of the child's world we do not mean, as we sometimes assume, the one real world in our particular aberration or incomplete view of it as seen through childish eyes. We mean our common world, but as grasped in the child's manner and responding to and therefore *being*—in relation to him—according to that manner. There are no things in themselves, says Piaget, as Kant had said. There are only things-in-relation-to. Our world, then, and the child's world are not related to one another as better to worse, truer to more mythical. At most, if we have kept the outlines of childish comprehension, the relationship is one of more inclusive to less inclusive. In a clear sense, then, the world is just the objective counterpart of some mentality or mentalities, and it mutates with such mentality.

Evolution gave Piaget the concept of adaptation which, when taken into the analysis of perception and intelligence of the developing child, closes the gap between the mind as active and the mind as passive. In doing so, as the foregoing suggests, Piaget also refuses to let perception and intelligence be polarized items in mental growth. One thing is clear about child development: although the development pulses, climbs rapidly, hits plateaus, and so on, it is continuous. Thought is thought in interaction, not stalled in the internalizing or externalizing role. The intimacy between perception and intelligence makes it plausible to suppose that what is said of perception and thought is true of intelligence generally. Indeed Piaget holds a broad view of intelligence and gives us definitions which cover so much that the term loses much of its flavor. He says that intelligence is

> only a generic term to indicate the superior forms of organization or equilibrium or cognitive structuring . . . the most plastic and at the same time the most durable structural equilibrium of behavior . . . essentially a system of living and acting operations . . . the most highly developed form of mental adaptation . . . the indispensable instrument for interaction between the subject and the universe when the scope of this interaction goes beyond immediate and momentary contacts to achieve far reaching and stable relations.[13]

This sweeping declaration gives us more feeling than precision. Intelligence is functional, operational (not in Skinner's sense of the word), and somewhere high up in the scale of flexibility and comprehensiveness. We are then a bit dashed to read on the same page that we are prevented from determining where intelligence starts; it is an ultimate goal, and its origins are indistinguishable from those of sensory-motor adaptation in general or even from those of biological adaptation itself.

What then are we to say of this sensory-motor stage and the intelligence which it nourishes? From one angle of Piaget's vision, intelligence is rooted in the most basic biological adaptation, below which lie only hereditary schemata awaiting differentiation through diversity of object contact. Nonetheless, the tightness of the sensory-motor circuit probably ought to warn us against any firm invocation of the idea of intelligence at this stage. Since we know such sensory-motor actions to be partly the soil from which intelligence springs, we can hardly avoid thinking of the needs of a more articulate, comprehensive, and reflexive mental operation as "already there." Such an implication lies in Piaget's startling (in the light of much of the above) phrase, "sensory-motor intelligence." [14]

"Intelligence" is justified because of the curious restlessness of equilibrium and adaptation in the child. In order to avoid teleological language (why?), says Piaget, adaptation must be defined in terms of "equilibrium between the action of the organism on the environment and vice versa." Adaptation is simply the "equilibrium between assimilation and accommodation." [15]

What Piaget directs our attention to is equilibrium. He is curiously reticent about indicating another factor: while the phases of growth themselves may be understood as equilibrations, with subequilibrations within, the phases are not *permanently* self-stabilizing but are followed by more complex equilibria which supervene and modify, largely replace, or absorb the earlier ones. "Gradually" is a word that appears everywhere in Piaget. He wants no thought of a leap from one phase to another, nor indeed a lock-step passage of all developed resources—however gradually—to parallel new phases in every department of mental growth. Nonetheless, his treatment of growth is saturated with the clear evidence that equilibria are replaced in the growth years by gropings and experimentations that rightly should be identified as disequilibria. Plainly Piaget is directed by his habit of thinking in terms of continuity but is perfectly aware of the characteristic inherent instability in growth—what we have dubbed "restlessness." We shall shortly see that perception and intelligence are best differentiated in terms of the types of errors to which they are prone. But they may also be differentiated, genetically commingled as they are, in terms of their aims. Here Piaget willingly turns to the teleological language whose avoidance led him to use the word "equilibrium" in the first place. Perception, habit, and memory, elementary cognitive functions,

> extend it [equilibrium] in the direction of present space (perceptual contact with distant objects) and of [temporally] short range reconstructions and anticipations. Only intelligence, capable of all its detours and reversals by action and thought, tends toward an *all-embracing equilibrium* by aiming at the assimilation of the whole of reality and the accommodation of it to action, which it thereby frees from its dependence on the initial *hic et nunc*.[16]

At most, then, "equilibrium" refers to a balance within the stage itself but not necessarily of the stage within the stages of a growing person. True to his Bergsonian convictions, Piaget believes that even the highest equilibria are action oriented, just as perception is: "intellectual operations whose highest form is found in logic and mathematics, [these] constitute genuine actions, being at the same time, something produced by the subject and a possible experiment in reality." [17] The last phrase is reminiscent as well of Kant's insistence that the categories through which we understand have meaning only in relation to a possible experience and cannot be used by pure reason, which would like to pass beyond all such bounds.

For all the stages (three of them) of growth and their subordinate phases there are several constants, all originating in biological adaptation and all eventually modeled on it: (1) assimilation and accommodation, the counterpoised elements of adaptation; (2) the equilibrium between the two; (3) the joint growth of perception and intelligence, with emphasis shifting from the former to the latter, but by way of supplement—noncompetitively; (4) the plainly exhibited but often unnamed shift through which one equilibrating pattern is superimposed on another in a definite sequence (see pages 221–236); (5) a closely related constant, which should be regarded almost as a specification or even definition of (4): what Piaget calls a "décalage." This is the use of a type of pattern or cognitive structure in some stage for other aspects of perception and action in the same stage ("horizontal décalage") or from one stage to the next ("vertical décalage"). These temporal displacements, as one translator calls them (the word means literally "unwedging" or "setting off"), are thus essentially the transfer of schemata.[18] (6) Lastly there is organization, the interior aspect of what appears as adaptation, when it is viewed from the side of the external environment.

THE STAGES OF GROWTH

In the main there are three stages of growth between birth and age fifteen; (1) the sensory-motor stage, from birth to two years; (2) the stage of conceptual intelligence and concrete operations, roughly from two to eleven years; and (3) the last stage, formal operations, from eleven to fifteen years of age.[19] The actual ages at which the stages occur, like those of the phases within them, vary a bit, but the stages are well defined nonetheless.

THE SENSORY-MOTOR STAGE

We shall follow the early phases of growth in one of Piaget's best balanced and most comprehensive works, *The Construction of Reality in the Child*. Piaget's observations could hardly be more intimate: they are of his own children, Jacqueline, Lucienne, and Laurent. Since the aspects of development observed in this book are rather hard and factual, namely the emergence of the concepts of object, space, time, and causality—in short, the Newtonian universe which even in its simplest forms serves us so well for practical purposes—we will also want to follow the child in terms of his less intellectual and less vigorous side. For this we will use *Play, Dreams, and Imitations in Childhood*.[20]

Clearly, the first stabilization in a world that William James described as a "buzzing, blooming confusion" is that of objects. The child finds the nipple and/or the thumb, then loses them. As early as the second day he searches for the breast "that escaped him." On the third day he searches systematically for it, and by the beginning of the second month the same thing happens vis-à-vis the thumb. And in this same month comes the expectation of similar experiences from similar things, e.g. a rattled tea kettle presented again silently is turned toward repeatedly, in expectation of a noise. The place where a picture was last seen is attended to until the picture appears again.[21] Plato's fundamental form of "similarity" thus surfaces early in a child's action—but primarily as a mode of action, of course.

The young infant in his earliest phase of the imitation-play-dream continuum wakes at night, one day old, and hearing other babies crying, raises his own cry. Other noise stimuli do not provoke this reaction.[22] By the middle of the third month he imitates sounds which he spontaneously generates himself, but he does not imitate sounds he hears but has never made himself. Movement imitation follows a similar course. Later, at three to six months, novel movements are "prehended" and "assimilated," after a period of responsive but nonimitative actions of an unfamiliar sort.[23] Sometime after six months a new phase emerges. The infant invents a sound and giggles with delight when it is imitated by someone else. This imitation may be regarded as socialization of emotions and also as a recognition of the similarity relation. A seen and grasped object is dropped and searched for as if the touch had been a learning action. Later—around nine months—a glimpse of a part of the lost object will serve to identify it.[24] Piaget calls this "reconstitution of invisible totalities." It might safely be regarded as a tangible root of the symbolic capacity that is to appear later; in genuine symbolism the arbitrary sign stands for what is signified rather than the part's standing for the whole. The child now is beginning to move from imitation of movement with parts of himself he can see to imitation with parts he can feel, e.g. from imitation of hand movements to imitation of eye movements. Around ten or eleven months, volunteered eye blinking is "imitated" in the child by opening and closing of mouth or hands. Not until fourteen months does a straight imitation of opening and closing of eyes occur in Lucienne.[25]

We pause here to note that the sequences Piaget discovers he discovers repeatedly, but they do not always "date" the same and they may be impeded along the way by some idiosyncratic development. Piaget thinks, for example, that Lucienne might have learned direct eye-movement imitation earlier had she not fallen into the mouth-movement substitute for eye opening and closing. What is important is the emergence of certain general skills and expressiveness in a sequence of gradual growth, each stage, as Aristotle said of the *telos* of nature, being "for the sake of the next."

Early play and imitation are closely related but distinguishable. They seem to have an undergirding of desire for constancy, the constancy between motor action and sensory response, between noise invented and noise repeated by the experimenter. The latter is in a sense the very opposite of imitation. It is a pleasure, in the child, of finding "the world" imitating him. The desire for constancy also shows up in the child's delight in the presence of a familiar face or access to a persistent object. This, at any rate, seems to be the trajectory of the sensory-motor stage: the desire for constancy (a particular form of equilibrium) that brings the child and his world into ever more complex harmony, each as both active and passive.

Roughly, this stage of two years falls into six phases, with imitation or appropriate use of "hereditary schemata" (such as crying when others do) as the first. In phase two the child will imitate "responsively," so to speak, only in answer to an imitation of something he's done.[26] In phase three the infant definitely imitates, beginning with voluntary motions of his own that he can see and later proceeding to those which he cannot—eye motions, sticking out tongue, etc. It is also the phase at which the child experiences what Piaget calls "Groos' pleasure of being the cause." The fourth phase, from roughly eight to twelve months, is marked by both playful use of learned schemata— routines of manipulation—and perfection of them for their own sake. Thus the first stirrings of means-end discovery arise. The well-rehearsed routine can be subordinated to more elaborate ones (an example is removing an obstacle in order to grasp the object behind it). Phase five involves routines of a much more complex character, genuine control of means-ends relationships. Piaget experiments successfully with breaking complex movements down into lesser parts that would please any Skinnerian. Moreover the child himself experiments with discovering new means. Phase six is that of "deferred imitation"; whole routines may be imitated the day after they are witnessed—the tantrum of a visiting child, a skeletonized imitation of a sibling's bath routine, and so on. There is the making here, Piaget feels, of representation and language, since language must be the kind of indicator which can be "on tap" at any time and abstractly represents or designates what one may later wish to use. Analogously, the object is brought under control in such a way that its properties are remembered and exploited.

In the early phases the infant is content to let the object be a series of discontinuous appearances and to show some anticipation of its re-

turn at the point where it disappeared. But by phase three the child
looks at the vanishing point and experiments with a brief searching
action (where did it go?) instead of merely *waiting* (when will the interesting thing happen again?). Action is beginning to take over. A
part of an object now stands for the whole object, but not—Piaget
thinks—as complete, rather as being made as it emerges. For example
the infant removes a blanket to see a partially obscured object better,
but does not remove it from a completely obscured object, even if
the latter is felt through the blanket. The fourth phase further bears
out Bergson's contention that perception is a guide to action, but in a
Piagetian form, namely that the development of action is a development of perception. Here the child will use action to reveal an object
he has seen hidden. But he always returns to the disclosure routine;
even if he observes the object being hidden elsewhere he will not disclose it there, but go back to lift the cover where it first disappeared!
In the fifth phase the child of thirteen or fourteen months goes to any
place he has seen the object disappear, but if he has not watched the
procedure of its being obscured he does not search. The "unobserved
displacement" cannot be imagined. The object is solid enough, but its
context of action to disclose is still pretty rigid and pretty *learned,*
rather than experimental. In the last phase, say at nineteen or twenty
months, the object is detachable from context and is searched for per-
sistently and imaginatively.

One further matter of interest to any teacher is: What is happening
to the self as it is conscious of itself and others? These too seem to be
linked with constancy. Jacqueline, at twenty-three months, regards her
image in the mirror as somehow some other person, not herself, and
her sister (thirty-one months) in a new bathing suit as not her sister.
At thirty-five months Jacqueline is "afraid" of a photograph of herself.
At thirty-nine months, two different red insects are regarded as the
same insect at different times.[27] All slugs are referred to as "the slug,"
apparently in different manifestations. Questions like "How could the
same slug get so fast from there to here?" evidently involve a physical
control of the universe in excess of the very young child's understanding. Thus a certain price is paid for stability, for the reliability of objects (by the way, how would *you* tell one red insect from another?)
that lingers well into stage two.

THE STAGE OF PREOPERATIONAL REPRESENTATION AND CONCRETE OPERATIONS

In his analysis Piaget deals with infant growth in conception of
objects, space, time, causality, force, imitation, play, and dreams.
We have chosen imitative play as the parameter of feeling in the in-

fant, and object synthesis as the cognitive parameter. The developing cycle of assimilation of what is perceived and the accommodation to it revealed in action comprise, in Piaget's terms, adaptation. But "adaptation" here has a somewhat passive ring to it, and the child's actions, which are in a strong sense the primary data for analysis, imply something more than mere adjustment. Adjustment is not a technical term in Piaget. We use it to refer to the compliant aspect of a child's development. For Piaget, there is a generative, creative, novel-reactive aspect as well. Piaget is suspicious of philosophical quarrels about freedom, teleology, creativity, and the like, and he usually avoids the terms. He wants to keep the psychic distance that characterizes the good observer. His humane sensitivity to these things is chiefly wrapped in the word "organization." This is the complementary notion to adaptation. It refers, a bit ambiguously, both to the child's view of the world in perception and conception and to his use of the world in action. If there is any sense in the notion of the world-as-it-simply-is, this is—at best—a late notion in the development of intelligence. The early concept of the world is of the world-as-it-is-in-relation. There is no object-as-is, but only object-as-it-is-capable-of-being-understood-by-me-currently. In the same stage we shall follow the increase of the datum "me," which thus far has been unemphasized. The reason is clear: there is relatively little of the definite "me" through the first stage.

What is striking in the second stage is the rise of self-consciousness. Our approach to this second stage will be to emphasize the subject-object/self-and-world differentiation as it matures. Even in the first two years we have seen strong signs of this differentiation. The case of being able to imitate hand movements before eye movements shows the shift from the child's early dependence on the body as observed to the more controlled concept of the body as lived. This is a shift in subjective subtlety. Yet it is a shift away from egocentrism, says Piaget. In the introduction to *The Construction of Reality in the Child* he writes a powerful passage that might well be memorized by any philosopher dealing with the problems of self and self-consciousness:

> Through an apparently paradoxical mechanism whose parallel we have described *à propos* of the egocentrism of thought of the older child, it is precisely when the subject is most self-centered that he knows himself the least, and it is to the extent that he discovers himself that he places himself in the universe and constructs it by virtue of that fact. In other words, ego-centrism signifies the absence of both self-perception and objectivity, whereas acquiring possession of the object as such is on a par with the acquisition of self-perception. . . .

> The transition from chaos to cosmos . . . is brought about
> through an elimination of egocentrism. . . .[28]

These words would have been espoused heartily by Rousseau. Strike "possession of the object" and put in "understanding of other persons," and you have a rich band of thought that extends from Kierkegaard to Erik Erikson and Richard Jones. Self-consciousness has a good start by the end of the second year, for at this point the child has language, mobility, and manipulative powers in considerable control. The on-coming stage, two to eleven years, is variously treated by Piaget. Piaget sometimes splits it into two subdivisions—two to seven and seven to eleven—and sometimes into three—two to four, four to seven, seven or eight to eleven or twelve.[29] In the latter case he designates the subdivisions *preconceptual, intuitive,* and the phase of *concrete operations* respectively. Piaget has done less work in the two phases preceding "concrete operations" than anywhere else, but the observations are highly suggestive. What the child brings to his understanding of the world is his heightened self-awareness. Three types of explanation occur in these years before seven or eight: artificialism, animism, magic. Each is anthropomorphic. The child has discovered his parents' efficiency in producing things he wants: [30] "natural phenomena are very early related by the child to adult activity." The twenty-month-old child already attributes atmospheric mist to Daddy's pipe; the thirty-five-month old says of dawning light, "They've put the light on outside." Agency is human agency; mechanical cause doesn't exist. But as the child's world widens, agency may become more remote. The forty-nine-month-old child experiments with the idea of babies as coming from the woods or a shop; sixty-three months suggests a factory. Sixty-seven months has a giant moving the sun from behind a mountain.

This last remark carries us over into animism, the conception of the world as invested with psyches, spirits. The sun drops down into the lake to bathe and is hiding, for the child of forty months. Sixty-two months makes a Greek remark: "Look at the trees over there. They're alive, because they're moving." [31] But as she is getting close to seven, Jacqueline in one ten-day period claims that the sun and the moon don't feel or know anything, that the sun "knew when it was fine," and that thrown rocks don't know when they are rolling. At fifty-one months, the car, slowed by a herd of cattle, "knows what it has to do." This animistic phase is one of the most striking features of child mentality. Technically, it is supposed to be replaced as maturation proceeds, but who has not seen a man kicking a flat tire or himself cursed the rain?

The previous two manifestations of anthropomorphism are interpretive, explanatory. To this extent they are mental adaptations resulting from assimilating data and accommodating them to already existing understanding, but there is an organizational outcome which returns to the world in the form of action. This action can be self-directed, like that of Jacqueline who, at four and a half, wants to like chimney sweeps but is afraid of them and invents magic routines to bring about the change in herself! Or she invents another routine to make the soup taste good. And at five and a half she devises a somewhat grander scope for her powers: she causes the dark and the light of day to come.

But nonmagical manipulations in the period from two to seven have a curious inflexibility about them. And just how different the child's comprehension of the world is has to be seen to be believed. Suppose we put the same number of beads in two jars of identical size and shape. The four- or five-year old then sees them put into jars of unequal shape. Even though he sees that no beads have been added or subtracted, he will hold that the taller container now has more in it because it is taller, or that it has fewer because it is thinner. By repeated changes of the dimension the child will "deduce conservation." Piaget dubs this period (four to seven) intuitive, presumably because the child does not reflect much, though he can be made to. Even up to seven years, a child will say that a box of wooden beads, most of which are brown and a few of which are white, has more brown beads than wooden ones, the intuitive "more" fastening on the brown-white comparison rather than on the class-inclusion relationship. He is narrowly "centering," in Piaget's vocabulary. Similar following of rigid routines can be seen in the child's inability before four or five to predict the order in which a serially disappearing group of three objects will reappear if they are brought back the way they went; and not until about seven can intuition be "articulated" to the point where a series of three balls, running in a circular path of which half is hidden, can be expected to reappear in reverse order if their motion is reversed while they are in the hidden part of the path.

This inflexibility is understood as the outcome of schemata which are image representations of a simplified sort in the order that the child focuses on his experience or has it presented to him. He cannot, without training or development, reverse the operation he has learned, even though he can transfer the schema of one instance to another. And his preference for one particular schema, e.g. "tall" as suitable for "more," will sometimes be carried to great lengths. So far as we know, Piaget does not put the point in the following way, but the presentation employs his concepts and is faithful to his observations: The child of four to seven has flexibility in exploration and manipulation, inventiveness in explanation of natural phenomena, linguistic suppleness in expression. But he is tied to a conservative idea of agency as anthropomorphic and methods of grouping and ordering that stray but little beyond what has been successful in the past. His methods and some presuppositions are not easily challenged, even by what are manifestly —from the adult point of view—infirming or disconfirming experiences. In short, the child's egocentricity persists in the form of reading himself and his preferences into a physical nature which he will discover later is indifferent to them.

What about moral development? In *The Moral Judgment of the Child* Piaget gives us a picture of the child's sense of morality.[32] He develops it as a sense of rules and follows it as it is reflected in the child's attitude toward games. Not until about three does the child even have much sense that play can be ordered by rules. Up to that point—in general—he makes up temporary rules and conforms or possibly "rebels," but with little sense of what or why a rule is. Around three there is clear imitation and intent to imitate, even a sense of properly imitating. But the child makes moves or plays in a way that betrays his egocentric impulses, usually not realizing that he is "going against the rules," following preferences and writing himself into the objective (or at least intersubjective) situation. The genuine social sense does not appear until seven or eight years, the last phase of stage two.

The culmination of the second stage runs from seven or eight to eleven or twelve. Piaget calls this the phase of "concrete operations." It is the point at which the child not only begins to understand moral reciprocity (as opposed to moral obedience) but can control his action in accordance with that ideal. He has not only images that he imposes on the world but conceptual grasp as well. This stage is remarkably close to Locke's description of how any sensory input yields us only particulars, e.g. a particular obtuse triangle. Only by transcending the localized peculiarities of any single image of a triangle—obtuse, equilateral, acute, etc.—do we come to the concept of triangle. So also the child in this somewhat misleadingly called concrete-operational phase disengages himself from particular sequences as given to how they must be. Before age seven (roughly) he could not envisage that balls *A*, *B*, and *C*, halfway around a circular route, would be in reverse order when the motion was reversed, but with *B* maintaining a constant relation—"between"—to *A* and *C*. Some time after age seven he climbs to this new level of understanding. We notice that the reciprocity of these envisaged and observed states corresponds neatly to the reciprocity required for social behavior. Piaget rarely preaches, but there is an implied lesson here that cannot be emphasized too much: Not only should we expect only a gradual and tested meaningfulness for the cumulative emergence of mature reason, we should also not expect the emergence of intelligence to be sound or significant unless accompanied by its moral counterpart. Indeed, there is a famous citation from Piaget that applies here: "Logic is the morality of thought, just as morality is the logic of action." [33] Piaget explicitly believes that even at this relatively early age (well within our six-year primary school), schools should exploit these social functions, tied as they are to intellectual development, in joint projects that depend on the exchange of ideas. [34]

Piaget's view of the child of seven is that he recapitulates in his own development the development that underlies much of Western thought.

> We can, however, refer to the striking resemblances between the beginnings of rational thought in the child of from seven to ten and in the Greeks. We find, for example, explanation by identification of substances (stars which are produced by air or clouds, air and earth coming from water, etc.), by atomism resulting from this identification and the use of the ideas of condensation and rarefaction, and even the exact explanation of certain movements by reaction of the air (ἀντιπερίστασις) used by Aristotle. [35]

We may, he goes on to say,

> assume the same genetic mechanisms which account for the development of the thought of the child of today were in action also in the minds of those who, like the pre-Socratics, were just emerging from mythological and pre-logical thought. . . .
>
> . . . We shall therefore adopt Jung's central idea of primitive symbolic thought independent of the mechanisms of repression and censorship. [36]

What we can extract from this comparison is the naturalness of certain modes of explanation. If it is used to deprecate Greek civilization, we might then have either to reject Piaget's implicit commitment to the parallel character of moral and intellectual development or else deprecate the Greek moral insights as well, showing how ours are superior. The prospect is not irresistibly tempting. An even more useful surmise is that the growth of intelligence means the absorption of older and earlier forms of thought, rather than the destruction or rejection of them. This is certainly the lesson to be learned by watching how the child develops his concept of force. This development consists in a gradual depersonification of the physical world, which—in a sense—enables him to personify himself. In previous phases of the second stage, the child's self-consciousness took the form of seeing spirits like himself in the world about him. Now his self-consciousness gradually loosens its hold on this egocentric self-consciousness and moves toward what Piaget calls "self-perception." In the passage from

The Construction of Reality in the Child quoted on page 225, he says, "Egocentrism signifies the absence of both self-perception and objectivity, whereas acquiring possession of the object as such is on a par with the acquisition of self-perception." [37]

We can hardly follow the phase from age seven to eleven through all its manifestations; Piaget's work here is vast. But we can profitably follow the above themes in some representative observations and see how they fit into the category of assimilation and accommodation. A child of six and a half says of the sun that "he wants to give us light"; another six-and-a-half-year old says that clouds "feel cold, so they walk," and an eight-year old clings to the same idea.[38] Still another eight-year old says they are alive. In general, the shift is from anthropomorphism to animism, a more sophisticated conception. Physical factors now begin to appear as more or less deterministic, even as the entities they control are not wholly deanimized, in the movement of clouds, heat, air pressure, or wind.[39] A backward child of nine still talks of the sun's wanting to do things, but for the normal nine-year old, clouds, stars, lightning are related to one another without anthropomorphic or animistic cement; and for an eight-and-a-half-year old the sun "goes by itself." [40] But the animistic interpretation retreats slowly. The movement of flowing water is the outcome of a force in the water, a push, drive, or thrust, sometimes from the other water behind it. Only around ten or eleven does the general conception of "heavy"—so directly seen in a dropped pebble—also cover the disguised weight as exhibited in the downflow of a stream.[41]

Piaget summarizes as follows: "The idea of force is of internal origin and it is by transference that we attribute force to the things around us," as Maine de Biran had urged.[42] But Piaget stresses that this is only true from the point of view of behavior. The trouble with de Biran's presentation of this matter is that it assumed an intuition of the "I" as causally effective, and from this there is an attribution of causal effectivity to external things. Piaget agrees with critics who point out that the "I" is not intuited but only reached by reflection. As a matter of fact, Piaget says, "The 'I' is slowly built up through childhood rather than immediately given at the outset of conscious experience." [43] No such intuition is present if we keep the point of view of "consciousness" rather than that of "behavior." Nor is there any transfer.

There is simply assimilation of the world by the ego "I"; and there is consciousness of the product of this assimilation before there is any consciousness of the "I" as a seat of force. Only by means of a derivative process does the mind [!] come to dissociate the "I" from the world around it, and in the measure that this dissociation takes

> place. . . . consciousness of self is the result, as it were, of carving consciousness out of the object. . . . this object is conceived by means of motor schemas which the conscious subject precisely does not localize in the "I". . . .[44]

The entire growth of the child can be interpreted as a reaching out into the world: "Originally the child puts the whole content of consciousness on the same plane and draws no distinction between the "I" and the external world." [45] This is what Piaget, somewhat misleadingly for American ears, calls "realism," the conviction that everything is equally real. From this position the child moves to (1) objectivity, the ability to realize what comes from oneself and what comes from an external reality; (2) reciprocity, the capacity to extend equal value (not just as important but also as true) to other points of view (the child up to eight may persist in saying that the clouds or the stars are "following us," never bothering to ask whether or not they also follow other people going in the opposite direction); and (3) relativity, the understanding that nothing the mind isolates has independent existence; that "heavy" and "light" are not qualities but relations depending on reference; clouds move entirely because of the wind external to them. They are not substantial things with power within.

The implications of these developments for the moral development of the child have been partly touched on. Egocentricity ideally turns into genuine self-perception and world perception, both of which it facilitates by dispelling itself. One interesting phenomenon remains to be mentioned. Along about ten or eleven, the child begins to use the language of obligation to get at the idea of necessity. The wheel *must* turn when turned; water *ought* to move when released; heavy things *have* to drop—their heaviness makes them. But after this age, after the withdrawal of animation and artificialistic and magical accounts from the course of nature, the child is left with the generality of laws. Nonetheless, he is at a loss to explain the necessity. Piaget says that "moral necessity becomes logical necessity." [46] This is an easily misunderstood claim. First, "logical necessity" does not mean, for Piaget, a basic, inescapable set of premises from which all else can be deduced. He means the rational feeling we have that not only are there general laws that describe all types of physical events, but that these laws themselves must cohere, be comprehensive and on principle unifiable into one logical order. What he is saying is that when one withdraws will and emotion from his perceptions of nature, these then become properly invested in the "I." All that is left is logical order as the ideal of generality. We may add to this the child's knowledge, by now, of the moral objectivity, moral reciprocity, and moral relativity of the social world, analogous to those of the perceived world.

THE STAGE OF FORMAL OPERATIONS

The second stage was called that of concrete operations. We have followed the child's concept of force and self principally through that period, and thus have illustrated but little Piaget's reason for the name he chose. Much of his work was done with physical concepts, such as weight, size, and number. The work focused on basic notions of conservation, reciprocity, transitivity of these constants. Speaking briefly of these, we may say that the child pieces his progress together a bit at a time. He passes from the flow of water and the fall of the pebble to the common idea of weight, but not until he has begun to get some idea of conservation. At seven the child will recognize the conservation of material in two bits of clay made into very different shapes, but the same child will deny conservation of weight up until nine or ten years old. And when this notion is gained, conservation of volume may still be denied up until eleven or twelve.[47] The question of volume is particularly difficult, and an hour's reading of the latter part of *The Child's Conception of Geometry* [48] will raise a serious question in any reader's mind as to whether or not the (to the authors at any rate) highly attractive development of the "new math" is proceeding on good experimental grounds. The point of this observation, and the sample of facts from the wealth of work in this area which Piaget and others have done, is to indicate that a kind of equilibrium of equilibria must underlie the formal stage of eleven to fifteen. There must be equilibrium of assimilation and accommodation to what is in hand—these clouds, that water, this cause, and so on. Or maybe clouds, water, causes, though these generalizations are more easily named than achieved. But now, what about clouds, rain, and water jointly? It is one thing to have good generalization within each group, but what about generalizations about them collectively, e.g. the water that cools the wind which causes the clouds to rain? Is it true that if A is heavier than B and B is heavier than C, A is heavier than C? The root of the discovery of the answer lies only in experience, evidently, and does not swiftly come. At eight a child will not agree that two weights that are equal to a third are equal to one another. The world is still whimsical about weights (not about amount of material, we saw). Up until eleven or twelve a "particular logical form is still not independent of its concrete context." [49]

By eleven or twelve the child is getting into a position where he can transfer schemata of relations and relations of relations to new situations. Transitivity, reversibility of relations, and more complex kinds of "seriations"—i.e. groups of organizing groups—are open to him. Complex seriations that require category shifts are not available, e.g. $A + B = B$, where A is a subset of B. A tangible case of this relation would be the problem of the wooden beads, most of which are white and a few brown. We have seen that even up to seven the child will say there are more brown than wooden beads. Between seven and eleven he can see "wooden" as the more inclusive class, to which the subset *A* (white) adds nothing in number. The point is that he sees this *concretely*. Between eleven and fourteen he moves to the generalized symbolic systems. The generalized statement would be:

$$A \text{ is a subset of } B$$
$$C \text{ is a subset of } B$$
$$C \text{ is not a subset of } A$$
$$A > C > O$$
$$\therefore B > A$$

Six years old sees that $A > C$ and maintains illogically that $A > B$. He cannot evidently compose the uniform class "wooden," which is not so evident as "white" and "brown," out of those two classes. Furthermore, he apparently tends to think of "greater than" as an attached property rather than a transferable relation. He is passing from the world of the actual to the expanded universe of the possible. The early phases of the transition from concrete-operational to formal-operational understanding—eleven or twelve to twelve or thirteen—are very like those from preoperational to concrete operational. Preoperational thought (two to six or seven) is characterized by a desire to schematize, but with somewhat whimsical results. Yet the whimsies in general can be referred back to egocentrism. Several instances of seeing slugs result in their all being manifestations of the same slug. Mountains, on the other hand, change as you go. Shadows thrown in a room are mysteriously the outcome of the activities of shadows outside the room. What happens is (to use terms that Piaget does not) a stability (equilibrium) of the image which is the outcome of drawing several image instances into one preconcept which is then rectified into a concept proper, albeit a "concrete" one—that is, one whose range is confined to the actual. The preoperational child is caught in the discontinuities of existence. His first major effort is toward an equilibrium that renders the world reliable, and success does not come all at once. His thought is time-bound in two ways: discontinuities of order at first overwhelm his capacity to assimilate and hence to accommodate. Secondly, he cannot reverse a line of thought, return to the starting point, or hold several elements in his reasoning before him in a single *Gestalt*. Youngsters between two and six (and later too!) get into fierce arguments partly because they can't remember the issue or proposals they made at the outset. The transition is effected by just the separation of the me and the what-happened-in-my-experience from one another. With this disengagement from the world the child gains, as we have seen, both self-perception and world perception. The disengagement is not in any sense a withdrawal; it is, if you like, a disentanglement. The transition from concrete operations to formal operations is very like this, save that now the child is no longer bound to actuality. Before, he was time-bound, later concrete-bound. In terms Piaget might not care for, there is a further transcendence, by way of the understanding of form, which opens the realm of the possible.

We are obviously not to suppose that somehow the child's imagination has not been functioning up to this point or that there has been no make-believe or fantasy or dreaming. But these functions, so closely connected in the young child with the sense of reality, have gradually become separated from that sense. Extension beyond the actual here is thus neither flight from the actual nor an alternate to it, but an explanation through and beyond the concrete structures which are embodied in the actual. It represents also a new stage of the power to predict and control experience. It represents the re-establishment of the ego's identity as agency in the world. This equilibrium "surpasses by far the equilibrium of concrete thought." [50]

The new hallmark of the eleven-to-fifteen stage is the power of abstract thought, formal operations, and hence an advance of control from the actual to the possible but still under the guidance of rigorous thought. The child before the age of seven needed freeing from egocentricity. With the freedom comes the rational, concrete-operational phase. This child is confined to the actual, however. The passage to adolescence is thus a new freedom, freedom from the concrete. We recall that the main distinction between perception and intelligence is the confinement of the former to a relatively short span of time and a sensorily based given. Adolescence is the flowering of intelligence beyond perception.

What of the inner life and life in relation to others? It is a platitude to say that although there may be a great new equilibrium of thought, there is also at least a risk of disequilibrium in emotional growth. We are nearing the end of Piaget's splendid resources, but he is neither unknowing nor mute on these matters. We turn to a joint work with Bärbel Inhelder for help here.[51]

It is precisely the liberation from the actual that lies at the heart of the emotional problems. The egocentricity of previous phases is what might be called perhaps not a constant, but a rhythmically recurring orientation. It characterizes any phase at the advent; as the phase develops, equilibrium is approached and a new objectivity and a new subjectivity jointly materialize. How does the egocentricity of adolescence function? In terms more warm than Inhelder and Piaget would like, the surge of power that comes through the liberation of intelligence from perception is like heady wine. There is a

> failure to distinguish between the ego's new and unpredicted capacities and the social and cosmic universe to which they are applied. In other words, the adolescent goes through a phase in which he attributes an unlimited power to his own thoughts so that the dream of a glorious future or of transforming the world through Ideas (even if this idealism takes a materialistic form) seems to be not only fantasy but also an effective action which in itself modifies the empirical world.[52]

The passage is a reminder of Bergson's insistence on the action-oriented character of perception. And we recall further Piaget's conception of intelligence as ranging beyond the domain—as well as the sheer givenness—of the actual. Is it too much to say that the powers of intelligence which reveal the domain of the possible and the general are in disequilibrium, provided no actualization of them is undertaken? The suggestion perhaps speculates a bit beyond what would seem secure to Inhelder and Piaget, but it is important to notice also that adolescence is a time of increased physical strength, coordination, and what can only be called physical ambition. There is a superabundance of energy, typically, which will not fit into old patterns.

Another factor is at work in the described equilibrium. Piaget calls the decompression of the egocentric features of any phase "decentering." In the case of the adolescent gregariousness materializes in the form of joining action groups, political groups, summer camps (more likely European than American). Within these groups there is a notorious tendency toward conformity, but there is also an "intellectual decentering." If you test a theory against the theories of others, you may discover its "fragility." These groups are, in a sense, transitional, however:

> The focal point of the decentering process is the entrance into the occupational world or the beginning of serious professional training. The adolescent becomes an adult when he undertakes a real job. It is then that he is transformed from an idealistic reformer into an achiever. In other words, the job leads thinking away from the dangers of formalism back into reality.[53]

In short, the new reality principle has two spokesmen, the test of other minds and the discipline of the practical. Parallel to these developments and indeed standing on the affective aspect of them is the enhancement of the "interindividual" feelings by the appearance of social feelings—e.g. feelings about large groups and institutions. Piaget speaks of a study conducted with A. M. West showing that the relatively narrow scope of the younger child's (up through eleven) cognitive reach is devoid of feeling about nationality, patriotism, and the like.[54] His feelings cover family, residence, language, and some customs. But these all have an immediacy about them that is analogous to that of concrete operations with tangible things.

CRITICAL EVALUATION

In an essay on Freud, Jerome Bruner points to Freud's power as dramatist and as deepener of our sense of human nature, rather than as theorizer with whom we must agree or disagree. Piaget is in a similar position. If the vision he gives us were to be estimated in terms of diversity of children studied, for example, we might find it hard to believe that he had done much beyond studying the social embryology of knowledge through a peculiarly limited period of time. Thousands of pages of Piaget's work are provided by his close observation of just his three children. They are a tiny segment in a small country of a bourgeois segment of a vast stratum of children. And surely the humaneness of their father has meant at least a kind of womb or cocoon in which almost idealized developments occur. Think of the familiocentric life of the Swiss, the paternalism of a country which has long been a standard bearer of freedom yet extended the federal franchise to women only in 1971. One is reminded of that highly provincial segment of rather high-strung Viennese ladies and others very like them who helped to propel Freud toward far-reaching theories. But Freud had male patients and non-Viennese and he searched history for confirmations of his theories. So also Piaget worked with other children in Switzerland and in France as well. Further, he took pains to work with some retarded children, even as Freud extended his analyses to the "psychopathology of everyday life." Yet in the end, the sample is pitifully small and can hardly be said to satisfy the normal demands of a theory of such generality. It is true that in physics only a handful of molecules have been studied and from such study a vast molecular theory has sprung. But molecules are (relatively) simple creatures and reasonably well behaved. Neither of these guarantees of stability is present in persons; indeed, quite the contrary is the case.

We must, accordingly, value Piaget on other than scientific grounds in spite of the many canons of science which he follows: close observation, recording of exceptions, tentativeness and revisability of theory. His art lies in the rare intuition for discovering the essential, so that a small sample is widely significant. Aristotle spoke of great tragedy as aiming for the "universal in man." Piaget has just that capacity to discover the universal. He provides us insight that resonates with our memories of our own childhood and of our own children. He brings the puzzling facts about children that confront any teacher into rational order. It is not too much to say that one can hardly imagine a teacher reading Piaget who is not humanized in the process, although a teacher presented with the subriot that characterizes ghetto schools may, while reading Piaget, have a faint sense of unreality. Perhaps we should admit that every statistic which Piaget gives for the age when so-and-so happens, each stage and phase, might be shown to be false in broader surveys, through more cultures and at different times. What would be lost would merely be a reliable table—not unlike those used by engineers—a kind of technical guide to how children normally proceed in the growth of intelligence in the twentieth-century French-speaking world. Piaget is himself not unaware of the provincialities of his work. He writes that it is likely that the development of Greek children was

> behind our own. Thus the age of 11–12 years may be, beyond the neurological factors, a product of a progressive acceleration of individual development under the influence of education, and perhaps nothing stands in the way of a further reduction of the average age in a more or less distant future.[55]

All that a nervous system can do, he continues, is to "determine the total possibilities at any given stage: A particular social environment remains indispensable for the realization of these possibilities." [56] Piaget thus joins those who refuse to identify human evolution with biological evolution.

Further work in circumstances more variegated than those of Piaget's subjects almost surely would show the relativity of his age groupings and perhaps often enough of his manifestations of intellectual growth. As we have seen, he is well aware of the cultural and social factors that enter intellectual development. But what would be conserved constitutes Piaget's more lasting contribution: the uniqueness of the phases of developments and the periods they comprise. This is the empirical generalization of Rousseau's intuition that the child's world is distinctive, composed of a series of enlargements of meaning which, though they lead to adulthood, are intrinsically worthy for their own sake, not merely imperfect gropings toward adulthood. Piaget has shown, although our language might disturb him, not only that the development of children warns us *not* to impose meanings upon the child which are inappropriate to his level of understanding, lest the continuity of development abort or become deformed, but that each stage in the child's development is a preparation for the next. This is exactly what Aristotle said is true of all action in nature: it has a *telos*. This *telos* is not to be anthropomorphized into purposiveness, nor mechanized into mere causal sequence. A telic element has a rational direction, which does not necessarily prescribe an end (unless we conceive of time as circular), and yet is not a mere sequence. In a telic order the phases of the order fit into one another, so that what follows prerequires what precedes it in a way more complex than merely being the outcome of it—though it must surely be that as well. Piaget is specifically wary of teleological language, since the easiest analogue or point of entry into teleological thought is by way of human purpose, and to attribute conscious reflective purpose to the course of nature is to fall into talk that has no scientific meaning: it cannot be submitted to objective test. Yet the order he discerns is a functional order, and not merely a cause-and-effect one.

This problem in Piaget leads us to another closely related one, in its briefest form of more apparent interest to philosophers than to educators or psychologists: What is the real nature of the external world? Piaget has exposed very well the relativity of worlds to the stage of intelligence involved. The world is never just the world, in the case of the child. It is the world of seven to eleven, and so on. Piaget constantly speaks of the "construction" of the world, even of the universe.[57] We recall the passage cited earlier from *The Origins of Intelligence in Children:* "Things are never known by themselves." [58] In the conclusion of the same work Piaget says,

> Objectivity does not therefore mean independence in relation to the assimilatory activity of intelligence, but simply dissociation from the self and from egocentric subjectivity. The objectivity of experience is an achievement of accommodation and assimilation combined, that is to say, *of the intellectual activity of the subject,* and not a primary datum imposed on him from without.[59]

We have emphasized the portion above which places Piaget close to the Kantian view and vigorously against that English tradition which regards informational comprehension of the world as the result of the conjoining of signals from an external source. Eight or nine pages later he becomes very explicit on this point:

> In other words, knowledge could not be a copy, since it is always a putting into relationship of object and subject an incorporation of the object to the schemata. . . . *The object only exists with regard to knowledge, in its relations with the subject. . . .* [This is not a mimicking of a ready-made reality.] *The object is not a "known quantity" but the result of a construction.*[60]

We must look at this later passage with a bit of care. The former clause we have emphasized speaks of the object vis-à-vis knowledge, i.e. as known; the latter speaks of the object unqualifiedly *as is.*

It is proper to press Piaget on these matters because of his lifelong occupation with epistemology. As we noted above, his initial entry into child development was undertaken because of his epistemological concerns. He shows a strong rejection of the copy theory of knowledge (of Locke, for example), an insistence that objects are always objects as known to intelligent subjects, and a dislike of the idea of an independently existing ready-made reality. It is therefore with something of a jar that we encounter the following:

> . . . two points of view are possible in the study of intellectual evolution.
>
> The first of these is to choose a system of reference and agree to call "external reality," reality such as it is conceived to be during one of the stages of mental evolution. Thus it would be agreed upon to regard the external world reality as it is postulated by contemporary science, or contemporary common-sense. From this point of view, the relations of child thought to the external world would, in fact, be its relations to the universe of our existing scientific thought *taken as the norm.* . . . And this would be Psychology. . . .
>
> Or else, the attempt to regard any system of reference as absolute can be abandoned. Contemporary common-sense or even contemporary science may be regarded as stages among other stages, and the question as to the true nature of external reality left open. And this would be Theory of Knowledge. . . .
>
> For our part, we shall confine ourselves to psychology . . . [and by the "external world"] we shall in future mean the world as it is viewed by science. . . .[61]

These words were written forty years ago, twenty years before the appearance of the three volumes of the as yet untranslated *Introduction à l'épistémologie génétique.* In volume III of this work, Piaget says,

> Even the most realistic physicists, like Planck, acknowledge that the conquest of the real is only an ideal. A necessary ideal, they add, and we are only able to know by taking account of our position as observers of physical thought: but this necessity constitutes, therefore, a simple intellectual obligation felt by the physicist, to try to arrive at the given of experience, independent of all "anthropomorphism," that is, of all intellectual egocentrism. It does not consist of any indication of the direction to follow, because the givens which are not external to me are those which give rise to the maximum of deduction on the part of the subject himself, and this in conformity to the characteristic mental structures of the level of his historical or individual evolution.[62]

What is most important here are the phrases "intellectual egocentrism" and "anthropomorphism." In no language should these terms be interchangeable. Their use here leaves a gap in Piaget's thinking.

"Intellectual egocentrism" places the stamp of the ego (as "center") on all experience insofar as it is intellectually significant. Anthropomorphism means literally making things or seeing them in human form, i.e. as though they were human. It is egocentric to say that a man is evil because he dislikes me. It is anthropomorphic to say that the sea abuses driftwood and then casts it aside. The reason that Piaget uses the terms interchangeably here is that the egocentricity of his six-year old takes an anthropomorphic form: there is a giant moving the sun the way I move my ball, but also—and this is egocentric only by extension—the way Daddy moves the couch. Again the adult Greeks would not really be classified as intellectually egocentric, but they were rather anthropomorphic about their gods—as we are. Finally, in the study of children it is essential to be anthropomorphic, since the children are anthropoi-to-be; but it is fatal to be egocentric.

This last point carries us over to a brief view of modern developments in the *theory* of development. The people, after all, that Piaget is talking about are "realistic physicists." What they want, says Piaget, is to avoid certain types of blunder, but such avoidances do not dictate some specific "direction to follow." The data that the physicist investigates, he seems to intimate, are not the only data that are "external." Anything is external to me which, within my stage of development, allows me great power of intellectual control ("deduction"). The obvious safeguard is the correcting power of the external, when I err. The danger is in reading myself into the data I observe.

It is this quasi-scientific cast of Piaget's mind that has gained him so much insight. And his humanistic refusal to accept only the "hard data" of the physical sciences as having a monopoly on what is external shows in his being a fine psychologist. But precisely because the investigation of stages of emotional development is an open invitation to being egocentric (not just intellectually egocentric), Piaget tends to stay away from looking at the development of children with the exclusive or primary emphasis on the emotive, the evaluative, the conative. Yet there is much to show that the origins of cognitive development are roots thrust deep into the emotional life, both in ontogenesis (it is the child's feelings and not his thoughts that we are first aware of) and in phylogenesis (many linguists urge that the origins of language are in feelings, imperatives, mandates, and evaluations, rather than in description, intellection, etc.). This difference, clearly present between Piaget and Freud, persists in the difference between Erikson and Bruner. A less well-known figure is Richard Jones, who hopes for a synthesis of the two views. We will profit from a brief comparison of these views.

NOTES

1. See R. S. Brumbaugh and N. M. Lawrence, *Philosophers on Education,* Boston, 1963, Chapter 4.

2. *Introduction à l'épistémologie génétique* (3 vols.), Paris, 1950, vol. I, pp. 12–18. See also *The Child's Conception of Physical Causality,* trans. M. Gabain, Paterson, N.J., 1960 (hereafter cited as *CCPC*), p. 196; also p. 119, the remarks about Greek conceptions of force.

3. See *Philosophers on Education,* Chapter 4.

4. *Matter and Memory,* trans. N. M. Paul and W. S. Palmer, London, 1911; *Time and Free Will,* trans. F. L. Pogson, London, 1910; *Creative Evolution,* trans. A. Mitchell, New York, 1911.

5. See especially the end of the introduction.

6. See especially Part III: "Of the Survival of Images: Memory and Mind."

7. *The Language and Thought of the Child,* trans. M. Gabain, New York, 1955; hereafter cited as *LTC.*

8. *The Construction of Reality in the Child,* trans. M. Cook, New York, 1954 (hereafter cited as *CRC*), p. xi.

9. *The Origins of Intelligence in Children,* New York, 1952; hereafter cited as *OIC.*

10. J. M. Baldwin, *Mental Development in the Child and the Race,* London, 1925.

11. *OIC,* pp. 6–7.

12. *OIC,* p. 8.

13. *The Psychology of Intelligence,* trans. M. Piercy and D. E. Berlyne, London, 1950 (hereafter cited as *PI*), p. 7.

14. *PI,* p. 87.

15. *PI,* pp. 7–8.

16. *PI,* p. 9.

17. *PI,* p. 16.

18. *CRC,* p. 359.

19. See *PI.*

20. *Play, Dreams, and Imitations in Childhood,* trans. C. Gattegno and F. M. Hodges, New York, 1952; hereafter cited as *PDIC.*

21. *CRC,* pp. 9–10.

22. *PDIC,* pp. 10–12.

23. See summary in *PDIC,* p. 25, and *CRC,* pp. 10–11.

24. *CRC,* p. 16.

25. *PDIC,* p. 39.

26. *PDIC,* pp. 56–57.

27. *PDIC,* pp. 224–225.

28. *CRC,* pp. xii–xiii.

29. See, for example, *Six Psychological Studies,* trans. A. Tenzer, ed. David Elkind, New York, 1947; hereafter cited as *SPS.*

30. *PDIC,* p. 245.

31. *PDIC,* p. 251.

32. *The Moral Judgment of the Child,* London, 1932; hereafter cited as *MJC.*

33. *MJC,* p. 404.

34. *MJC,* pp. 410–414.

35. *PDIC,* pp. 197–198.

36. *PDIC,* p. 198.

37. *CRC,* p. xii.

38. *CCPC,* p. 66.

39. *CCPC,* pp. 70–71.

40. *CCPC,* pp. 77, 80.

41. *CCPC,* pp. 100–102.

42. *CCPC*, p. 131.

43. *CCPC*, pp. 130.

44. *CCPC*, pp. 131–132.

45. *CCPC*, p. 242.

46. *CCPC*, p. 278.

47. *PI*, p. 147.

48. Jean Piaget, Bärbel Inhelder, and Alice Szeminska, *The Child's Conception of Geometry*, trans. E. A. Lunzer, New York, 1960.

49. *PI*, p. 147.

50. *SPS*, p. 64.

51. Bärbel Inhelder and Jean Piaget, *The Growth of Logical Thinking From Childhood to Adolescence*, trans. A. Parsons and S. Milgram, New York, 1958; hereafter cited as *GLT*.

52. *GLT*, pp. 345–346.

53. *GLT*, p. 346.

54. *GLT*, p. 348.

55. *GLT*, p. 337.

56. *GLT*, p. 337.

57. *CRC*, p. xii.

58. *OIC*, p. 7.

59. *OIC*, p. 367.

60. *OIC*, p. 375.

61. *CCPC*, p. 238.

62. Pp. 305–306; translations ours. Just these deductions beg the question.

10

A Dialogue: Bruner, Erikson, Jones

We are not likely soon to find another Piaget. His is a rare talent combining industry, insight, affection, and flexibility. In addition, Piaget knows how to synthesize the efforts of predecessors and to work with contemporaries. Furthermore, probably no future investigators will be able so well to disentangle the cognitive processes in human development from their conative counterparts. Such a luxury will likely be impossible since—with world unrest and the instant communication of it to everyone who is interested—the emotionally stable and protected learning environment which surrounded his children may well be a thing of the past. The tremendous challenge to values and feelings, which presses in upon us everywhere, is of the very texture of modern life. And though much of Piaget's work has been done in relatively value-stable circumstances, he is still very much a modern man. For him as for every modern educator the aim of the educational process is objectivity, mature stability, in the sense of a balance between self-understanding and understanding of the world.

The question now is, however: What do "self-understanding" and "understanding the world" mean? As we have seen, one dominant theme in Piaget treats the scientific ideal of a cognitive approach to the world as virtually a symptom of maturity. Nonetheless, he does not subscribe to physical reductionism. Correspondingly, self-knowledge seems to be what the "outer world" would demand: a recognition of the distinction between physical processes in the world and mental processes within ourselves, the separation of values from facts, the elimination of anthropomorphism in our view of nature, the sense of ourselves as setting moral rules and obeying them, and so on. Somewhat underplayed is the sense of the emotional structure of society, our feelings as inescapably tinting our cognition of "fact." Most importantly Piaget does not stress the deeper structures of our consciousness, emotional habits, and dispositions as intruding into our perceptual discrimination and our capacity to remember. In the case of memory, for example, most people remember little or nothing of the first two years of their lives. For Freud this is evidence of repression of early life, with its conflicts, struggles, early psychic disturbances, and so on. For Piaget there is no infantile amnesia; there is only a phase of not very sharp differentiation between self and world and hence very little in the way of a genuinely memorial self to recover.

In any case, the present weakening of the family's contribution to the growth and development of a child, together with the closer relation between school and society and the aforementioned media impact, makes it unlikely that the child of the future can be shielded from emotional problems while his intellect emerges. His sensibilities are extended and amplified. The new child's durability, if he can muster it, must be created out of something other than the comfort of deliberate emotional shelter. The modern dialogue revolves around the question of how much modern education can do—how much of a role it should play—in the education of the emotions. Alternatively— and this is by no means the same thing—how much should emotional development and cognitive development complement and/or be mixed with one another?

JEROME BRUNER

The best defender of the view that education should concentrate on cognitive skills is Jerome Bruner. His point of departure is Piaget's structures of development. He unhesitatingly modifies Piaget's substages, as Piaget did himself, and he moves smoothly from the descriptive emphasis in Piaget's work to a prescriptive emphasis in the need for modernization in curriculum. In so doing he essentially employs the pragmatic position of John Dewey, which refuses to separate values sharply from facts and finds no difficulty in looking to the course of "natural" development for general clues as to what a child's needs for growth are. Bruner does not bear down on this point, nor does he attack the general philosophical problem of which it is an instance, namely, how the "ought" can be derived from the "is," or the nearly related problem of how to derive value from fact. Nevertheless, the presumption of deciding that there *are* phases of development, each requiring the next and each presenting peculiar opportunities for and limitations on educational expectations, presupposes the inherent *value* of these phases. We instruct children, then, only insofar as we are instructed by the nature of children. Clearly there are natural limits, at least in the order of the acquisition of cognitive skills if not in the actual amount of time that the average child should spend in each phase.

Bruner has constant recourse to the three stages which are the gross

heritage of Piaget's investigation. This is clear-cut in his treatment of tools and language. "Seen as amplifiers," he says, "tools can be conceived to fall into three general classes—amplifiers of sensory capacities, of motor capacities, of ratiocinative capacities." [1] These are respectively, of course, the sensory-motor, the concrete-operational, and the symbolic stages of Piaget.

As with other tools, so also are there phases in the development of that often so-called specialized tool, language. In one sense language is implicitly present even in the earliest stages. At one year children make recognizable identifications and evocations. But this is a stage, Bruner says, when "knowing is principally knowing how to do, and there is minimum reflection." [2] Furthermore, "The very young child uses language almost as an extension of pointing, and recent work shows that the likelihood of a word's use in the early linguistic career of the child is vastly increased if the object is either in hand or in direct sight." [3] From here on, there is an "internalization of language. In the transition from the second to the third year, the child experiments with grammatical structure. He imitates and corrects, in response situations with a tutor." [4] There is an internalization of language, moving from the "enactive" phase to the "iconic," from pointing, handling, and naming, to grouping, joining, and relating. In this iconic phase, running up to about eleven or twelve years, conservation experiments modeled on Piaget show that the child's grasp of conservation of transferred volumes of liquids is reinforced by his capacity to express the conservations linguistically. Typical statements about volumes rendered into different shapes are: "It looks different, but it really isn't." "It doesn't change when you only pour it." [5] These experiments, conducted at Harvard, exhibit the increased fecundity of the child's mind in the use of the notion of "likeness" or "similiarity." This is a growth in freedom: "Language provides the means of getting free of immediate appearance as the sole basis for judgment." [6] (He recalls Piaget's urging that as the physical world comes into sharper focus in the categorizing and classifying of elements in experience, the child also achieves better self-understanding.) The third phase of language, again as in Piaget, is the symbolic one, the free use of language qua language. An even greater freedom appears in the logical awareness and control of the possible, rather than confinement to the actual (over whatever broad spans of time).

Bruner has spent a fair portion of his professional time on the educational development of linguistic skills. His conclusions about the growth of language define his general position quite well. Language conceived as a tool evolves toward a goal of symbolic understanding, the achievement of mature "internalization." In general, the growth of knowing shows

> three parallel systems for processing information and for representing it—one through manipulation and action, one through perceptual organization and imagery, and one through symbolic apparatus. It is not that these are "stages" in any sense; they are rather emphases of development.[7]

Bruner goes on to explain that there are three systems of *skills* that correspond to three principal tool systems which are prerequisites for maturity: "tools for the hand, for the distance receptors, and for the process of reflection." His marked preference for the cognitive approach is evident in the very language he uses, e.g. "processing information." But even here he is not dependent upon Piaget for more than the major categories. Thus, though he clearly holds that perceiving and thinking are processes which "run their course," he nowhere leaves us with a sense of fixed periods for development, as Piaget sometimes does.[8] He says of mental growth that it goes by "spurts," and that "the steps or stages or spurts" are "not very clearly linked to age."[9]

Bruner, then, lies somewhere between Piaget and Skinner but a bit closer to the former. Although Piaget often prefers to let his data speak for themselves rather than be dropped into prefixed categories, we get the impression from him of a fairly regular emergence of phases and subphases in the child's intellectual growth, closely associated with chronological age. Still these data are contextual and likely speak as much for the culture and even the cultural stratum as they do for anything firmly built-in in the youngster merely waiting for release. To take a particularly pressing point and a painful one: What of the native capacities of blacks? There seems to be no way of getting an answer from Piaget. We might well use his methods profitably, but could we surround the black child with the same warmly supportive social surroundings in which Piaget's children live? However, Bruner is not primarily interested in emotional warmth; he is more concerned with the deprivation of opportunities for the learning of basic skills. Deprivation experiments with mammals, in which lost "opportunities" in the development sequence of the young result in defective adult animals, are suggestive models for analogous problems with human children. With children,

> The principal deficits appear to be linguistic in the broadest sense—the lack of opportunity to share in dialogue, to have occasion for paraphrase, to internalize speech as a vehicle of thought. [The resultant defect in basic linguistic skills stunts future develop-

ment appearing, for example, in] the increasing difference of intelligence with age between such culturally deprived groups as rural Southern Negroes and more culturally privileged whites.[10]

Bruner is here emphasizing the "alloplastic" features of education (those which mold the child from the "outside") and incidentally making a strong case—he recurs again and again to "basic skills"—for something like the three R's, although hardly for the old method of teaching them. The extreme case of alloplastic influence is, of course, Skinner's brand of "conditioned reinforcement." The extreme case of "autoplastic" influence is Rousseau's rearing of Emile with very little direct instruction. But, says Bruner, what is often missed is that "one *teaches* readiness or provides opportunities for its nurture, one does not simply wait for it." [11] Furthermore, "There is an appropriate version of any skill or knowledge that may be imparted at whatever age one wishes to begin teaching—however preparatory the version may be." [12] Bruner noted in his presentation at the Woods Hole Conference of 1959 that Piaget's associate Bärbel Inhelder recommends Grades 1 and 2 as a training ground in the "basic logical operations" used in science and mathematics: "There is evidence to indicate that such rigorous relevant early training has the effect of making later learning easier." [13]

In spite of his refusal to confine some type of learning to some particular age, chronological or whatever, he has little enthusiasm for Skinner's extension of laboratory manipulation of animals into the classroom shaping of children. On the contrary, he remarks of rats raised by his children in the "chaos of a human habitat" that they showed greater development of animal intelligence than the rats "who lived in the gray atmosphere of the laboratory." [14] Deliberate controls are bad enough. There are as well "latent controls," against which we are rather unable to defend ourselves:

> What I should like to propose at this point is not that we seek to manipulate patterns of child training for achieving official forms of control over man's behavior. [We need instead defense against controls that are] likely to be dangerous to the future of democratic society. Whoever is sick with the fear of rejection, whoever has formed too strong and transferable an identification—he is the potential victim of forms of control that make men unfree.[15]

In the same essay Bruner says, "It is not surprising that writers who are fond of fantasies about social control, like my colleague B. F. Skinner in his novel *Walden Two,* encourage themselves with tales set in a neatly arranged, benign, but nonetheless utterly monopolistic utopia." [16]

Bruner's mention of a "transferable identification" shows a clear sensitivity to the inward lives of persons and the problems of integration of personality which are so strikingly investigated by Erikson. His preference for the cognitive is not really a bias or a prejudice; it is a kind of professional bent, concentrating on a dominant aspect of education. The above passages with their mention of fear, rejection, identification, and fantasy are not just concessions to another aspect of human life.

Bruner mentions his own earlier phase of psychological inquiry, in which he was much impressed by the role that motivation plays in perception.[17] His turning to the dominantly cognitive aspects of perception was a reaction to that phase. Nor has he dropped his interest in motivation. In a not frequently noted essay, "On Coping and Defending," he cites several painful cases of motivation deprivation that arise from motivational inhibition: the youngster with a mongoloid sister who takes all the family's attention is one such case.[18] If he succeeds at school, that justifies the family's behavior; his family doesn't need to pay attention to him. If he fails, he gets criticized both at home and at school, but at least he is not ignored. So he fails. He is defending against the intrusion of education that would insure psychological indifference in his family. Again, a boy yelled at for failures refuses to try to answer problems rather than risk error. His therapeutic tutor encourages yelling in return until the shouting becomes a reciprocal game with the dysfunctional fear eliminated. "Coping" means handling a rough situation, "defending" means preventing it from arising. If the failures of education are intolerable, the student will prevent education from arising. It is the distinction, he says elsewhere in a pungent metaphor, between playing tennis and fighting hard not to be dragged onto the court.[19]

Bruner is much aware of the role of education in revealing the world of feeling. Anyone who tabs him merely as a cognitivist should read his *On Knowing: Essays for the Left Hand.* Here he writes a vividly appreciative estimate of Freud as imagist. In a chapter on "Art as a Mode of Knowing" he argues that any impulse can be turned to art, acknowledging the limitations of logic in aesthetic production.[20] Further, he looks to Erikson for help in understanding the innards of men in the fiction of Camus, Fitzgerald, Conrad, and Romains. Elsewhere he emphasizes the educational function of having young children studying tragedy.

Thus Bruner is well aware of the role of motivations and emotional disturbances and blockages in education. He knows that the materials of art and literature, with their context of feeling, are indispensable in education. What, then, does his cognitivism come to? He gives a good answer, ironically, in some comments on a point made by the architect

Pier Luigi Nervi.[21] Nervi remarks that the age of speed limits what you can build. A wagon road can meander, a superhighway cannot.

> It may well be the case that not only are we entering a period of technological maturity in which education will require constant redefinition, but [specific technology may change so fast] that narrow skills will become obsolete within a reasonably short time after their acquisition.[22]

The problem is the problem of the aging of skills in a technological society. Technology tends to cancel the specific skills by which it reaches toward others. Early computer people, in some cases, might just as well know how to make buggy whips. Currently, for example, aerospace experts of high caliber have no place to go in the wake of congressional cutbacks in financing giant supersonic aircraft. The loss —to embroider Bruner's theme a bit—is of these people not just to society and to employment but to their own self-respect. The Piagetian notion here is adaptation, in this case to a swiftly moving, superhighway society. Bruner's cognitivism rests then on a preoccupation with the kind of thoroughgoing knowledge which objectively underlies the great variety of human skills, existing and to come: knowledge of language, science, mathematics.

Clearly, a good case can be made for the emphasis on these skills. Indeed, we should perhaps call them superskills (Bruner is not guilty of this brassy term), since they overarch particular skills. To have a firm grasp on them is to be polyadaptable (nor of this one, either) and not likely to be caught in a swiftly changing present. Since any skill can be taught, in some form, at any age, it must be a continuing presence in all that a developing child might learn. This indeed is exactly what Bruner holds.[23] There will be certain "spiral" axes, like those of literature, science, and number, up which the path of learning goes.

Language/literature, science, mathematics—to these Bruner returns again and again.[24] He warns us against the "fantasy" of trying to take a metaphorical car at seventy miles per hour into any curve save a conforming arc.[25] And he looks back on the "life-adjustment" courses era of American education with a pity amounting to distress.[26] These courses were reluctant to "expose the child to the startling sweep of man and nature for fear that it might violate the comfortable domain of his direct experience. . . . Education seeks to develop the power and sensibility of mind."[27] Yet elsewhere he says that it is not the function of psychologists "to decide upon educational goals."[28] Clearly this does not mean that education should have no aims. And the previous citation insists on at least some exposure of the child to the "startling sweep of man and nature." Education aims at basic understanding of man and nature. Nature may be at least approached through science and mathematics, though some (including the authors) might regard this as a narrow-gauge railway. What of man? Does literature carry the whole burden? Not likely in this age.

The answer to all of the above questions is suitably embodied not so much in a doctrine as in what Bruner himself describes as an "unfinished course," his "Man: A Course of Study." [29] What is decided upon in this course of study is not a definite outcome—"a goal"—so much as a broadening of perspective—"an aim," or better, perhaps, a "purpose." This purpose is the exploration of three questions: "What is human about human beings? How did they get that way? How can they be made more so?" [30] The course, which has been assembled and produced by Educational Services Incorporated (now Educational Development Center), is addressed to children at the fifth-grade level. It includes sections on language, both animal and human, on tool making, on social organization, and so on. Fifteen films, nine of them on the Netsilik Eskimos, are used as supplemental materials. The program also includes the use of games, related to what the children have learned, as elicitative devices. We will come back to one of the Netsilik films in the third part of this chapter, since it is a point of departure for some critical discussion by Richard Jones. The point is, Bruner has returned to his early concern with motivation in perception, broadening the conception of cognitive skills to include the empathic excitement that comes of the study of "primitive" man whether as forbear or as contemporary. The result is—by all reports—a highly successful experimental course and one in which, as we shall see, the aspect of feeling and that of cognition are closely interconnected. Jones will argue that the involvement of the student is beyond what is often anticipated and that it exhibits still another dimension in education. But in any case Bruner has exhibited, in his own way, the point which Piaget makes so well: Knowledge of the world (in this case the social world on which Piaget concentrates very little of his attention) and self-knowledge go hand in hand.

ERIK ERIKSON

As a writer Erikson is an almost perfect complement to Piaget. Where Piaget writes in sustained works, often with a battery of associates, Erikson writes, largely by himself, in papers or short studies which are later revised, enlarged, and fused into book-length studies. Both men follow an outline of the stages of development which has served them through several decades, albeit with changes in emphasis and alterations of detail. Piaget forges his own categories, whereas

Erikson's are extensions and imaginative modernizations of Freud's categories combined with many of his assumptions as well.

In emphasis and point of view, also, the two are complementary. Piaget, aware of the conative elements in development, has largely concentrated on cognitive studies in the areas of perception, intelligence, and the more observable features of morality. Erikson, equally aware of the role of cognitive development in the growth of the child, has devoted himself to the processive and pendularly regressive emergence of personality.

Finally, the two men are almost too neatly opposed in background and growth. Piaget began life as a naturalist, publishing at the age of ten, and came—by way of an early dilemma about the world of nature and the knowledge of nature—to the study of children. There he stayed, with numerous forays (e.g. his lengthiest work) into epistemology, occupied with child development—which he had intended to be a four or five-year affair in his pursuit of a genetic theory of knowledge. And Piaget stayed mostly in French Switzerland where he was born. His life seems to have been set in the kind of relative emotional calm that makes it not only feasible but realistic to regard the growth of intelligence as the emergence of the self.

Erikson, on the other hand, was a child of crisis from the beginning.[31] His Danish parents separated before he was born. His mother went south to Germany, to Karlsruhe, fell in love with her son's pediatrician (Erik was three years old), and later married him. Young Erikson took his Jewish stepfather's name for a while; his first paper was published under that name: Erik Homburger. Thus were fused together the identity crisis of the young Dane reared in a foreign land with the help of a stepfather, and the identity problems of a wandering, feared, and outcast race. Erik, art student and artist, wandered literally and figuratively for several years. In Florence he met Peter Blos, at that time a writer, later to become a child psychologist. Blos, part of a cluster of Americans intimate with the Freuds in Vienna, persuaded Erikson to come help him open a school there, funded by one of the American families. The school was run in a very open fashion, "progressive" in the better sense of the word. Many of the children were in analysis, as were their parents. Eventually, Erikson himself was analyzed by Anna Freud, but he recalls insisting that he must remain an artist. At last his interest in the visual led him to the study of dreams. Soon he was not only teaching school but also studying clinical psychoanalysis and working in a Montessori group, where he especially examined children's use of space. He married in 1929. His wife joined the school, whose recesses were often arranged so that Joan Erikson could nurse her baby.

Thus did the artist become educator and psychoanalyst. Yet Erikson's work on education per se is small. The technology of the classroom, the development of curricula, the phases of cognitive development have occupied little of his time, and sometimes it seems that he takes cognitive development as much for granted as Piaget does conative development. There is thus a double problem in writing about Erikson: first, we must address his work somewhat to formal education, whereas he does not; second, because his work is multifaceted and full of significant detail, one must write either much or little about him. We shall have to follow the latter plan, hoping that readers will somehow sense his genius and go to his works themselves. Erikson is clearly a twentieth-century giant. We give him in a microportrait.

Erikson at one point defines the educative uniqueness of human beings, one principal development in his thought that goes beyond Freud. En route he touches on our relation to and use of animals, the relation between mind and body, and the underlying concern of all education with value. We quote the passage in its entirety as a point of departure for our brief inquiry:

> *Care* is a quality essential for psychosocial evolution, for we are the teaching species. Animals, too, instinctively encourage in their young what is ready for release, and, of course, some animals can be taught some tricks and services by man. Only man, however, can and must extend his solicitude over the long, parallel and overlapping childhoods of numerous offspring united in households and communities. As he transmits the rudiments of hope, will, purpose and competence, he imparts meaning to the child's bodily experiences, he conveys a logic much beyond the literal meaning of the words he teaches, and he gradually outlines a particular world image and style of fellowship. All of this is necessary to complete in man the analogy to the basic, ethological situation between parent animal and young animal. All this, and no less, makes us comparable to the ethologist's goose and gosling. Once we have grasped this interlocking of the human life stages, we understand that adult man is so constituted as to *need to be needed* lest he suffer the mental deformation of self-absorption, in which he becomes his own infant and pet. I have, therefore, postulated an instinctual and psychosocial stage of "generativity" beyond that of genitality. Parenthood is, for most, the first, and for many, the prime generative encounter; yet the perpetuation of mankind challenges the generative ingenuity of workers and thinkers of many kinds. And man *needs* to teach, not only for the sake of those who need to be taught, and not only for the fulfillment of his identity, but because facts are kept alive by being told, logic by being demonstrated, truth by being professed. Thus, the teaching passion is not restricted to the teaching

profession. Every mature adult knows the satisfaction of explaining what is dear to him and of being understood by a groping mind.[32]

Several things that amount to credos, but not undefended ones, appear here. (1) The development of animal behavior is not a very good model for human education. Animal education of animal behavior, although instinctive, brings about a "release"; there is thus postulated a certain prepacked interior which in normal growth develops, that is, unfolds. (2) We are then led to ask: What is in man that must be released? *Hope, will, purpose,* and *competence.* Only the last of these can come under the heading of cognitive instruction. The first three lie in that vague and vital area which is felt evaluatively rather than as sensory fact. With a knowledge of what is peculiarly human we can use the ethological models to understand our own relation between parent and offspring.[33] (3) The releaser is man himself, as educator, fulfilling not only a function which his offspring needs but his own basic "need to be needed." If he reaches out to others less than that, he falls shy of adulthood, into a stage of confinement of interiority to self-preoccupation, "his own infant and pet." (4) The genital phase of Freud may thus mark some maturity of sexual orientation, a role of creativity supervening upon that of biological procreation. This is the "generative" instinct. Perhaps without deliberately meaning to, Erikson has answered a troublesome question that may be asked of any doctrinaire Freudian: how to account for the great teachers and thinkers who have had no families (Jesus) or left them (the Buddha) or have lived much outside them (Socrates). Little beyond the familiar magic word "sublimation" is normally available. One might answer: their generativity went beyond genitality.

Closely connected with Erikson's generative instinct is his epigenetic account of human development. The generative phase is itself the seventh of eight stages (preceded by young adulthood—"genitality"—and followed by maturity—"ego integrity"; see chart on page 256), and it is that stage in which the desire to reproduce matures into giving to others something in addition to animal existence. On cue from Erikson we may as well call it the "teaching phase" and have done.

We reproduce Erikson's developmental chart in its earliest form, from *Childhood and Society.*[34] It is a chart of eight "identity crises," also called "nuclear conflicts." [35] The course of these crises, each of which could go either way and therefore has a pair of names for it, is dubbed "epigenetic." The term harks back to an ancient controversy in embryology, antedating microscopic knowledge: Is the embryo already present in the sperm, or does it develop out of structureless, primordial material? "Epigenesis" was the name given to the latter view, "preformation" to the former. Epigenesis turned out to be closer, in

ERIKSON'S STAGES OF HUMAN DEVELOPMENT

		1	2	3	4	5	6	7	8
VIII	Maturity								Ego integrity vs. despair
VII	Adulthood							Generativity vs. stagnation	
VI	Young adulthood						Intimacy vs. isolation		
V	Puberty and adolescence					Identity vs. role confusion			
IV	Latency				Industry vs. inferiority				
III	Locomotor-genital			Initiative vs. guilt					
II	Muscular-anal		Autonomy vs. shame, doubt						
I	Oral-sensory	Basic trust vs. mistrust							

what it denied, to the truth. But before it was done, epigenesis wound up embracing certain aspects of the preformationist theory. This fact is evident in Erikson's account of the epigenetic principle. "Somewhat generalized, this principle states that anything that grows has a ground plan, and that out of this ground plan the parts arise, each part having its time of special ascendancy, until all parts have arisen to form a functioning whole." [36]

The difference between Piaget's theory of development and that of Erikson is quite clear. In cognitive matters Piaget evidently regards the course of development as sequential, linear. Intellectual and perceptual development is a kind of ladder you climb, a progressive revision of formerly held views. It is true that he seems to sense a kind of ingathering in the very young child, but as soon as hand and eye coordination are evident, the child's behavior at first and then his language later indicate a replacement of his former views as well as an enlargement of the scope of his questions. Generality, precision, objectivity, these are the directions along which cognitive development occurs.

For Erikson development is quite another matter. It is not linear, except that there is a temporal sequence of crises in average development. Each stage, in a rationale that is hard to describe but which resonates with our experience, fits into the next. But emotional experience, the sense of value, attitudinal variation, and all the rest are cumulative. Many people remember the animistic phase in their view of nature. Few hold to it now. We revert to this animism at just that point where our emotions are aroused, but not our cognitive beliefs. One kicks the jammed door, curses the rain on the picnic, indulges in baroque arabic profanity at the gas gauge whose lie is discovered twenty miles from a gas station. Such reversion, which overwhelms cognitive stability, is a form of regression, in Freudian terms.

Regression is a return to some emotional age which has been passed through but badly or incompletely. A structural metaphor will do here, but it ignores the cumulative character of emotional maturity. A tall structure with defects will begin to totter as we build it higher. The whole may come tumbling down if we cannot somehow reach down to the earlier layers and shore them up, strengthen them. Regression, in one light then, can be regarded as a sheer survival gesture, a kind of homeostatic effort to correct a psychic imbalance in the accumulating personality. Widely diverse schools of neo-Freudian psychoanalysis lean on this kind of metaphor to bring about some of the most striking human repair. Medard Boss in *Psychoanalysis and Daseinanalysis* tells of his discovery that he must enter the patient's world not merely *however* psychotic that world is but because it *is* psychotic, *cognitively* ridiculous, a prison of loneliness. In one case he took a violently ill professional woman back to her infancy—or rather went there with her, cradled her between his legs, let her nurse on a bottle repeatedly. When she had completed the infant phase denied her by her overbearing father, she returned to normal life.[37]

Speaking simply, everyone regresses in some degree at some times. The mere presence of a regressive impulse or action is hardly unhealthy. No one is sickened to see a seven-year old on hands and knees playing with his three-year-old brother. Nor does one suppose that a seventeen-year old who sulks for want of the family car has suffered a personality collapse. But what *is* indicated is that perhaps the task of integration is never complete, always present. As Erikson says, "The personality is engaged with the hazards of existence continuously even as the body's metabolism copes with decay." [38]

If we think then of the conative development of children as being cumulative, with the past perhaps never composed of phases which have reached an ideal perfection, the diagram not only indicates where the cognitive educator may find himself blocked but—more constructively—defines the inner life and nuclear problems of a student of any given age.

With classrooms even in good schools crammed with too many students there is likely to be little time for assessing the personal struggles of the nine-year-old student. But what can be done is to choose materials appropriate to the problems in life style for youngsters of a given age. Not even Jones wants to turn the healthy classroom into anything like a psychiatric clinic, but it should be evident that where cognitive progress is undertaken with no attention to the problems of feeling and evaluation appropriate to a given age group, education may be working against itself, killing interest rather than harnessing it, or cooperating with it, or even mayhap enhancing it. In the catch phrase of current student complaint, it may lack relevance. This is not the tactical relevance of world problems but the strategic relevance of personal development. This theme is the one which preoccupies Richard Jones, although he should not be saddled with our statement of it, and we must shortly turn to a brief exposition of that theme.

We conclude this section with a brief consideration of what Erikson calls the "Eight Ages of Man," together with some relevant remarks from Erikson on Piaget and on education. Were Erikson's work finished, his wisdom at an end, and this a book exclusively on human nature, the present treatment of him would be absurdly brief. He appears here because he supplies the point of view and the basic schematic which has affected many theoreticians of education, and because he warns us implicitly of the dangers of education largely devoted to compliance, performance, skill, and information.

The heart of the heavily cognitivist position is in the identification of the public world of common sense and its rarefied offspring, the "physical reality" of the physical sciences, with reality in general. Here Erikson makes one of his firmer departures from Freud, with his customary grace in showing that even the path of departure is in Freud's writings, albeit in embryo. What he is criticizing is the conception of an autonomous "outer world." The phrase appears in his citations of other authors.[39] Of this he says:

> Maybe our habitual reference to man's world as an "outer world" attests, more than any other single item, to the fact that the world of that intuitive and active participation which constitutes most of our waking life is still foreign territory to our theory. This term, more than any other, represents the Cartesian strait jacket we have imposed on our model of man, who in some of our writings seems to be most himself when reflecting horizontally—like a supine baby or a reclining patient, or like Descartes himself, taking to his bed to cogitate on the extensive world.[40]

He continues with a reference to a once-remarked but not followed-up distinction in Freud between *Realität* and *Actualitaet*. It is in the *act* of *Actualitaet* that Erikson finds the complement to the reality principle of Freud.

> Reality, then (to repeat this), is the world of phenomenal experience, perceived with a minimum of distortion and with a maximum of customary validation agreed upon in a given state of technology and culture; while actuality is the world of participation shared with other participants with a minimum of defensive maneuvering and a maximum of mutual activation.[41]

Here Erikson joins squarely with modern phenomenology: the life world is observation *and* participation, reflection *and* act; split it at your peril.

The chart, then, is a chart of action and participation, not so much in validation of views about the nature of the observed world but in the positing of a life style, in the contribution to a social reality. The basis is trust: "A lasting ego identity, we have said, cannot begin to exist without the trust of the first oral stage." [42] From there on out it is a question of whether the ego "is strong enough to integrate the timetable of the organism with the structure of social institutions." [43] In this first stage the beginnings of personality show in habits of sleep, feeding, and elimination. The untrusting child blocks, the trusting child "lets go" in all three. The first signs of autonomy turn up in random motion, the first signs of control of his environment in his "challenge" to be served.[44] The second stage is variously treated by Erikson.[45] In general, he emphasizes the potentially dangerous situation in cultures such as our own and Japan's where excessive interest is invested in early toilet training. In this "anal" phase there is a psychic component, the chance to begin the sense of free will, a "sense of self-control without loss of self-esteem." [46] But demands that he cannot meet may cause the infant to develop a "precocious conscience" and a helpless one. He may abandon himself to shame and doubt, the former creating a resolve to get away with things unseen, i.e. "unshamed." We may note in passing that Erikson might have called this "false conscience."

In the third stage the older preschool child is also viewed in the modalities of freedom of motion, language, imagination.[47] The freedom makes itself felt as intrusion, in space, in interruptions, in curiosity, by physical attack and (frighteningly to him) the thought of intrusion into the female body. For girls there arises at this time the highly rated discovery of having no penis. In this period also comes the division of the sexes into their respective forms of the castration complex. This is the stage at which initiative, ill-born, can result in guilt. The negative feeling in the second stage was one of shame, the sense of a flaw or a weakness in one's *being*. The negative feeling in the third stage is that of *doing,* or *having done.* And guilt in turn saps initiative, in extreme cases paralyzing it.

We pause here to consider another major departure of Erikson from Freud. We have deliberately underscored Erikson's emphasis on freedom—not the mere sense of freedom but its *Actualitaet,* as Freud called it in one passage. We may guess that Freud never developed *Actualitaet* as companion for *Realität,* since *Realität* fell under the iron law of scientific determinism.[48] The appearance of *Actualitaet* raises the scientifically unacceptable notion of freedom, that very freedom, however, which all psychoanalysis wants for its patients. In any case, Erikson's departure is firm.

> Clearly, the first insight, concerning the self-determination of free will, is related to the second [the polar experiences of William James], that is the abandonment of physiological factors as fatalistic arguments against a neurotic person's continued self-determination. Together they are the basis of psychotherapy, which, no matter how it is described and conceptualized, aims at restoration of the patient's power of choice.[49]

The fourth stage is the beginning of schooling. For the first time disciplined results are expected, with a more or less clear-cut institutional procedure to be met. The scene grows more complex, the child may want to go home to Mommy; something in the first three phases is wanting. Or he may wish to stay, but is more fascinated by play and playmates than strict "subjects." Or he may "fix" his identity on the performance of tasks, not necessarily with joy or even interest, but with a premature sense of being obliged. A liberal mixture of play is required—to break up the protocompulsion of the last-named reaction, or to remove the forbiddingness felt in the former two cases.[50] In this phase are born the roots of both conformism and rebellion. Not only is a liberal use of play required, then, but a teacher sensitive to individual differences.

It is in these school years that we find Erikson and Piaget necessarily closest together. We recall that Piaget notes the submission by the adolescent of his beliefs to his peers. This is the special and social form of the differentiation of self from world which leads to objectivity. This fifth stage—adolescence—has been the most engaging area of study for psychologists of all stripes. Erikson prefers to leave the boxes of his diagram largely open. He says it can be used only by those who can take it *and* leave it.[51] But "adolescence" is all but filled. The social dimension, as Erikson sees it, is vastly more complex but just as unavoidable as it is in Piaget. "Adolescence," he says, "is the last stage of childhood"; [52] he might have added, from his own analysis, "and the first stage of adulthood." Every kind of ambivalence results—in role and role-playing, in sexual intimacy or distance, about work, about leaders. There can even be, in some cases, a collapse of trust that produces violent regression clear back to the earliest stage of demands, with tantrums upon being frustrated. The impact of school on psyche raises an important question: how much can a school and its education ignore the psyche, or how well can the school confine itself to intellect and skill? When he was still in his twenties Erikson examined this question very provocatively.[53]

We have seen Erikson the artist become analyst by way of teaching in an open and Freudian-oriented school. This period of Erikson's life (he was then "Homburger," remember) was itself one of polar crisis. He was letting go of one aspect of life to embrace another, moving from the world of art to the world of children. It seems fair to say that his personal confrontation with the need to be needed and the need of children to be understood—not simply developed and informed—led him out of formal education and into child psychoanalysis. Finally, it is in this period that he married and the young couple had their first child, Kai. Thus Erikson entered as father into the world he already occupied as teacher: adulthood proper, which combines genitality with generativity. Let us see what his reflections on that experience are. The paper is "Psychoanalysis and the Future of Education." [54] He is twenty-seven and teaching. The time is 1930, eleven years after the Peace (if that is the correct word) of Versailles, a peace declared at the height of young Homburger's adolescent period. He is reviewing an episode at the school where revealing talk about legitimate rage and the ways of discharging it was followed the next morning by fighting between two older boys.

> In view of such experiences one would think that modern educa-
> tion must often stand abashed before its own courage, the courage
> with which it hopes to lead young people, by means of good will,
> toward a new spirit and future peace. It is psychic reality which
> forces itself through, and this the more unexpectedly and unpleas-
> antly the more it is denied. One can understand that many are
> panic-stricken and as it were, throw to the winds the ideal of the
> primacy of intelligence.[55]

Mere good will. It is irony that those who hope to find in the facts of the world and in their own good will sufficient power to lead people to peace lack facts about persons. In the language we discussed above, *Realität* understanding to be useful requires *Actualitaet* understand-ing.

But it is not merely the problems of behavior, the world cry for peace, and the blindness with which education proceeds, insufficiently armed with psychological understanding. It is that the primacy of in-telligence itself is threatened and rejected by a supposition of the au-tonomy of intelligence. Perhaps this is the best way to put it: the as-sumption of the autonomy of intelligence may in the end defeat the child's interest in intelligence. Cognitively disposed as Bruner is, this point comes through clearly in his "On Coping and Defending." It is one thing to hold that intelligence is reducible to nothing else, i.e. is *prime;* it is another to hold that intelligence stands alone, is autono-mous, *a law unto itself.*

Still more is involved. The child's world does not come in neat piles of thought and feeling, a little bit to be developed here and a little bit there. When the young child who has learned little about dissembling asks a question, the question has a double intention: it is cognitively aimed but conatively loaded. It is about the world, but it comes from within, and the interior is not the trim, orderly, intellectual searching which the adult has been taught to follow. The more inhibited the culture in which the question is asked (the child being always in some measure aware of this inhibition), the more likely is the question to be disguised or preceded by indirect ones that skirt or circle the subject. (Any Freudian who wants to analyze that sentence has our permission.) This fact accounts for Erikson's verging on what seems to be hyper-bole; he was writing in a still pretty inhibited Vienna and for colleagues who knew the situation well. Erikson spells out the concrete case of a seven-year old, in which the vital questions are postponed, delayed, half reached for, or disguised, with only small hints of the deeper problems for which there is both little language and likely only a shocked audience.

> For the teacher there remains another individual problem. He must not only appreciate sexual curiosity masquerading as desire for knowledge, but he must make the greatest possible use of it. The child never learns more than he does at the time of disguised curiosity. At this time *he learns with the cooperation of his affects . . . for he is learning now for the sake of the life he dimly divines and not for the sake of his lessons.*[56]

The principal emphasis is on the disguised sexual curiosity here, but certainly not genital curiosity per se. Rather we are told that the whole set of his affects is incorporated in his curiosity. A bit later Erikson paraphrases the whole unasked question behind many of this child's questions: "What about the desire and the fear of destroying, and the fear and desire of being destroyed?"[57] Not just *eros* but *thanatos.* We find this reduction to two terms extreme; we are suspicious of adult names given to protean, childish drives and impulses. But as labels for the termini of the spectrum of the conative-evaluative psyche, they dramatically underscore the fact that overt motives are likely to be firmly attached to deeper and more abiding ones.

The major resistance against this approach to education comes, of course, from society itself, the very people who once questioned just like the seven-year old and were heard without what Reik calls the "third ear." The posture of social inhibition, noncontact between the old and young (surely one ingredient in any generation gap) is thus socially inherited and self-reinforcing. Erikson cites Freud:

> Certainly men are like this, but have you asked yourself whether they need be so, whether their inmost nature necessitates it? Can an anthropologist give the cranial index of a people whose custom it is to deform their children's heads by bandaging them from their earliest years? Think of the distressing contrast between the radiant intelligence of a healthy child and the feeble mentality of the average adult.[58]

The solution is neither good will nor love. Both experience and theory show that love increases guilt feeling. What is required is to make

> unconscious material conscious, and to prevent the accumulation of unconscious material by continuous enlightenment. Apparently paedogogy now faces a similar problem in the question of aggression, guilt and desire for punishment, and perhaps here, too, steps taken

toward suppression or liberation will not really touch the heart of
the problem.

Perhaps a new education will have to arise which will provide enlightenment about the entire world of affects and not only about
one special instinct which, in an otherwise entirely rationalized outlook of life, appears too obscure.[59]

Good will, then, is not enough, and love is not enough. Nothing less
than *candor* will do, plus one other ingredient which appears in the
early part of Erikson's essay: "One rule proved to be important,
namely, never to give more information than was asked for." [60] The
answer would seem to be dialogue, with the child asking and the adult
responding. But this is at seven, and the task is not easy.

Much of what has been cited from this first essay could serve as a
motto for Richard Jones's work. It seems likely that he has read it.
But there is a major difference. Jones often uses a nonpersonal third
party—Bruner's film on the Netsilik, for example. The curiosity-
provoking item is in a sense an artifice, but it is an objective referent,
and it combines conative and cognitive interest in a way natural to the
child's psychic posture. Finally, the Netsilik film is for ten-year olds,
more articulate and likely better balanced, on the average, than the
youngsters Erikson taught. So, often enough, the teacher asks the questions. But before turning to Jones, we must comment—though briefly,
since they soon run off the map of formal education—on the remaining stages of Erikson's Ages of Man.

The genital period of the young adult springs from erotic fulfillment and (ideally) moves from this sharing to social sharing. One
often wonders not at the ideals of the socially enraged eighteen-year
old but at how concrete he can be with no fulfilled mutuality of erotic
love to support him. Perhaps the political protest that flares violently,
only to subside shortly to almost invisible embers, is the analogue of
an equally short-lived series of puppy loves or adolescent infatuations.
The beginning violinist, analogously, may develop a pure tone relatively early; *sostenuto,* however, takes time, labor, love, and patience
to execute and to learn.

Freud, confessedly neurotic and all but compulsive about releasing
the world from its needless inhibition of sexual understanding, regarded the genital phase as the sign of maturity. Erikson discerns two
stages further, both of them significant for education but in the
broader sense. Genitality has an end which is erotic, but its function is
reproductive. He calls it, as we have seen, "generative." To generate
another generation is surely not to cease at the point of giving it biological life. We are, he says, the teaching species. We not only can but
must extend our act of generation to the continuous act of psychic cre-

ation. In biological terms, what is human is exosomatic, i.e. outside the body, lodged in the art, the culture, the science, and the language of a society. These sociocultural elements survive and flourish only through teaching. It is only the physiological inheritance which is endosomatic, inside the body. Shaw's playful slander on pedagogues might well be reformed: those who can teach, *create;* those who cannot, merely *make.*

The final stage, again ideally, is the last ambiguity: the crisis of integrity vs. despair. In the only chart that Erikson ever published with most of the boxes filled, the seventh and eighth stages are left blank for the "psychosexual" phase.[61] There *is* no purely psychosexual phase, beyond genitality, but there is much of life in these final two stages. In the column marked "Related Elements of Social Order," a single word appears for the eighth stage: wisdom. Teaching here is embodiment, educating by being an exemplar. And the last filled box, the one under the heading "Psychosocial Modalities," refers implicitly to the theme of integrity vs. despair: "To be, through having been; to face not being."

RICHARD JONES [62]

"We shall proceed with Freud out of Erikson," says Jones in his most recent educational study.[63] He might equally well have said Lawrence Kubie, for Kubie gives him his particular target—formal education—more than does either Freud or Erikson.[64] Indeed, of an early work by Jones, an anthology of writings on educational psychology which includes contributions by both Bruner and Kubie, Jones says that it is designed "to bring the two camps [Kubie representing "autoplastic" and Bruner "alloplastic"] into happier concert than I had observed them to enjoy." [65] And he has preceded his remarks by acknowledgment of the point in Piaget which we have already stressed, that self-knowledge and knowledge of the world are inseparably interconnected. But in Jones, this self and its knowledge are defined in terms of emotion, feeling, and imagination, at least as much as by concept formation or manipulation.

Thus Piaget's self-knowledge resembles the self-knowledge of Kubie and/or Jones only if one does not inquire too deeply into what is intended by "self." Piaget's self is the knowing self that learns to differentiate itself, a stage at a time, from the world it knows. There are successive sheddings of animism and anthropomorphism which permit

All quotations from *Fantasy and Feeling in Education* reprinted by permission of New York University Press from *Fantasy and Feeling in Education* by Richard M. Jones, © 1968 by New York University.

progress toward a mature cognitive stance, with scientific detachment occasionally appearing as the monitor if not the mentor. Piaget's self is, of course, also an agent, not merely a knower. In fact the knower begins as manipulator in the sensory-motor phase. Later he becomes a moral agent, submitting his inward assumptions and convictions to the outward test of his peer group. His peers function for him as a kind of human analogue to the corrective character of a physical world cogently experimented with. Both society and physical world are realities that curb our egocentricity.

The self in Kubie is hardly different—Piaget, after all, is not a poor observer—but it is more obscure, more a creature of emotion, imagination, and feeling. In this sense the self as an observable agent, which it is in Piaget, is only the most easily seen part of the self as a hidden agent, an agent which as often acts on itself as object as it acts on the outside world of things and/or people.

What sort of synthesis, then, are we to expect from this conflict of the deep-laid life of feeling and the demanding life of thought? The "best moments," says Jones, "in the Kubie School [come] when the experimenter is mindful that expressions of fantasies and emotions in school rooms are means and not ends, that the conditions which make such experiences appropriate should also make them relevant." [66] The worst moments, he says, occur when the experiment "regresses" to its clinical origins. (An example of the clinical posture is failure to distinguish between anxieties that lead to learning and those that block it.) From a purely clinical point of view anxiety is always an undesirable item in mental life. But in a classroom an anxiety may provide unusual teaching opportunities. Conversely, in Bruner, the approach is at its best when it recognizes "emotional loadings" as "opportunities for deepened learning"; the worst moments arise at the point when the teacher has to abandon her well-understood "bagful of potential pedagogical tricks" and feels she has "little insight into the child's conative life which, for the moment, may have taken over." [67]

Self-knowledge. overflow of the conative life, neutrality of cognitive aspects of learning, psychic isolation in the middle of educational community: these are the topics (though not necessarily by those names) with which Jones is concerned. In our exposition we will focus on two direct encounters which illustrate the quality of his educational theories. The first was a self-knowledge psychology course which he taught at a tradition-bound New England preparatory school for girls.[68] Jones met the class for weekly forty-five-minute sessions of instruction directly followed by eighty minutes of free discussion in which no holds were barred provided the action was all verbal. The second encounter was a use (in more depth than anyone quite intended) in a public school summer enrichment session of Jerome Bruner's "Man: A Course of Study." The first was for seniors, some of them eighteen and a bit uptight. The second was pitched at the fifth-grade level and had a sharper cognitive focus than Jones gave to his high school sessions. The Bruner course gave the youngsters a common objective focus in a film and coordinate reading matter; also, the fifth-grade students had accumulated less in the way of defense mechanisms against the intrusion of alien personality than had the high school seniors. The social stratum in both cases was distinctly "comfortable" middle class, allowing good comparison (but also preventing results from being generalized to less "privileged" children). Nonetheless, the two groups of students presented different problems.

The experimental class with the private school seniors concerns us less for several reasons. (1) It was frankly modified group therapy, which the school gave credit for but which no college would accept; the discussion sessions tended to use psychotherapeutic interchange as an end in itself—the very thing Jones finds least acceptable in Kubie. (2) The alternation of cognitive and conative teaching was something of an impediment to both; the girls found it difficult to shift gears from one to the other.[69] (3) All too often the shortness of the sessions of conative encounter foreclosed discussion just when it was becoming most productive. (4) Though the girls, who were nearly of one chronological age, varied widely in their emotional age, the reader finds it hard to assess this variation; a student's contribution to the discussion is usually labeled simply "G," with the result that personalities are blended into the homogeneous group which was (perhaps too strongly) the leader's ideal. Clearly he wanted to preserve individual privacy in his public account.

Much was uncorked in these sessions, including hostilities of almost every kind—even, at times, those which came close to collective Freudian transference. Yet—and this is something of a disappointment from the Freudian point of view—the catharsis of having a common enemy, the instructor, did not particularly seem to increase group unity or decrease group friction. (Group unity, to be sure, was but one of several aims.) Occasional unity, or at least commonality, did emerge in these sessions. In addition, the taste and flash of honesty often appeared. The reader also senses the girls' relief on finding that strange and shameful feelings and dreams are remarkably common and remarkably alike. In general, the reader often has the sense that he is watching a room of children of about two and a half in the stage of "parallel play." The place of toys is taken by feelings, but the atmosphere is the same: neither isolation nor genuine sociality. The antisocial factors seem to be inhibitions and distrusts rather than hostilities per se. The

diapason sounds· in the discussion are those of wariness, very briefly
broken by spurts of impulsive fear and anger. The reader may come
away thinking that Jones overestimates both his failures and his neutrality.[70]

The other encounter is much more illuminating. What the senior
girls gained was invaluable: some self-knowledge and knowledge of the
socially other. These are also the aims Jones hoped to achieve for the
fifth-grade children with Bruner's "Man: A Course of Study." What
Jones sees in the use of Bruner's course, particularly its films, is a
chance to redefine both the self and the other along lines not restricted
to isolated cognitive comprehension. "Our hope," says Bruner of
"Man: A Course of Study," is "to lead the children to understand how
man goes about explicating a world, making sense of it, and that one
kind of explanation is no more human than another." [71] Jones has
taken this as license to demand that insight and outsight be given
joint—if not equal—roles among educational determinants.[72]

Jones's investigation and demonstration of the deep structure of educational response through the teaching of Bruner's course took place
in a voluntary, leisurely paced summer school. The context is an able,
even distinguished, group of teachers. The sequence of study is important. Not everything was Bruner, man, and Eskimos. In between segments of the course the students went to Miss Greenfield for dance.
She sounded the tocsin:

> I am growing increasingly disturbed over how the new films must
> be affecting the children in their regular classes. I have no objec-
> tion to helping them to express their feelings about violence and
> death through the medium of the dance. Sometimes they do it
> beautifully. But the theme is becoming monotonous. Is there no
> way to channel these interests into thought and fellow-feeling *in* the
> classroom, before they come to me?
>
> I would like to think that I have something to add to this curric-
> ulum and not that I am merely being used as a random outlet for
> unused feelings.
>
> . . . Film has the power to exaggerate—the face, the hands, the
> body, the emotions. Thus the focus of the great documentary films
> has always been on basic activities, simplicities of being in nature.
> . . . The exaggerations of the media have always been modulated,
> however, by the use of black and white and by narrated interpreta-
> tions, both of which remove the viewer from actuality and offer a
> point of view. The new films are in vivid color and are silent. I
> presume these features are in the interests of authenticity and I
> must not quarrel with them. But the children who come to me
> from your classrooms are not yet trained anthropologists, looking
> for details of the what and how of the tools being used. As yet they

have nothing to vitiate the vivid registration of their senses that an animal has been killed. Moreover, you are apparently giving them nothing with which to assimilate these facts or with which to make them credibly remote. Else *I* as their dance teacher could sometimes have other images with which to work. Everyday it is violence and death.

What have we come to when we act as though a child is not made curious and aroused by the sight of a naked baby at a mother's breast or the breaking of a dead seal's back? When we see a beautiful actress in the cinema do we come away talking about the shape of the knife with which she ate or the kinds of shoes she wore or the way her hair was arranged? No, we remember the act of eating and its particular emotional significance in the setting of the drama, the expression of her hands, the way she walked, the beauty of her ankles, her facial expression, etc. Perhaps on their fourth viewing we focus on technological details. How can you deny that a young child who sees the breaking of a seal's back will remember this longer and more deeply than the method of retrieving the animal, the season of the hunt, or even the difficulty of finding a seal hole. You must have found a way because I hear you complaining that the children are uninterested in your classes. My complaint is that they are *too* interested in mine. It is always death or violence —sometimes beautiful, but it is boring me.[73]

A stunning comment, and it tells the whole story. Efforts were already being made to tap at least some of the children's high charge of feeling for cognitive purposes. But in addition they were offered expressive release and enactment in what was apparently a frequent free exercise in dance composition. These efforts were so complex that they are difficult to summarize; the reader should examine them for himself.[74] The original film featured (1) the killing and slaughtering of a ring seal (one of the three principal protein sources of the Netsilik), including a bloody ritual snacking of raw liver from the still warm seal, on the ice, before the seal is dragged back to the igloo for further ritual dismemberment, blood sharing, and preservation; (2) breast feeding; (3) the abandoning of a grandmother too old to follow the nomadic journey with her duffel; (4) the deliberate and fatal exposure of a girl baby born into a group with too many girls during a season of poor hunting; (5) the feeding of a fish eye to a baby; (6) the brutal pounding to death of the first-kill seagull by a young boy, who is then warmly received by his mother.

The brunt of the whole exercise is borne not only by the children, whose emotional conventions are less stabilized and formalized than our own, but also by their teacher.[75] Indeed, the teacher must share in some degree the children's anxiety and face as well the powerful sec-

ond-order anxiety of being unable to handle it. Here the drama becomes complex. The teacher's way out must be assistance with the
child's way out, in the form of a solicitation of free expression of the
students' *emotional* comprehension of what they cognitively must accept.

For Jones the ambiguous nub of the whole matter is anxiety. He
takes our basic conviction that "one state of mind does psychological
harm to children" and mitigates the claim a bit: "Or, more precisely,
the defensive excesses of thought, feeling, and behavior which we tend
to develop against chronic expectation of anxiety." [76] He is convinced
that anxiety can be used effectively in the classroom if it is handled
discriminatingly. For example, disagreeable feelings aroused by the film
are allowed to take their course in compositions describing a disagreeable experience the child remembers.

Freud says neurosis is the normal lot of man. Jones is a shade sub-
tler: anxiety is rooted in being human. The preconditions of anxiety
are those of being human.

> (1) Our instincts, while strong, are not specific; (2) we languish in
> immaturity for an extremely lengthy period; (3) we must adjust our
> behavior to social environments of bewildering complexity; and (4)
> we are equipped with an oversized cerebral cortex which incessantly
> constructs hypotheses about the ambiguities attending these—
> hypotheses as to what our instincts of the moment are seeking, hy-
> potheses as to what our competence of the moment will support.[77]

Freedom is not without its price. The necessities of the "outside"
world are complex, those of the "inner" world are equally demanding.
To bring the two into harmony requires an imagination whose products are not necessarily secure, agreeable, or even tolerable. "By virtue
of being human, in other words, we are always imagining, and we are
sometimes alone and helpless in the process. When we are all of these
simultaneously—imagining and alone and helpless—we are in a state
of anxiety." [78] Jones goes on to explain that anxiety proceeds from internal rather than external sources. The usage is strained, of course.
We may either fear for or be anxious about an overdue friend, a sick
relative, etc. It might have been better if Jones had defined anxiety in
terms of the self as object rather than as agent, since—in a sense—all
emotional life at least inculpates the inward self, almost by definition.
Emotions are differentiated at least as much by what they intend, what
they are pointed toward, as by what they arise from.

Nonetheless, Jones's analysis is formidable. Imagination is the spontaneous extension from something that is or has been to something
which has not. If it has no power of action to express it or actualize it,
it is helpless. If it has no commerce with *sympatico* selves, who will at

least mirror it and play with it, it turns back upon itself and is alone. For all the questionable route, the conclusion is strikingly accurate. And the cure is: be less alone, less helpless, or less imaginative. But imagination crushed to earth will rise again. And when it does, an unsatisfied longing proper to a given age will show up later as a regressive block—a stubborn demand to get the groundwork of personality well founded before proceeding, as in Medard Boss's patient mentioned on page 257. The block will appear and effectively stop the cognitive process or render it a meaningless routine, "irrelevant." The reduction of aloneness can be accomplished, at bottom, by declaring yourself. Say "Ugh" at the raw-flesh-eating. It will be echoed by your classmates. Discuss the diversity of your opinions also. As a result of comprehending the very commonality of the problem—whether or not a solution is reached—the sense of alienation and isolation will be reduced. And by bringing the emotions to reflective understanding you also gain control over them; you are no longer helpless before them. Spinoza said it all compactly three hundred years ago. An emotion which is not understood, he says, is a "passion." That is, one is passive, helpless, before it. Spinoza was neither Christian nor puritan. Emotions he expected, but not as masters. Although Jones often modifies "mastery," a somewhat Nietzschean notion, to "use," a rather more distinctively American one, the point is still "Don't be driven blindly by feelings." When we are so driven, we find the cognitive life a secondary matter. For oldsters this means a routine, but for youngsters it means something irrelevant.

However, helplessness is not the prime ailment—after all, who is not helpless, ultimately? The aloneness is more vital, more bad: "Reduction of feelings of aloneness is the common denominator of all forms of psychotherapy." [79] But the situation which the psychologist seeks to alleviate is one which the teacher ought to seek to improve. "It follows that a therapist's methods seek to reduce aloneness and helplessness, and that a teacher's methods seek to increase the polar opposites: community and mastery." [80]

To this end of improvement the teacher will not be afraid to permit situations which threaten the child, or, therefore, to create a risk of anxiety, if the threat entered into provides the child with the possibility of *communalizing* the anxiety and/or *mastering* it. Jones's final words on this subject are a shade milder: "share" and "use." [81] "Threat" is "stimulus," "anxiety" is what arises from it, and even the latter is tolerable if it takes the form of a challenge that can reasonably be met. [82]

The major focus of research, then, is how to cultivate and use imagination for the increased mastery of subject matter. Educational, not

clinical, research must answer this question.[83] The reasons are clear:
clinical work is alleviative, educational work constructive.

Up till now our presentation of Jones has largely been an explication intended to arouse the reader's interest in and approbation of an
educational viewpoint that can hardly be ignored. At some points education pivots on the conative side of learning. At others the pivoting is
clearly cognitive. Educated emotions facilitate educated minds. At the
very least, blocked emotions are brakes on the wheels of education. At
other points, however, nothing is so rewarding as cognitive achievement or liquidation of factual ignorance. For instance mastery of intellectual or bodily skills can do much to evaporate the little pools of in-
security that sometimes trickle into torrents of confusion and distress.
Salvation from distress through athletic, intellectual, or creative
achievement does much to attack helplessness and to reward imagination. The playing fields of Eton perhaps were not the seedbeds of empire, but no one left them without an improved sense of objectivity.

What is really at stake, however, is not the questions "Should we do
it?" or "Must it happen?" but "Who does it, when, how, why, how
often, how long, etc.?" Our cautionary critique can hardly enter into
technology, especially where good empirical data are so hard to come
by. On the other hand these data will hardly be acquired by a careful
effort to follow past procedures. In a word, blunders will be made and
the cost may even be high. The alternate risks may be higher, since
there is hardly any denying the demands of the feelings generally to be
heard and to be acted upon; early emotional stress may be healthier
than later emotional inadequacy. Analogously a broken leg at sixteen
may heal in six weeks; at forty it may take twice as long or more. Our
critique is confined to two limitations that qualify Jones's observations.

The first has already been hinted at. The economic and social
strata of the students with whom he has been in direct contact are quite
narrow. Bluntly, much of America just isn't there—in particular
the urban millions who are less likely to be shaped tomorrow by the
upper-middle class than they are to shape it. It may be the case that
Newton, Massachusetts, youngsters (or senior girls in a private school)
are somewhat stirred up by the sight of a nude baby nursing or a seagull stoned to death in a lengthy, nonutilitarian ritual, or by the deser-
tion of a supernumerary baby or elder. Urban youngsters, however,
who carry knives to school in order to assure a return or who don't
want to report a body in a vacant lot because the fuzz might think
they're involved with the local pusher will have different immediate
sources of anxiety. Such youngsters will be harder to reach, and they
will be able to use cognitive enrichment of the standard sort less read-

ily. And for some young man who, as substitute teacher, has been rightly told, "Don't try to teach anything. Just keep order if you can, and above all, *never turn your back on the class*," Jones's work may seem a little unreal. It is not that Jones's observations do not apply or are not likely to. Rather, his stratum of encounter is among children and adolescents who stand to make immediate cognitive gain out of conative education. In the great public educational stockades of the city, the cognitive benefits may be less ready to hand, and the school as institution of social therapy may be more of a living need than we realize. But conversely, by a perverse acclimatizing of school age children to a kind of premature self-sufficiency in the jungles of the city, we may be able to reach such youngsters *only* by heavy emphasis on useful skills that show immediate prospects of reward, particularly in the way of gaining a competitive advantage over peers. We cannot see— speaking as authors of this study—how you could know whether these alternatives are exclusive or how they could be made to be complementary. Only shrewd and devoted experimental work would supply clues. In brief, the force of Jones's theories, since they are also theories of a technology, is strongest for the type of data it reflects upon, and these are necessarily restricted.

The other problem that arises in connection with Jones's work pertains to education within or without the classroom and has to do with the heart of his theory. The case he makes for emotion, feeling, and imagination as conatively deployed seems to us extremely important. Conative education likely never did proceed by itself successfully. It may be that in the past we derived emotional growth from a simplified environment. The older environment lacked the capacity to bring instant pictures of terror, agony, distress, famine, misery, brutality, waste, corruption, and war into the lives of those presently helpless to ward them off or effect any change in them before they become mature. The quintessential nightmare is impotence before horror. Or it may be that the family structure and its relative immobility provided complementary nourishment, so that the schools could concentrate on cognitive skills. Or again, it may be that value stability was maintained against the multiple intrusion of immigrative and diversified cultures, by relatively homogeneous ethnic groups. Probably at least these three elements cooperated. The family now is less a well of resource and less a wall of protection, and its mobility diversifies its collective perceptions. Instant horror can be had by the flick of a switch, and you can take your choice: fact or fiction or the unhappy blend that leaves you cognitively addled as well as conatively deformed. Finally, the interpretation of a highly variegated cultural accumulation produces extreme value relativism, which can easily be the antechamber to meaninglessness. The most evident victim of these as-saults is the conative self. We do not think, nonetheless, that the semitherapeutic relief and/or the honesty of self-revelation and un-blocking, nor even the providing of cognitive materials for affective evaluation, can possibly carry the full load of conative need.

There are at least four types of value: utilitarian, aesthetic, socio-moral, and religious. Of these, Jones concentrates his attention on the third, with sharp emphasis on ego maturation. Moreover, utilitarian values there are aplenty, even though they often enough lack a criteri-ology. That is, are some usefulnesses better than others, and if so what standards do we employ in finding this out? Broadly, how useful is the category of use? We are presented with two other kinds of value, reli-gious and aesthetic, which are "useful" where *use* is not.

Our separation of church and state has led us to a tradition which separates religious values from political values. The interpretation of religious teaching, however, as likely leading to church oppression seems to us gratuitous. It was in reaction to the church's intrusion in political life that we knew that church and state should go their sepa-rate ways. Religion may well be another matter, and we have some sympathy for those who think that the religion of scientific material-ism should, in justice, be met by equal time, and in the schools, for spiritual values. One may even muster a quite secular uneasiness about able psychologists who insist on talking about ideas "in the head," or about how the "cerebral cortex . . . incessantly constructs hy-potheses." [84] But this issue can hardly be quickly settled, and the overwhelming momentum of the law requires of society that religious education be realized otherwhere than in the public schools.

We are left with what is still a vast area, aesthetic education—education in the creation, criticism, and appreciation (these last two are *not* the same) of art, painting, dance, music, architecture, poetry, and the rest. These subjects are still regarded as embellishments, ancil-lary pleasures, special activities—in short, secondary. The present fate of self-knowledge is the constant fate of aesthetic feeling and aesthetic creativity, namely, to be regarded as something that one probably also ought to think about and—admittedly—in some rare cases as being of paramount importance.

It is false to think of aesthetic creation as a mere expression of emotion. It is false to find its primary significance in what it psycho-logically reveals. It is false to think of it primarily as Piagetian adapta-tion, accommodative or assimilative. In fact, aesthetic creation is dis-rupting, not adaptive; assertive, not accommodative; and it generates a reality, rather than assimilating one. It seems vital to being human. It will be seized on even by a chimpanzee, with time and materials at his disposal.[85] It was the triumph of the Aurignacian culture which produced incredible cave paintings about 13,000 B.C. It bodies forth a reality, adding to the world, and especially the human world. Its comprehension and reception belong as much to a genuine reality principle as to any matter of fact or any self-recognition and self-understanding. It stands apart from religious value and social value, occasionally colliding with them. The education of the emotions is much neglected, but the conative extends over the *whole* field of value. In this field the worth of oneself, the knowledge of one's feelings and what they are for, and the imaginative conquest of aloneness and helplessness is a vital portion. The context of this domain, however, is the rest of the field of value.

NOTES

1. Jerome Bruner, *Toward a Theory of Instruction*, Cambridge, Mass., 1966 (hereafter cited as *TTI*), p. 81.
2. *TTI*, p. 27.
3. *TTI*, p. 14.
4. These conclusions are borne out by the work of Roger Brown. See V. Bellugi and R. Brown, eds., *The Acquisition of Language*, Monographs of the Society for Research in Child Development, No. 29 (Chicago, 1964), pp. 79–92.
5. *TTI*, p. 16.
6. *TTI*, p. 16.
7. *TTI*, p. 27.
8. *TTI*, p. 3.
9. *TTI*, p. 27.
10. *TTI*, p. 29.
11. *TTI*, p. 29.
12. *TTI*, p. 35; compare Jean Piaget, *The Psychology of Intelligence*, trans. M. Piercy and D. E. Berlyne, London, 1950, p. 47.
13. Quoted in Piaget, p. 47.
14. *On Knowing: Essays for the Left Hand*, New York, 1965 (hereafter cited as *OK*), pp. 142–143.
15. *OK*, pp. 141–142.
16. *OK*, p. 134.
17. *TTI*, p. 3.
18. *TTI*, pp. 129–148.
19. *TTI*, p. 4.
20. *OK*, p. 68.
21. *TTI*, p. 31.
22. *TTI*, p. 32.
23. *TTI*, p. 35.
24. See, for example, *OK*, pp. 97–111, 122; *TTI*, pp. 19–20, 29, 37.
25. *TTI*, p. 32.
26. *OK*, p. 115.
27. *OK*, p. 115.
28. *TTI*, p. 23.
29. *TTI*, Chapter 4.
30. *TTI*, p. 74.

31. We are indebted for this biographical material to Robert Coles, *Erik Erikson: The Growth of His Work*, Boston, 1970.

32. *Insight and Responsibility*, New York, 1964 (hereafter cited as *IR*), pp. 130–131.

33. Erikson is undoubtedly thinking of Konrad Lorenz, among others, who investigated animal postnatal imprint and discovered that in the brief period after a gosling is hatched, it becomes attached to the most dominant animal figure in evidence, electing it, so to speak, "mother." Lorenz thus became mother to a whole gaggle of European graylag geese.

34. *Childhood and Society*, New York, 1950; 2d ed., 1963 (hereafter cited as *CS*), p. 247.

35. See especially *CS*, pp. 247 ff.

36. *Identity, Youth and Crisis*, New York 1968 (hereafter cited as *IYC*), p. 92.

37. Trans. Ludwig Lefebre, New York, 1963, Chapter 1.

38. *CS*, p. 247.

39. *IR*, p. 163.

40. *IR*, pp. 163–164.

41. *IR*, pp. 164–165.

42. *CS*, p. 245.

43. *CS*, p. 246.

44. *IYC*, pp. 95, 96.

45. Compare *IYC*, Chapter 3, and *CS*, Chapter 8.

46. *IYC*, p. 109.

47. *IYC*, p. 115.

48. Compare *IYC*, p. 229.

49. *IYC*, p. 154.

50. *CS*, pp. 258–261; *IYC*, pp. 122–135.

51. "The Problem of Ego Identity," *Psychological Issues* I (1959): 119; hereafter cited as "PEI." Reprinted from *Journal of the American Psychoanalytical Association* IV (1956): 56–121.

52. *IYC*, p. 154.

53. *CS*, pp. 261–263; *IYC*, pp. 128–135, 154, 165–172.

54. First read before the Vienna Psychoanalytic Society in April, 1930; published as "Die Zukunft der Aufklärung und die Psychoanalyse," *Zeitschrift für Psychoanalitische Pädagogik* IV (1930); trans. and reprinted in *Psychoanalytic Quarterly* IV (1935): 50–68; hereafter cited as *PFE*.

55. *PFE*, p. 67.

56. *PFE*, p. 62; emphasis ours.

57. *PFE*, p. 63.

58. *PFE*, p. 68.

59. *PFE*, pp. 67–68.

60. *PFE*, p. 51.

61. "PEI," p. 166.

62. Richard M. Jones was until recently Professor of Clinical Psychology and Public Practice at Harvard University and Director of Psychological Services for the Commonwealth of Massachusetts. He left these jobs to help plan and set up an experimental school, Evergreen State College, in Olympia, Washington, where he is presently teaching and serving as Coordinator of the Human Development Program.

63. R. M. Jones, *Fantasy and Feeling in Education*, New York, 1968; hereafter cited as *FFE*.

64. For Kubie, see particularly his articles "The Forgotten Man of Education" and "Research in Protecting Preconscious Functions in Education," both in Richard M. Jones, ed., *Contemporary Educational Psychology*, New York, 1966 (hereafter cited as *CEP*), pp. 61–71, 72–88.

65. *CEP*, pp. 14–15.

66. *CEP*, p. 15.

67. *CEP*, pp. 15–16.

68. R. M. Jones, *An Application of Psychoanalysis to Education*, Springfield, Ill., 1960 (hereafter cited as *APE*), p. 3.

69. Jones has indicated to one of the authors that the two-track approach—academic class/nonacademic group—had exactly this difficulty and some others as well, namely that it was difficult not to drift into an exploitation of the encounter phase of the course in order to acquire psychological data.

70. *CEP*, p. 227. The word "responsible" in this passage surely should be "responsibility."

71. *TTI*, p. 89.

72. *FFE*, pp. 55–86 *passim*.

73. *FFE*, pp. 43–44.

74. *FFE*, Chapter 3.

75. Jones never seizes the fine opportunity to ask what an Eskimo would think of an American film that shows a man cutting scores of others to ribbons with a machine gun or of a real-life scene where blacks starve in view of the dome of the Capitol Building in Washington, D.C.

76. *FFE*, p. 70.

77. *FFE*, p. 70.

78. *FFE*, p. 70.

79. *FFE*, p. 80.

80. *FFE*, p. 77.

81. *FFE*, p. 86.

82. *FFE*, pp. 70 ff.

83. *FFE*, p. 85.

84. *FFE*, pp. 61, 70; it is either a mind, or better a person, who constructs such hypotheses, through (no doubt) cortical activity.

85. Desmond Morris, *The Biology of Art*, London, 1962.

INDEX OF TITLES AND PROPER NAMES

Cross-references enclosed in square brackets appear in the Index of Terms, Topics, and Themes.

INDEX OF TERMS, TOPICS, AND THEMES

Cross-references enclosed in square brackets appear in the Index of Titles and Proper Names.